British Rearmament
and the Treasury:
1932–1939

To my Parents

British Rearmament and the Treasury: 1932–1939

G. C. PEDEN

Department of Economic and Social History
The University, Bristol

1979

Scottish Academic Press
Edinburgh

Published by
Scottish Academic Press Ltd.
33 Montgomery Street, Edinburgh EH7 5JX

ISBN 0 7073 0229 3

Printed in Great Britain by
R. & R. Clark Ltd., Edinburgh

Contents

Acknowledgements

My thanks are due to Dr. C. J. Bartlett, for suggesting the subject of this study, and to Professor N. H. Gibbs for wise counsel while I was undertaking the research; to Mrs. Catherine Charlton, Mr. George Oram, Sir Thomas and Lady Padmore, Sir Edward Playfair, Lord Trend and Sir John Winnifrith for granting interviews; to Dr. Bartlett and Professor Gibbs, again, and to Professor C. Blake, Mr. Vernon Bogdanor, Mr. Brian Bond, Sir Norman Chester, Mr. A. A. Lonie, Dr. A. P. Madden, Mr. Peter Sinclair, Mr. G. N. von Tunzelmann and Professor D. C. Watt for reading drafts and commenting on them; to Dr. G. K. Fry, Sir Noel Hall, Mr. Nevil Johnson, Dr. R. A. C. Parker and Dr. John Rawson for information or ideas; to Viscount Caldecote; Baroness Vansittart; Churchill College, Cambridge; the Military Archive Centre, King's College, University of London; the National Maritime Museum, Greenwich; H.M. Treasury; the University of Cambridge, and the University of Leeds for access to documents; to the Controller, H.M. Stationery Office, for permission to reproduce copyright material held in the Public Record Office, and Lady Liddell Hart for permission to reproduce copyright material from her late husband's papers; to the Scottish Education Department and the Institute of Historical Research for funding, and to Mrs. Sheena Rhind, the typist, for coping good-humouredly with my handwriting and amendments. The responsibility for errors is, of course, the author's.

G. C. PEDEN

University of Bristol

Abbreviations

A.D.G.B.	Air Defence of Great Britain
ADM.	Admiralty document in P.R.O. of series and number indicated
A.D.R.	Air Defence Research
AIR.	Air Ministry document in P.R.O. of series and number indicated
A.M.	Air Ministry
A.R.P.	Air Raid Precautions
CAB.	Cabinet Office document in P.R.O. of series and number indicated
C.I.D.	Committee of Imperial Defence
C.I.G.S.	Chief of Imperial General Staff
C.O.S.	Chiefs of Staff (Sub-Committee of C.I.D.)
C.P.	Cabinet Paper
D.C.M.	Ministerial Committee on Disarmament
D.C.M.(A.F.)	Ministerial Committee on Disarmament dealing with Air Defence
D.M.	Defence Matériel Division (of Treasury)
D.P.(P.)	Defence Plans (Policy) Committee paper
D.P.(P.)C.	Defence Plans (Policy) Committee
D.P.R.	Defence Policy and Requirements Committee paper
D.P.R.C.	Defence Policy and Requirements Committee
D.P.R.(D.R.)	Defence Policy and Requirements (Defence Requirements) Committee paper
D.P.R.(D.R.)C.	Defence Policy and Requirements (Defence Requirements) Committee
D.R.C.	Defence Requirements Committee
E.A.C.	Economic Advisory Council
E.A.C.(E.I.)	Economic Advisory Council's Sub-Committee on Economic Information paper
H.C. Deb.	House of Commons Debates
H.L. Deb.	House of Lords Debates
N.C.	Neville Chamberlain papers
N.C.M.	Ministerial Committee on London Naval Conference paper
P.A.C.	Parliamentary Committee of Public Accounts
P.C.E.	Public Capital Expenditure Committee paper
PREM.	Prime Minister's Office document in P.R.O. of series and number indicated

P.S.O.	Principal Supply Officers
P.S.O.C.	Principal Supply Officers Committee
S.A.C.	Strategic Appreciation Committee
T.	Treasury document in P.R.O. of series and number indicated
T.E.E.C.	Treasury Emergency Expenditure Committee
T.I.S.C.	Treasury Inter-Service Committee
W.O.	War Office document in P.R.O. of series and number indicated.

'Gouverner, c'est choisir'
        M. PIERRE MENDÈS-FRANCE

I

Introduction

Sir James Rae, a senior Treasury official in the Nineteen-Thirties, once remarked that if he had a penny for every time the Treasury was damned, he would be a very rich man.[1] If Sir James's estate had received a penny for every time the Treasury has been damned by historians, his estate would still be growing. Historians of British rearmament in particular have tended to be free with phrases like Treasury 'tight-fistedness', and 'Treasury meanness',[2] although not every historian has accepted at face value complaints by servicemen that all would have been well if only their particular department's expenditure had not been curbed by the Treasury. D. C. Watt, for example, published a useful counterblast to the 'Air Force view of history', showing how the Treasury had been used as a scapegoat for deficiencies in the R.A.F. which were really the responsibility of the Air Staff.[3] Nevertheless, the adverse comments on the Treasury quoted above have been published since Watt's article, so it seems that the Air Force – and indeed the Army and Navy – views of history are still influential. This is not surprising, since politicians, air marshals, generals and admirals are more prone to writing memoirs than are civil servants.

The public did not have long to wait for the first authoritative denunciation of the Treasury's influence on rearmament. Mr. A. Duff Cooper, three weeks after his resignation as First Lord of the Admiralty from Mr. Neville Chamberlain's Government in October 1938, wrote an article in the London *Evening Standard* claiming that rearmament was being retarded by the 'paralysing hand of the Treasury'.[4] As one who had been Financial Secretary to the Treasury in 1934–5 and Secretary of State for War in 1935–7, before becoming First Lord, Duff Cooper's views commanded attention and respect. At a time when great deficiencies in Britain's defences had been highlighted by the Munich crisis it was easy to believe that more could have been accomplished if Treasury control had not been maintained over defence departments' expenditure during the rearmament programme.

Defeat on land and the threat of invasion in 1940 brought criticism to a new pitch. The polemic *Guilty Men* – a book written by three journalists in a weekend – demanded to know why the 'best soldiers in the world' had been driven from Belgium, and attributed defeat to lack of equipment. Although conceding that Chamberlain, while Chancellor of the Exchequer in 1931–7, had consistently recognised the need for rearmament, the joint authors claimed that it had been Treasury policy 'in war as in peace ... to ensure that expenditure should be strictly limited', and included in the indictment of those responsible for defeat both Chamberlain and his successor at the Exchequer, Sir John Simon; as well as the then Permanent Secretary of the Treasury, Sir Horace Wilson.[5] *Guilty Men* was no work of history, but historians who had experienced the events described therein were often brought to similar conclusions. Sir John Wheeler-Bennett, for example, writing in 1948 of the constant conflict between the service ministers and the Treasury in 1937 and 1938 as to the degree of expenditure necessary for rearmament, commented: 'The full realisation of the gravity of the situation seemed to be wanting; there was a refusal to admit the inexorable argument of fact'.[6]

With the publication of Sir Keith Feiling's by no means unsympathetic biography of Chamberlain in 1946 it became clear that the Treasury had feared that rearmament expenditure would lead to inflation, leading in turn 'to the loss of our export trade, a feverish and artificial boom, followed by a disastrous slump and finally the defeat of the Government'. Memories of high unemployment in the inter-war years made such fears seem groundless, and it seemed all the more unfortunate that Chamberlain, even as Chancellor, had been, in Feiling's words: 'the moving spirit (in the Government), so that his individual view on the point of danger and the financial limits was reflected in the measures brought to Parliament'.[7] Moreover, it became apparent from Feiling's book that not only had expenditure on rearmament been limited by the Treasury, but also that Chamberlain, while Chancellor as well as while Prime Minister, had sought to influence priorities as between the armed services. Subsequent historical research has confirmed this fact, and there has been a tendency to conclude, in the words of one historian, that the Treasury's influence had been 'excessive, dominating the arguments of the Chiefs of Staff and the Foreign Office'.[8]

Little has been written by former members of the Treasury to counter the critics. Simon's memoirs did nothing to suggest that the Treasury had made any positive contribution to rearmament. Sir Warren Fisher, the Permanent Secretary of the Treasury and official Head of the Civil Service throughout the inter-war period, on the other hand, wrote an article in 1948 in which he described the rearmament programme announced in 1936 as a 'façade' and 'ludicrously unsubstantial', and in a letter to *The Times* in 1942 claimed that 'from 1933 onwards ... with one or two others (he) had never ceased warning successive Governments of the dangerous implications of Hitler's accession to power and urging the vital necessity of rearmament'. Sir Richard Hopkins, who, as the Second Secretary of the Treasury was Fisher's deputy for finance, was more restrained, and published no more than a bland introductory note to a volume on wartime economy, in which he made no comment on pre-war rearmament. Lord Bridges, the Treasury official most involved from 1934 to 1938 in day-to-day dealings with defence departments, published work describing the Treasury and Treasury control, but dealt with these subjects in general terms only.[9] Consequently, the Treasury's case has gone by default.

It is worth recalling that the conclusion of peace in 1919 marked the beginning of a period of intense political pressure on British governments to reduce the country's armed forces. Conscription, adopted as a wartime expedient, was abandoned, and not readopted until the spring of 1939, so that the size of the armed forces was limited to what could be raised by voluntary recruitment. The Navy and Air Force were, on the whole, successful in attracting recruits, but the Army was much less so, and for most of the inter-war period was below establishment. An even more important restriction, however, was the popular demand from 1919 that the government should reduce what were then considered to be high rates of taxation (the standard rate of income tax in 1919, 6 shillings in the pound, was about five times the pre-war level), and also to balance the Budget to prevent inflation (prices had risen rapidly during the war, and continued to do so during a brief post-war boom). Defence expenditure, and interest payments on the war-swollen National Debt, made up the greater part of the Budget, so that men of all political persuasions, be they Conservative businessmen seeking reductions in taxation, or Left-wing pacifists opposed to arms in principle, could agree on the need for lower defence Estimates.

How far defence Estimates should be reduced depended on the dangers of the international situation, and in 1919 the Cabinet decided that for the purpose of drawing up service Estimates it should be assumed 'that the British Empire will not be engaged in any great war during the next ten years, and that no Expeditionary Force is required for this purpose'.[10] This 'Ten Year Rule' was used by the Treasury to persuade defence departments to accept lower Estimates, which were reduced from a total of £604 million for the three services in 1919 to £111 million in 1922.[11] Subsequently further defence economies were made, but these, though painful to the services concerned, did not succeed in bringing the Estimates below £103 million in 1932, the inter-war nadir of defence expenditure.

The reduction in Britain's defence services was begun without waiting for any international agreement on the limitation of arms, with the important exception of the limits imposed by the Allies on Germany in 1919.* A major problem of British foreign policy in the inter-war

---

* By the Treaty of Versailles the German army was limited to 104,000 men, and the navy to six small armoured vessels, six light cruisers and 12 destroyers. No submarines, and no military aircraft, were allowed. No fortifications were allowed west or 32 miles east of the Rhine.

period, therefore, was that of persuading other powers to agree to limit their armed forces to levels which would afford Britain and her Empire reasonable security. Despite the long-term potential threat of air attack on the United Kingdom, and the enhanced importance of keeping the Low Countries in friendly hands, the view of the British Government in 1920, and later, was that, because of the world-wide extent of the British Empire and of Britain's maritime trade, Imperial defence, including that of the United Kingdom, must continue to rest on the basis of sea power.[12] The war had eliminated the German navy as a factor to be considered for the time being, and the growth of the French and Italian navies had been stunted on account of priority given to land warfare, but the years since 1914 had seen a rapid growth in the navies of the United States and Japan, and both these countries had large post-war naval construction programmes. Moreover, whereas Britain had been weakened economically and financially by the war, the American economy had grown stronger than in 1914, so that Britain was ill-placed to engage in a naval arms race with the United States. The possibility of war with the United States could be ruled out, and Japan was, for the time being, an ally, but it was a question whether Britain's prestige could survive her eclipse as the world's leading sea power.

Consequently, in 1921 the Government accepted eagerly the invitation of the American President, Harding, to take part in a disarmament conference in Washington. The American proposals made at the conference included the suspension of capital ship* construction for ten years, and the fixing of the relative strengths of the American, British and Japanese navies at 5 : 5 : 3. The British Naval Staff was alarmed at the prospect of completing no new capital ships for ten years, as the Royal Navy had only one such vessel designed with the benefit of wartime experience, whereas in 1920–1 four American capital ships were launched, and two Japanese capital ships were completed. A compromise was reached whereby only three of the new American ships were completed, and Britain was to build two new ones, but otherwise no more would be built by the three powers, or by France or Italy, for ten years. Of existing capital ships Britain and the United States would retain a total of 525,000 tons each, Japan 315,000 tons, and France and Italy 175,000 tons each. All other capital ships of the five powers were scrapped. Much smaller totals for aircraft carriers on a comparable basis were also agreed.

In addition to these quantitative limits, it was agreed that new capital ships should not exceed 35,000 tons displacement or carry guns of calibre greater than 16 inches, and that new cruisers should not exceed 10,000 tons or carry guns of more than 8 inches. Further agreement could not be reached at Washington, or at the Geneva Naval

* The term 'capital ship' included battleships and battlecruisers.

Conference of 1927, and it was not until 1930 that the first London Naval Treaty limiting cruisers, destroyers and submarines was signed by Britain, the United States and Japan – but not by France or Italy, who could not agree on limits between themselves. The Japanese accepted limits of 61 to 65 per cent of British or American strength in cruisers, 70 per cent in destroyers, but parity in submarines. All five major naval powers agreed at London not to build replacement capital ships until after 1936.

The Washington Conference of 1921–2 also attempted to settle political differences between the United States, Japan and Britain, and, indeed, it was this political agreement which made disarmament arrangements possible. There had been growing tension between the United States and Japan over conflicting interests in China and the Pacific, and consequent American dislike of the Anglo-Japanese Alliance. In deference to American (and Canadian) opinion, the alliance was allowed to lapse in 1922, and was replaced by a Four Power Treaty between the United States, Britain, Japan and France, whereby they agreed to common consultation to preserve peace in the Pacific area. These four powers, and five lesser ones, also signed a Nine Power Treaty affirming China's integrity and sovereignty. Finally the three major naval powers agreed not to build or improve naval bases in the Pacific – which in Britain's case affected Hong Kong, but not Singapore, where the Government had already decided to build a naval base.

The limits on the Royal Navy accepted at Washington and London have often been criticised, but it was not really the principle of parity with the United States which limited British sea power. The underlying cause was parsimony on the part of both Conservative and Labour governments, and such were the constraints of the annual Estimates that the Admiralty was unable to lay down all the ships it wished even when not restricted by treaty. In November 1924 the then Chancellor of the Exchequer, Mr. Winston Churchill, made a determined effort to reduce future defence expenditure, so as to expand (slightly) social expenditure within balanced Budgets. The Treasury believed borrowing for government expenditure to be impossible, given the need to reduce the burden of national debt and to keep foreign confidence in sterling, without which the gold standard, soon to be re-established, could not be maintained. Given balanced Budgets, and the desire on the part of Churchill and other ministers to reduce taxation, the choice was one between guns and butter, and the Cabinet preferred the latter. The Cabinet was guided in its choice by the view of the Foreign Office that war with Japan was unlikely so long as existing conditions prevailed in Europe, and in 1925 the Committee of Imperial Defence,* a sub-committee of the Cabinet, ruled that

* This committee was known as the 'C.I.D.', the abbreviation used hereafter.

'aggressive action against the British Empire on the part of Japan within the next ten years is not a contingency seriously to be apprehended'.[13]

The dispute in 1924-5 between the Chancellor and the First Lord of the Admiralty, Mr. W. C. Bridgeman, over future construction of cruisers was such as to make the latter threaten to resign, with every possibility that the whole Board of Admiralty would follow him. In the end there were no resignations, but only two cruisers were laid down in 1925, instead of the five asked for by the Admiralty, and the programme for future years was similarly reduced. To add to the ill-feeling between the Admiralty and Treasury, the Treasury set up the Colwyn Committee, comprising a businessman and two former Permanent Secretaries of the Treasury, to make a general study of defence expenditure, and the tone of the committee's strictures on the need for further economies was much resented in the Admiralty. As it happened, the United States did not build up to treaty limits either, and, in numerical terms, the Royal Navy remained the largest in the world down to the Second World War.

The other two defence services fared much worse. Attempts to secure international agreement on limitation of air and land forces failed, but hopes of such agreement remained until the failure of the Geneva Disarmament Conference in 1932-3, and even after. Success in these fields comparable to naval disarmament was always unlikely, given that aircraft, at a time when civil and military aircraft were almost interchangeable, and land weapons were more easily concealed than ships, and that more countries were involved than the five naval powers. Nevertheless, British governments in the Nineteen-Twenties never aspired to the same standard of air power as sea power. A scheme of 1923 to expand the Air Force's metropolitan strength was well under way by 1925, with about half the proposed 52 squadrons formed, but in 1925 the scheme fell a victim of Churchill's economy moves, and the date for completion was put back from 1928 to 1935, and greater retrenchment after 1929 imposed further delay. As a result Britain stood only fifth among the world's air powers when expansion of the Air Force came to be mooted again towards the end of 1933, and while this might not have mattered much while France was the only air power within striking distance of the United Kingdom, there was much truth in the remark of Sir Edward Ellington, Chief of Air Staff from 1933 to 1937, that 'when we resumed expansion in 1934 we had a much smaller basis on which to build than we should have had had Winston been as enthusiastic for expansion when Chancellor as he was when a critic'.[14] At all events Germany overtook Britain as an air power in 1935-6, and increased her lead down to 1939.

The British Army fared even worse than the Air Force. Denied the need to prepare an expeditionary force by the Ten Year Rule of 1919, the War Office was unable to resist successive cuts by the Treasury in the Army Estimates, which were reduced from £62 million in 1922 to £36 million in 1932. By 1933 the Regular Army, which had stood at 259,000 men in 1914 had been reduced by economy and short-falls in recruitment to 206,000, with very little post-1918 equipment.[15]

The justification for such unpreparedness was the belief, propounded by the Cabinet in 1919 and 1925, that there would be no major war for ten years. The Ten Year Rule was extended indefinitely in 1928, after Hopkins, then Controller of Finance and Supply Services at the Treasury, put forward a memorandum to the Chancellor advising:

> If a major war is to be judged to be as distant now as it was in 1925 ... there is a great deal to be said for obtaining a new ruling, otherwise as the critical date 1935 begins to come nearer both the War Office and the Admiralty will be hastening their preparations to attain perfection by that year.
> It would be useful in connexion with future Army Votes, and more particularly in connexion with future Admiralty votes, to consider whether the Cabinet might not lay down an assumption that at any given date there will not be a major war for ten years from that date – the assumption to stand until, on the initiative of the Foreign Office, or one of the Fighting Services, or otherwise, the C.I.D. and the Cabinet decided to abrogate or alter it.[16]

Churchill took the matter up with his accustomed vigour, and, despite a few dissenting voices in the C.I.D., he had his way. The C.I.D. recommended, and the Cabinet laid down, 'that it should be assumed, for the purpose of framing the Estimates of the Fighting Services, that at any given date there will be no major war for ten years'.[17] This was the Ten Year Rule in its strongest form, and the C.I.D. did not recommend its cancellation until March 1932, after Japan had invaded Manchuria the previous September.

There can be little doubt that advisers at the Treasury, even Fisher, who was an advocate of rearmament from 1933, must share a heavy responsibility for retrenchment at the expense of defence down to that year. The rigid financial orthodoxy of the Treasury in the Nineteen-Twenties and early Nineteen-Thirties set tight limits to government expenditure,[18] and in the Nineteen-Twenties Fisher shared the prevailing optimism about the international environment. In 1928, when a Treasury official argued for reductions in the service Estimates in the light of the renewed Ten Year Rule and of the Kellogg–Briand Peace Pact of the same year, Fisher commented: 'I agree with the argument that the present is a real opportunity to show our faith in the peace professions we have signed'.[19] On the other hand, financial orthodoxy at home and optimism about foreign affairs were hardly the sole prerogatives of the Treasury, being held by every British government of the period, and the majority of the electorate. In the words of Lord Chatfield, who, as First Sea Lord from 1933 to 1938, and Minister for the Co-ordination of Defence from 1939 to 1940, was a severe critic of

Treasury control: 'The Services were not really emasculated by the Treasury, but by successive Governments acting through the Treasury and its powerful organisation'.[20]

The consensus of historical opinion seems to be that by 1932 retrenchment had reduced Britain's defence services and armaments industry to a dangerously low level.[21] Be that as it may, one would be hard put to argue that Britain was in a worse position than Germany in 1932, despite covert breaches of the Versailles Treaty by the Weimar Republic. Britain fell behind Germany in the years 1933-8, in which period it has been estimated that Germany spent about three times as much for military purposes as Britain.[22] Since Germany had a greater national product than the United Kingdom, some disparity was to be expected, and a fairer comparison of the military effort in the two countries is the proportion of gross national product devoted to military expenditure, which can be given, very approximately, in tabular form:

Percentage of G.N.P. devoted to
military expenditure[23]

		U.K.	Germany
1932	...	3	1
1933	...	3	3
1934	...	3	6
1935	...	3	8
1936	...	4	13
1937	...	6	13
1938	...	7	17
1939	...	18	23
1940	...	46	38

Whatever the exact figures there can be little doubt that, so far as rearmament was concerned, what Churchill called the 'locust years' ran from 1933 to 1938. Furthermore, there seems to be a *prima facie* case for believing that the Treasury's advice to the Government in these years resulted in defence being restricted unduly. When in 1932 the C.I.D. recommended that the Ten Year Rule be cancelled, the Chancellor of the Exchequer, Chamberlain, insisted, and the Cabinet agreed, that this cancellation should not be taken to justify an expansion of defence expenditure without regard to the current economic crisis.[24] In the event the defence Estimates rose in 1933 to £107·5 million from the £103 million of 1932, but this no more than restored the 1931 level of expenditure. It was not until February 1934 that the Cabinet was presented with a programme drawn up by officials in the Defence Requirements Sub-Committee of the C.I.D.,* proposing the expenditure of an additional £77 million spread over the next five years, with a further £16 million in subsequent years.[25] Although the D.R.C.'s proposals amounted to no more than the completion of plans originally

* This sub-committee was known as the 'D.R.C.', the abbreviation used hereafter.

drawn up for the different services at various times in the 'Twenties – plans which had been frustrated by the Ten Year Rule and retrenchment – ministers spent five months considering them, before deciding to halve the Army's proposed allocation of £40 million. This reduction was very much at Chamberlain's instigation.[26]

Events in 1935 compelled the Cabinet to review the situation. German rearmament was openly proclaimed in defiance of the Versailles Treaty, and was clearly going ahead rapidly, particularly in respect of the Luftwaffe. The British Government responded with an acceleration of the expansion of the R.A.F., with a view to having an air force equal to that which Germany was believed to be creating, and further increases in all three services were already under consideration when Mussolini's attack on Ethiopia emphasised the growing dangers of the international environment to an Empire which already faced possible threats from Germany and Japan. Attempts to put a halt to the growing arms race had almost no success. Hitler's offer to limit the German navy to 35 per cent of the Royal Navy was accepted in the Anglo-German Naval Treaty of 1935, but Japan made it clear that she would not renew the Washington and London Naval Treaties when they terminated at the end of 1936, and a second London Naval Conference in 1936 failed to replace these treaties, since Britain and the United States would not concede Japan's claim that all three powers should have a common upper limit to the size of their navies, and Japan would not settle for anything less. In 1935 the British Government entertained hopes of an air pact between Britain, Germany and France on the basis of parity, but these hopes proved unfounded.

In November 1935 the officials of the D.R.C. recommended a rearmament programme which would require a total expenditure by defence departments of £1038·5 million in the quinquennium 1936–40. Ministers trimmed this total in February 1936 by £22·8 million,[27] although it was known that even under this programme Britain would spend much less on rearmament than Germany. At the end of 1935 Germany was estimated in Whitehall to be spending the equivalent of £500 million a year on rearmament outside her budget, and it was thought that this figure might double in a peak year.[28] In the same year British defence expenditure was £137 million, and in the rearmament programme decided upon in February 1936 the Government did not intend spending more than £225 million in what was anticipated would be the peak year (1938).[29]

The adoption of this rearmament programme was followed almost immediately by Hitler's occupation of the Rhineland in March 1936, which represented a further sharp increase in the dangers facing Britain. As other nations expanded their armaments, and as new weapons were developed, it became necessary both to accelerate the authorised rearmament programme and to make piecemeal additions to it. As early as February 1937 a white paper warned the public that 'it would be imprudent to contemplate a total expenditure on defence during the next five years of much less than £1500 million'. Indeed Chamberlain, still Chancellor, told Parliament when introducing the first Defence Loans Bill that same month that the figure of £1500 million 'could not be regarded as final or certain'.[30] This growth in rearmament planning was checked four months later, however, when Chamberlain, now Prime Minister, presided over a Cabinet which approved the recommendation of the new Chancellor, Simon, that new defence projects of major importance should be postponed until the defence departments' programmes had been reviewed as a whole in the light of the nation's financial and industrial resources. Simon further suggested that the figure of £1500 million should be taken as a maximum for the quinquennium 1937–41. This was the figure before Sir Thomas Inskip, the Minister for the Co-ordination of Defence who carried out the review of the defence programmes, and, following upon a report by Inskip in December 1937, the Cabinet decided to give first priority to the defence of the United Kingdom and its trade routes, and to economise at the expense of the Army's expeditionary force, which was no longer to be prepared on a scale necessary to support potential European allies at the outbreak of a war. Although the defence departments' 'ration' of finance was eased somewhat in February 1938 to an aggregate of £1570 million, policy remained unchanged until the spring of 1939.[31] Treasury 'rationing' of finance, and Inskip's review of policy, were of fundamental importance at a critical time.

On the other hand British defence expenditure rose rapidly in 1939 – the War office's peacetime Estimates doubled over the previous year's – and by the outbreak of war Britain's arms production had caught up with, or exceeded, Germany's in important aspects. For example, British production of aircraft in 1939 was not far short of the German figure for the year, and Britain's monthly production actually overtook Germany's from September.[32] Even more surprising, Britain's tank production was greater on the eve of war than Germany's although, as was the case with aircraft, Germany possessed more because of greater production in the past. Indeed, from the outbreak of war overall production of armaments was actually less in Germany than in Britain.[33] Certainly the quality of British aircraft and tanks in production in 1939 was uneven, some types being older designs kept in production to employ labour until newer designs were ready, but the overall production figures seem to suggest that more could have been done to prepare for war, or to deter Hitler, had only Britain's main rearmament effort been made earlier. From that conclusion it is a short step to assume that, had the Treasury not restricted defence expenditure, Chamberlain would have had a stronger hand to play at the Munich Conference in 1938.

In particular, Britain's failure to match German aircraft production between 1935 and 1939 placed a fearful responsibility upon statesmen who had been warned by 'experts' that air attacks would be devastating. Again, the Cabinet's decision in 1937 not to prepare an expeditionary force to support possible European allies from the outbreak of a war seems particularly foolish, especially in the light of what we now know about the German concept of *blitzkrieg*, which was based on a maximum concentration of frontline forces, and surprise, to achieve victory at the outset of a campaign, with a minimum of reserves. At the time, of course, the full power of the German panzers had not been revealed, and, indeed, at the time of the Rhineland crisis in 1936 the French army was stronger than the German, while even in 1938 and 1939 the German army was outnumbered, on paper, by the combined French and Czech or Polish armies. But the lack of an effective expeditionary force before 1939 left the British exposed to the taunt that they would fight to the last Frenchman.

It was certainly reasonable that military men should have been indignant about being kept short of funds, and the explanation which follows of why the Treasury acted as it did is not intended to imply that defence departments were wrong to ask for more money than they were given, indeed at times the departments might well have pressed for more than they asked for. Even so, it was the attitude of the Treasury which was crucial, and this book is an account of the influence of the Treasury on the decisions and actions of the Cabinet and the defence departments in the years 1932-9. The measure of 'influence' is taken to be the extent to which the Treasury caused ministers or departments to depart from courses which they otherwise would have followed regarding rearmament. If the Treasury's influence were not to appear to be wholly negative, it seemed to the author essential to ask what were the Treasury's functions; to identify influential personalities in, or associated with, the Treasury, and to try to understand what they were trying to do. The results of these enquiries are embodied in Chapter II, which also contains descriptions of how various key personalities were in harmony or clashed with each other, and of how men's relationships and importance changed in a few years of growing tension.

Problems in deciding what proportion of the nation's industrial and financial resources should be devoted to production of armaments provide the theme for Chapter III, which is a study in political economy in a period of uncertainty, and is not an attempt to estimate by how much more the Treasury might have relaxed the purse strings if there had been 'perfect knowledge' of when and where war would break out, and of how business confidence, and trade union attitudes, would alter as the country's danger and the economy's difficulties increased. Men's perceptions of the country's danger changed between 1932, when the need for economic recovery seemed paramount, and 1938-9, when war seemed imminent although not yet certain, and these changing perceptions are taken into account.

The Treasury's arguments for relating rearmament to the country's industrial capacity and international purchasing power led on to the problem of deciding priorities in defence policy, and the Treasury's advice and influence on the extent and timing of the various parts of the defence programmes form the subject of Chapter IV. The consistent theme in defence policy was the need to deter aggression while diplomacy removed possible causes of conflict, and the Treasury wished defence policy to take into account what industry could provide in the short term, and what the economy could maintain in the long term in peace, or during the likely duration of a war. Treasury views on what policy should be varied as costs and production problems increased: for example, from 1934 to 1937 the Treasury supported the Air Staff's attempts to match German bomber production, but once it seemed that British industry could not match German output under peacetime conditions, the Treasury put pressure on a reluctant Air Staff to give priority to defensive aircraft.

On the whole, the Treasury was successful in persuading the Cabinet to make decisions on priorities down to 1939, when the international situation became such as to lead ministers to discount financial warnings. On the other hand the Treasury was much less successful in persuading defence departments to abandon their own ideas as to priorities even after the Cabinet had laid down priorities which accorded with the Treasury's ideas. Thus the Air Ministry continued to aim at bomber 'parity' with Germany even after the Cabinet had directed that fighters should have priority; the Admiralty tended to exceed its authorised programme while pursuing its own ideas as to the size of fleet necessary to fight Germany and Japan simultaneously, and the War Office was reluctant to give as low a priority to the re-equipment of its field units as Cabinet decisions seemed to suggest. Chapter V discusses how successful the Treasury was in using the power of the purse to keep departments to its interpretation of Cabinet policy, and shows how selective use of Treasury control enabled the Air Ministry to have first call on such finance and new industrial capacity as was available for defence.

Conclusions to be drawn from this four-part analysis include that certain civilians in the Treasury – notably Chamberlain, Fisher, Hopkins and Bridges – exercised at different times and in different ways considerable and constructive influence on defence policy. The financial limits set to rearmament by the Treasury were not unreasonable, given industrial limits and a growing balance of payments deficit, and certainly there was a need for selective rearmament, and the financial limits were designed to force the Cabinet to decide which parts of the rearmament programme should be completed first. The difficulty experienced by defence departments in carrying out even those parts of the rearmament programme which received first call on finance suggests that weaker Treasury influence and control might have resulted in larger plans, but more incomplete forces, in 1939–40. Greater government control over private finance and industry would have made possible greater rearmament, but the Government of the day was unwilling to take the necessary powers, and Treasury advice was framed accordingly. The Treasury's advice is open to detailed criticism, but it played a vital role in forcing those responsible for defence policy to make choices which otherwise might have been avoided until forced upon them by events at a later date. This study in administrative, economic, military and political history shows how the Treasury's functions gave it a wider view of events than any one defence department, and even if one does not agree with the Treasury's interpretation of what it saw, the attempt to understand the Treasury view gives a new perspective on British defence policy in 1932–9.

II

The Treasury and Its Role

This chapter deals with the machinery of government as it existed in the Nineteen-Thirties from the point of view of showing how the Treasury could influence defence policy. The term 'Treasury' is taken throughout to mean the department of which the Chancellor of the Exchequer is the political head. Chamberlain was Chancellor for five and a half years before becoming Prime Minister in 1937, and there is no doubt that thereafter he retained a concern for the Exchequer which must have strengthened the hand of the Treasury. But although the Prime Minister had the official title of 'First Lord of the Treasury' it would be confusing to equate the influence of the Treasury with that of the Prime Minister, especially since Chamberlain departed radically from the 'Treasury view' on defence policy early in 1939, despite protests by leading Treasury officials. By the same token the term 'Treasury officials' is used only in connection with civil servants directly responsible to the Chancellor, and therefore does not include members of the Prime Minister's Office, or the Office of the Minister for the Co-ordination of Defence, although the pay of such officials was entered in the Treasury Vote in the annual Estimates.

The key questions in the formation of any defence policy are: what proportion of the nation's resources is to be devoted to defence, and how should resources devoted to defence be allocated between defence services? The first question is one of politics and economics, and it comes as no surprise to find that in answering it the Government leaned heavily upon the advice of the Treasury, as the central department of finance. Less obvious, but no less important, was the Treasury's influence on how the second question, on the allocation of resources, was answered. There was no Ministry of Defence before the war and the allocation of funds was negotiated directly between the Treasury and three independent defence departments. This gave the Treasury a co-ordinating function in interdepartmental policy-making, and even in individual departments' execution of policy. What follows shows how Treasury officials could become informed about defence problems, and which officials advised which ministers; also how the Treasury through financial control could force ministers and defence departments to make decisions, which otherwise might have been avoided, about priorities; how Treasury officials saw to it that departments followed priorities laid down by the Cabinet, and how interdepartmental competition for industrial resources was reduced.

It will become clear that the Treasury itself was not a monolithic body and that its policy as a department could not be created by a single individual. But before going into details of the Treasury's internal organisation it may be best to outline the constitutional position of the Treasury. Officially defence policy was co-ordinated through the C.I.D. with the assistance, on purely military matters, of its Chiefs of Staff Sub-Committee.* The C.O.S. submitted an annual review of the country's military position in the light of political information supplied by the Foreign, India and Colonial Offices. General policy was discussed in the C.I.D. with ministerial and military members taking an equal part, and its recommendations were forwarded to the Cabinet for approval. Each defence department was supposed to prepare its annual sketch Estimates in the light of the general policy approved by the Cabinet, and forward them, early in the autumn, to the Chancellor of the Exchequer for review in the light of the overall financial position. In fact decisions on high policy had often still to be made when the different departmental claims were forwarded to the Treasury, and the coat of policy might well have to be cut according to the cloth of finance. In the event of the Chancellor and the minister responsible for a department being unable to agree to a limit to that department's expenditure in the coming financial year, the matter would be referred to the Cabinet for arbitration. Defence expenditure always required Cabinet approval in principle, and Treasury approval in detail.

Although contact was maintained between the Treasury and the defence departments throughout the year, it was at the point when the Chancellor received the sketch Estimates that the formal process known as Treasury control might be said to begin. Treasury control involved both control of expenditure and control over establishments, but the former was the more important since policy was determined in the light of what finance could be spared. The Chancellor, advised by his officials, could criticise defence departments' proposals either on the ground that finance was not available, or on the merits of the proposals themselves. Since not all proposals included in the Estimates could be examined in detail by Treasury officials before the Estimates were submitted to Parliament in February, or at the beginning of March, it was customary for the Treasury to reserve some matters, especially new proposals, for further consideration, and if the Treasury later found it could not approve these proposals, the money allocated to cover them could not be spent, even although already voted by Parliament.[1]

Ministers responsible for defence departments were jealous of their constitutional right to take disputes with the Chancellor of the Exchequer to the Cabinet, and they resented any suggestion that Treasury

* Hereafter referred to as C.O.S.

officials had any independent authority. Fisher himself denied that Treasury officials constituted a separate power 'behind the thone', and claimed that instead of Treasury control it was right to speak only of the Chancellor's control of finance.[2] Treasury officials did, however, have the right to advise, to consult and to warn – and in view of their experience, and of fresh memories of the economic crisis of 1931, such warnings could not be lightly disregarded by ministers.

Moreover, in controlling expenditure Treasury officials had a responsibility to Parliament to ensure that public money was spent year by year as voted by Parliament, and a corpus of rules relating to expenditure by government departments had been built up since Gladstone's time by the Parliamentary Committee of Public Accounts,* in consultation with Treasury officials. Each defence department's Estimates were divided into Votes – for example, the Admiralty's Vote 1 covered wages, Vote 2 covered victualling and clothing and so on; savings on one Vote could be transferred to meet excesses on another only with the approval of the Treasury, and the Treasury could use this power, known as virement, only in urgent cases. Otherwise when a department wished to exceed its Estimates it had to ask the Treasury for a Supplementary Estimate which would then have to be submitted to the Cabinet and Parliament for approval. In this way Treasury officials were kept informed of how the Estimates were working out. The Treasury was also responsible in conjunction with the P.A.C. and the Estimates Committee for the rules relating to the placing of government contracts – and the fact that departments had to go to the Treasury for approval of certain contracts provided an extra check on expenditure.

The responsibility of ensuring that the taxpayer got the maximum value for his pound was not the Treasury's alone, for each department's permanent civilian head was also its accounting officer, with responsibility for financial criticism and control within his department. Each year the departmental accounts were subject to scrutiny by the Comptroller and Auditor General, an official responsible to Parliament and independent of the Treasury, and the permanent civilian head of each department had to explain any anomalies in the accounts to the P.A.C. Lord Bridges observed that when the Treasury asked a department if some proposed expenditure had been fully worked out, the premonition of what kind of figure the permanent civilian head of that department would cut before the P.A.C. was a powerful inducement for that department to work out its proposals more carefully.[3] Being an element in parliamentary control of expenditure strengthened the authority of the Treasury, while at the same time placing upon its officials an obligation to abide by the rules of public finance.

* Hereafter referred to as P.A.C.

Ministers and the Treasury

Although the Treasury was the Chancellor of the Exchequer's department, the Prime Minister's title of 'First Lord of the Treasury' was not an empty one. The Permanent Secretary of the Treasury might tender advice directly on his own initiative to the Prime Minister, and the files of the Prime Minister's Office show that Fisher did so from time to time. The Minister for the Co-ordination of Defence, a post created in 1936, also received advice from Treasury officials from time to time, and any attempt to explain the influence of the Treasury at the ministerial level must consider the interplay of the roles and personalities of the men who held the post of Prime Minister, Chancellor of the Exchequer and Minister for the Co-ordination of Defence.

This interplay was reflected in the close links maintained between Treasury officials and officials in the Prime Minister's Office and the office of the Minister for the Co-ordination of Defence. Fisher and Wilson, the Prime Minister's 'confidential adviser', had long enjoyed a relationship of great mutual trust and confidence, which developed into a feeling of real affection. It had been Fisher who had brought Wilson out of the Ministry of Labour to become Chief Industrial Adviser to His Majesty's Government, at the Board of Trade, and who later, in 1935, had sent him to the Prime Minister's Office.[4] Once established in the Prime Minister's favour, however, Wilson was in no way dependent on Fisher. Bridges' work in the Treasury dealing with defence expenditure involved some contact with Mr. H. G. (later Sir Graham) Vincent, secretary to the Minister for the Co-ordination of Defence, and they were on sufficiently close terms for Bridges to address Vincent as 'Dear Tubby'.

At the ministerial level roles varied with personalities, and the key character was that of Chamberlain, Chancellor of the Exchequer from November 1931 to May 1937 and thereafter Prime Minister. Neither of his predecessors as Prime Minister, Mr. Ramsay MacDonald or Mr. Stanley Baldwin, had provided dynamic leadership, the former being in failing health by 1933, and the latter being past his prime when he took over in June 1935. As Chancellor, Chamberlain fought for the Treasury view in the Cabinet with all the authority of heir-apparent to the premiership, and, being self-confident and prone to seek his own solution for problems, he was prepared to take the initiative in considering the problems of defence policy.[5] His successor, Simon, on the other hand, had no such prospects of future political patronage, and the Treasury files give no hint of Simon making an original contribution to strategy. Indeed one wonders why Chamberlain appointed to the Exchequer a man whom he himself had once described as able to summarise the pros and cons of a case but 'temperamentally unable to make up his mind to action when a difficult situation arose'.[6] Simon never disagreed with his Prime Minister's views on defence, even when his officials did so, so that Chamberlain continued to be the man whom Treasury officials had to convince if they were to influence policy.

It was natural that the mutual bonds made over almost six years should have been slow to dissolve, but having the Prime Minister's ear was not in itself enough. The Treasury still had to make its case in the Cabinet, and here the Treasury may not have benefited from Chamberlain's accession to the Premiership. As Chancellor Chamberlain was described by one Cabinet colleague as a 'human dynamo . . . alert and brisk of speech', and he was praised by a First Lord of the Admiralty for his grasp of detail.[7] Simon, on the other hand, on accepting the Chancellorship admitted to having no special knowledge of national finance, and as late as July 1939 he does not seem to have felt himself to be the complete master of his brief. In that month Hopkins was asked to come before the Cabinet to explain the Treasury's views on the economic consequences of rearmament. A few weeks later Wilson and Bridges gave Hankey the impression in a conversation that Simon had 'very much deteriorated'.[8]

Of the junior Treasury ministers – the six men who successively held the office of Financial Secretary in the years 1932-9[9] – little need be said so far as their work in the Treasury was concerned. The post had a traditional pre-eminence among the junior ministerial posts and was a test of parliamentary competence, since the Financial Secretary acted in Parliament as the lieutenant of the Chancellor of the Exchequer and had to answer questions on a wide range of subjects. It is not surprising, therefore, that the post was usually a step towards promotion; but any Financial Secretary who had executive ambitions was apt to find the post profoundly frustrating, since the tradition of the time was to exclude him from the formation of major policy. He was briefed how to answer debates and questions, but if he disagreed with those briefs he had little chance of getting his way. This certainly applied to rearmament policy, though, as the volume of C.I.D. business rose in 1938-9 the Financial Secretary occasionally sat in on C.I.D. sub-committees, with a Treasury official at his side, to state the Treasury view.[10]

The fact that a Cabinet minister had once been Financial Secretary might, or might not, be significant. Mr. Leslie Hore-Belisha was Financial Secretary from 1932 to 1934, and thereafter he was very much a Chamberlain man, which was no doubt one reason why Chamberlain appointed him Secretary of State for War. But a former Financial Secretary need not be his former Chancellor's satellite. Duff Cooper, who was also a Financial Secretary during Chamberlain's chancellorship, disagreed constantly with Chamberlain, both as Secretary of State for War (when Chamberlain was still Chancellor) and as First Lord of the Admiralty (when Chamberlain was Prime Minister). The personal relations which Hore-Belisha developed while at the Treasury were not necessarily conducive to greater Treasury control over War Office expenditure. During 1937–8 Fisher and Hore-Belisha were so close that their relationship was described by Wilson as an 'affaire'.[11] Hore-Belisha certainly consulted Fisher as well as Chamberlain before making changes in the Army Council, and Fisher was in favour of Sir Cyril Deverell's replacement as Chief of the Imperial General Staff* by Lord Gort in December 1937.[12] On the other hand Sir James Grigg, himself a former Treasury official, who in the 'Thirties was working with the Government of India, complained in January 1938 that 'Fisher is in Hore-Belisha's pocket. ... Now that Fisher has adopted Hore-Belisha as his own the Treasury aren't much of a front line of defence for us' (in resisting War Office proposals which would increase Indian defence expenditure).[13] Grigg was exaggerating, but Fisher had written to Hore-Belisha saying that: 'If there is at any time anything you think I can do, you can count on me, Bless you, Warren'.[14]

Another minister with whom Treasury officials might have direct dealings was the Minister for the Co-ordination of Defence, a position of Cabinet rank created in February 1936, partly, if not wholly, it would seem, to appease those critics of the Government who called for the creation of a Ministry of Defence. The Minister for the Co-ordination of Defence, however, lacked a department and had no executive powers or jurisdiction over the apportionment of the available resources between the three Services.[15] Officially the new minister's functions were to reduce the pressure of work on the Prime Minister by acting as his deputy as chairman of the C.I.D. and thus having an oversight over strategy, while also taking over from the President of the Board of Trade as chairman of the Principal Supply Officers Committee, the C.I.D.'s sub-committee co-ordinating the supply arrangements of the three services. Chamberlain admitted that there was some truth in Churchill's criticism that the new minister might be so occupied with supply problems that he would not have time to attend to strategy, but went on to say that he (Chamberlain) did not believe that the minister 'should himself be a strategist', but that he should 'see that strategical problems are fairly and thoroughly worked out by the strategists'[16] – a remark which may give an insight into the Chancellor's conception of of own role and that of his department with regard to defence policy.

Both Chamberlain and Simon saw Sir Thomas Inskip, the first Minister for the Co-ordination of Defence, as a man who could work with the C.O.S. without causing friction or stirring up inter-service rivalries.[17] According to Inskip's successor, Lord Chatfield, as soon as he (Chatfield) took office in January 1939 Simon wrote to him saying that Inskip had worked closely with the Chancellor to cut down the service

* Hereafter referred to as C.I.G.S.

Estimates, and that it was hoped that Chatfield would do likewise. Chatfield refused.[18] As for Inskip's role, Chatfield's evidence is borne out to some extent by the official files, but it would be fairer to say that Inskip tried to reconcile the diverging views of the Treasury and the defence departments by consensus and consent. Chamberlain, while Chancellor, did speak of it being 'necessary to handle (Inskip) firmly', but Inskip was no tool of the Treasury. It is true he was advised by Treasury officials while reviewing defence policy in 1937-8 with a view to limiting future expenditure by the defence departments, but Hopkins observed before the Minister's report that 'it is impossible of course at present to prophesy Sir T. Inskip's conclusions', and after the report Bridges commented that 'it is by no means as satisfactory a report from our point of view as we had hoped for'.[19]

Much of what follows concerns advice given by officials to ministers, and it is worth stressing the obvious constitutional point that responsibility for decisions lay with ministers, and that ministers did not always follow officials' advice. Personality counted for much, and there is no doubt that the dominant personality among ministers was Chamberlain.

The Treasury Officials

Immediately prior to Fisher's appointment as sole Permanent Secretary in 1919 there had been three joint Permanent Secretaries in charge of the Treasury, and even after his appointment the Treasury continued to be organised for a time not as one department but as three, with three Controllers responsible respectively for Finance, Supply and Establishments. Each Controller had the status and pay of an official head of a major government department, and, while Fisher had general powers of co-ordination, supervision and direction, the Treasury Minute of 1919 conferring these powers made it clear he was not expected to concern himself with the detailed work of the Controllers. Under this system the Permanent Secretary's position was, in Fisher's words, 'deliciously vague, floating somewhere rather Olympian'.[20] In 1927, however, a first step was taken towards a more centralised organisation when two of the departments, Finance and Supply, were combined under one Controller, Hopkins. Then, in 1932, the then Controller of the Establishments Department became Permanent Secretary at the Home Office, and Fisher took the opportunity to abolish the rank of Controller, and to convert the Treasury into a unified department. Hopkins was given the title of Second Secretary, and he retained the status of a head of department, and acted as the Permanent Secretary's deputy for financial matters. The work formerly done by the Controllers was given to less prestigious Under-Secretaries.

But it would be wrong to think of the re-organisation of the Treasury in 1932 as giving Fisher a monopoly of official influence. The work of the Treasury was more than he alone could comprehend. He publicly admitted that financial technicalities were beyond him, and Hopkins felt quite free to tender advice contrary to that of Fisher to the Chancellor on financial matters. The Under-Secretaries had personal access to the Chancellor, and might communicate directly with other ministers provided that Fisher and Hopkins knew what was going on. Treasury officials referred all important decisions to the Chancellor for ministerial authority. In such cases a memorandum would be prepared by the junior Treasury official who knew most about the matter, and the memorandum would be forwarded, with comments, by one of the Under-Secretaries to Hopkins. Hopkins would then consult with Fisher, unless a purely financial issue were at stake, and the memorandum would be modified in the light of their deliberations and forwarded to the Chancellor with their comments. The emphasis was on teamwork, and usually there would be a good deal of informal discussion.[21]

Hopkins thus emerges as a key figure. He seems to have been exceptionally able as well as respected and well-liked. Sir Roy Harrod described him as unique in his generation in his ability to meet Keynes on the latter's chosen ground of economics without Keynes having the better of the argument. Although Keynes' and Hopkins' views were widely divergent at the beginning of the 'Thirties, Keynes admitted that Hopkins did understand public finance. A classics scholar at Cambridge, Hopkins had been grounded in public finance during twenty-five years in the Inland Revenue, which he entered as a first division clerk in 1902. He was chairman of the Board for five years before he was transferred to the Treasury.[22] To his colleagues Hopkins was known as 'Hoppy'. He is remembered 'with affection and great respect as a kind but reserved man of formidable intelligence, with a sceptical view of human motives which saved him from quick enthusiasms. He was not an innovator like Fisher, but his experience, his intelligence and his capacity for taking up, developing and above all expressing in simple but compelling terms ideas which others may have originated, made him the most influential of advisers'.[23]

Fisher left Hopkins to run most of the Treasury machine while he himself concentrated on what he considered to be the most important issues. Fisher once told the P.A.C. that 'if you suggest [Hopkins'] brain works quicker than mine I should agree', and added that the official Head of the Civil Service had 'a lot of other things to do besides departmental Treasury work',[24] and, indeed, Fisher had been much absorbed in the Nineteen-Twenties with reform of the Civil Service. The work of the department – which was very much smaller than the present Treasury – was divided between eleven divisions plus a Financial Enquiries Branch. Each division was headed by a principal assistant secretary or an assistant secretary, and the divisions were grouped according to their function under one or other of the Under-

Secretaries. Sir Frederick Phillips supervised the work of the two divisions dealing with Finance, together with the Financial Enquiries Branch. Mr. J. A. N. (from 1938 Sir Alan) Barlow supervised the work of the divisions dealing with Supply; and Sir James Rae supervised those dealing with Establishment questions.*

Phillips was invariably consulted on financial matters. He has been described by a former colleague as having the manner of a none-too-genial bear, but also as a most able administrator and a brilliant mathematician. To Keynes 'F.P.' was

> a character ... with his bulky frame, his great head and his disconcertingly direct gaze over the top of his spectacles. ... If a point was good he took it without wasting time: if it was bad his premonitary rumble foretold a plain and incisive criticism. ... To watch him sweep together a scattered argument, pose the essential issues, and express a cool constructive judgment upon them was a lesson. ...[25]

Phillips was the architect of the Budget. For his calculations of what would be available for defence Phillips relied upon estimates of future revenue at a given rate of taxation supplied by the Inland Revnue and H.M. Customs Intelligence Branch, made in the light of forecasts of future trade trends supplied by the Board of Trade. Government loans were handled jointly by Hopkins and Phillips, in consultation with the Bank of England, and its Governor, Mr. Montagu Norman, so that when, from 1935, Fisher advocated a defence loan, he had to leave it to Hopkins and the others to decide how much could be raised.

The effects of rearmament and borrowing on Britain's balance of payments had to be considered. Here Phillips' most senior lieutenant was Mr. S. D. (later Sir David) Waley, the principal assistant secretary in charge of the division dealing with overseas finance. Waley has been described by former subordinates as a man who attracted great devotion. He had enormous technical capacity, with an intuitive, elliptic mode of thought, and never allowed growing balance of payments difficulties in 1937-9 to depress him.[26] His tiny division was typical of the small scale of the Treasury's organisation – in 1938 overseas finance was dealt with by Waley, a principal and two assistant principals. The Treasury also maintained a number of financial attachés abroad, with one each in Washington, Paris, Berlin and China.

Advice might also be forthcoming from another of Phillips' lieutenants, Mr. R. G. (later Sir Ralph) Hawtrey, the assistant secretary in charge of the Financial Enquiries Branch. Like Phillips, Hawtrey had read mathematics at Cambridge, and his understanding of economics was what he had derived from his work as a Treasury official. Unlike Phillips, Hawtrey was not concerned with day-to-day administration – the Financial Enquiries Branch amounted to no more than a little room inhabited only by himself and an assistant. Treasury officials

* See Appendix I for organisation chart.

would forward queries to Hawtrey from time to time, but there was no pressure of business, and he was free to contemplate problems of economics and to write a number of books on the subject. In 1928–9 he had been given leave to lecture in economics at Harvard University, and his reputation was such that he has often been regarded as an academic economist. Fisher described Hawtrey's work as 'metaphysical', but in 1937, before a Treasury Organisation Committee, Phillips stated that he could not do without him. Hawtrey, Phillips explained, understood professional economists in a way that he did not, so that as well as giving advice on his own account Hawtrey made intelligible what other economists were advising.[27]

In fact Phillips understood professional economists well enough to become an advocate within the Treasury of ideas culled from economists on the Economic Advisory Council's Committee on Economic Information, a body designed to bring together official and informed outside opinion.* The Treasury officials on the committee were Phillips and Sir Frederick Leith-Ross, who held the title of Chief Economic Adviser to His Majesty's Government. Too much should not be read into the latter's title, however, as Leith-Ross himself described it as a misnomer, in that his duties principally involved representing Britain in international negotiations. He had a seat in the Board of Trade as well as the Treasury, and although he had been Deputy Controller of Finance prior to his appointment as Chief Economic Adviser in 1932 he was no longer concerned in departmental business after that date. He did, however, tender advice from time to time.[28]

Barlow became Under-Secretary with responsibility for Supply in 1934, his predecessor, Sir Ernest Strohmenger, having moved on to become Deputy Chairman of the Unemployment Assistance Board after only two years in the Treasury. Barlow himself was a newcomer to the department, having previously been the Prime Minister's Principal Private Secretary, and before that he had been at the Ministry of Labour. He was an easy-going, popular man, who appeared not to contribute much by way of original thought, but Sir Christopher Bullock, the former permanent Secretary of the Air Ministry, was too harsh when he described Barlow (and Vincent) as 'little more than good clerks'. If Barlow appeared to add little more than his initials to memoranda on defence this was because the compiler of the memoranda, Bridges, his subordinate, left little more to be said.[29]

Of the Supply divisions working under Barlow one only dealt with the Votes of the defence departments. This was '5D', whose full

---

* The Economic Advisory Council (hereafter referred to as E.A.C.) had been set up during the Depression to be an economic counterpart to the C.I.D., but had ceased to meet in full session by 1932. Its Sub-committee on Economic Information continued to submit reports through the Cabinet Secretariat.

range of functions in July 1936 included: policy and matériel questions relating to the Navy, Army and Air Force; and supply questions relating to civil aviation, colonies, C.I.D., contracts, Dominions, foreign services, Home Office (for air raid precautions), India Office, the Middle East, and many other matters, such as deceased and distressed British subjects abroad.[30] There was little logic to this grouping of functions, and at the beginning of 1937, as Hopkins noted: 'the increase of work in the international sphere . . . made it desirable . . . that some steps should be taken as a matter of urgency to relieve the resultant pressure on the staff of 5D, particularly its Head', and a new division, 5BD, was created to take over 5D's functions relating to the Empire (except Indian defence) and foreign services.[31] In April 1938 5D was renamed Defence Matériel Division, or D.M.

The man in charge of 5D, or D.M., from the autumn of 1934 to the summer of 1938 was Bridges, a man destined, like Hopkins, to rise to the top as Permanent Secretary of the Treasury. The years 1932-8 saw Bridges rise from the rank of a principal at the Treasury to the post of Secretary of the Cabinet. One of his duties as head of 5D was to brief the Chancellor for meetings of the C.I.D., offering comments on memoranda by the defence departments. The outstanding quality of his work early attracted Chamberlain's notice, and Chamberlain made a point of getting to know him. Chamberlain described Bridges as a 'man of exceptional ability and brilliance and possessing attractive personal qualities', an opinion that has been echoed by two of the men outside the Treasury who worked most closely with him, Lord Swinton, Secretary of State for Air, 1935-8, and Lord Ismay, who was appointed Secretary to the C.I.D. at the same time as Bridges went to the Cabinet Office.[32] Bridges' grasp of defence problems, and Chamberlain's regard for him, made the head of 5D much more influential than an assistant secretary or principal assistant secretary would normally have been, but this influence was not resented in the least by his superiors, and Bridges enjoyed a friendly and informal relationship with Hopkins.[33] When Bridges left to become Secretary of the Cabinet in August 1938 Simon noted in his diary: 'A fearful loss to me and to the Treasury, for he has every aspect of rearmament at his fingers' ends'.[34]

Bridges' subordinates also held him in the highest regard. He was shy, but his enthusiasm for his work was infectious, and seldom can leadership have been given with so little conscious effort and so much success. He was quite unconscious of the high standards he set, and at the end of a long session of discussion or drafting he would often refer to the episode as 'great fun'.[35] At the same time he was fully aware of the human factors behind the figures in which he was dealing. He himself had served as an infantry officer on the Western Front from 1915 to 1917, when he was severely wounded, and, twenty years later, while reviewing defence expenditure, he noted:

I have still sufficiently vivid recollections of the days of 1915 – when our gunners, when called upon for help by the front-line infantry, used to tell us that they had only a couple of rounds per gun per day – to have nothing but the strongest sympathies for an Army insufficiently supplied with munitions.[36]

The work done by 5D increased enormously from 1934 onwards, and this was reflected in a growth of the division's exiguous staff. When Sir John Winnifrith – then a raw assistant principal – joined 5D in 1934 the division had only three officials of the administrative grade dealing with defence expenditure: Bridges himself (then an assistant secretary), Mr. G. E. A. Grey, a principal, and Winnifrith. This, Sir John commented, was the perfect co-ordinating machine, since each of these officials knew what each of the defence departments was doing.[37] But the volume of work quickly increased, and before the end of 1935 Grey was dealing with Army, Air Force and C.I.D. work, while Mr. E. E. B. Speed, a principal who had served in the War Office, dealt with the Navy. By 1937 there were three principals, each dealing with a different defence department: Grey handled Air Ministry matters; Mr. (later Sir) Edmund Compton, who had replaced Speed in 1936, handled War Office matters, and Mr. T. L. (later Sir Leslie) Rowan, handled Admiralty matters.[38] Both Compton and Rowan were to become well-known civil servants – Sir Edmund as Comptroller and Auditor General, and, later, as Britain's first 'Ombudsman', or Parliamentary Commissioner for Administration (in 1967), and Sir Leslie as Churchill's wartime private secretary.

Of Bridges' predecessor in charge of 5D, Mr. R. A. Grieve, little need be said. Grieve suffered a breakdown in June 1934 before the defence programme had got under way, and it was this accident which brought Bridges to 5D. Bridges' successor in August 1938 was Mr. B. W. (later Sir Bernard) Gilbert, an able principal assistant secretary, who, however, inevitably lacked Bridges' familiarity with defence questions. Nevertheless Gilbert impressed his superiors and in 1939, along with Waley, he was promoted to Under-Secretary when Barlow and Phillips were promoted to the newly-created post of Third Secretary (a change designed to relieve Hopkins of part of his work-load).

There was one other Treasury division which dealt with defence questions. This was 8D, which was headed by Bridges from April 1934 until early in 1935, when he was relieved of the double burden of running two divisions. 8D was one of six divisions under Rae, the Under-Secretary dealing with Establishments. 8D dealt with personnel questions of the defence departments, but unlike 5D, it was not concerned with overall defence policy. For example, when the War Office decided to mechanise the cavalry it was 5D which considered the merits of the proposal and its implications for defence expenditure,

while 8D was responsible for considering the War Office's proposals for
new rates of pay and conditions of service to accompany the change
from horses to armoured vehicles. 8D reviewed these proposals not
only on their merits as a means of attracting a new type of mechanically-
minded recruit, but also from the point of view of the possible implications on the recruitment and wage bill of other departments. If Army
mechanics were to be paid more, the claims of equivalent grades in the
other services had to be considered. 8D and 5D kept closely in touch
with each other, and members of the two divisions met informally
once a day in a 'tea club' within the Treasury.[39]

The men who advised the Chancellor on defence policy were an
élite. The department's advice on how much finance could be found for
defence was formulated, after consultation with Fisher, by Hopkins
and Phillips, while Fisher, Hopkins, Barlow and Bridges (and later
Gilbert) discussed how that money could be spent. To this group
should be added Mr. J. D. B. (later Sir Donald) Fergusson, Chamberlain's Principal Private Secretary from 1931 to 1936, whom Chamberlain much admired. Fergusson was a very forceful character, and was
very close to Fisher.[40] When briefing the Chancellor on defence
questions he seems to have reinforced Fisher's arguments. The original
minds at the official level in the Treasury so far as the military aspects
of defence policy were concerned were Fisher and Bridges, but Hopkins
too was important on account of his ability to analyse other people's
arguments.

The Treasury and the Committee of Imperial Defence

As noted above, the official machinery for inter-service co-ordination
was the C.I.D. Treasury participation in the C.I.D. organisation ensured that Treasury officials were kept informed about defence policy
even as it was being evolved, and although for much of the time
Treasury official representatives acted only as observers, they briefed
the Chancellor of the Exchequer who could, and did, criticise the
defence departments' policy proposals and suggest alternatives at
ministerial meetings. The C.I.D. itself, with a permanent panel of
about a dozen Cabinet ministers together with the C.O.S. and the
Permanent Secretary of the Treasury, was on the large side to be an
effective committee, and its detailed work was done in sub-committees.
Since executive decisions were taken in the Cabinet or in Cabinet
sub-committees there was a tendency for the main C.I.D. to become a
'rubber stamp' for its sub-committee's proposals. C.I.D. sub-committees proliferated during the 'Thirties, and by the end of 1937 there
were over 50. Hopkins for one thought that while no doubt there were
many things for which committees were essential, C.I.D. sub-committees, with their advisory function, were 'not the means to speed and

decision in action' and were 'apt to relax the individual's sense of responsibility'.[41]

Holding together the maze of sub-committees was the C.I.D. Secretariat, headed until he retired in July 1938 by Sir Maurice Hankey, who was also Secretary to the Cabinet. Hankey had been the C.I.D.'s Secretary since 1912, and his unrivalled experience meant he was much more than just a secretary. He drafted the report which was accepted almost in its entirety by the Cabinet in February 1936 as the rearmament programme, and his advice seems to have weighed heavily with Inskip when that minister drew up his influential report on defence policy in 1937. Hankey and Fisher were intimates, but they could also be rivals for the ear of the Prime Minister, and in 1934 Hankey resorted to *argumentum ad hominem* when he wrote to Baldwin that Fisher's judgement was not to be relied upon in view of the latter's ill-health.[42] The rivalry went back to Bonar Law's premiership, when Lloyd George's machinery of government was being dismantled, and Fisher had tried to have Hankey and the Cabinet Secretariat brought into the Treasury, subordinate to himself. Hankey had defeated this move and had retained the right to tender advice on his own initiative to the Prime Minister.

Fisher supported Hankey and the C.I.D. organisation against public criticism early in 1936, even although Chamberlain complained that Hankey was 'a terrible reactionary' on the subject of new methods of defence co-ordination.[43] Hankey stood firmly against the idea of a Ministry of Defence because, as he later frankly admitted, such a minister 'would come between me and the Prime Minister'.[44] By February 1936, however, even Hankey could see that the mood of the House of Commons demanded some sort of ministerial appointment, and he himself prepared the memorandum which paved the way for the appointment of a Minister for the Co-ordination of Defence. Hankey discussed the memorandum with Fisher, who approved it, subject to the new minister being a man who did not 'desire to make a place for himself' – possibly a hostile reference to Churchill – and who would not 'confuse mere activity as such with efficiency'. Fisher and Hankey were agreed that Lord Halifax was the right man, but the Cabinet preferred Inskip as a man who would increase the Government's debating strength in the Commons.[45]

According to Bridges, Hankey had become too self-important by the mid-'Thirties, but apparently it was not until near his retirement in 1938 that Hankey managed to get on the wrong side of Fisher.[46] In May 1938 Fisher took the initiative with Wilson in pressing for Bridges as a successor to Hankey. Hankey, however, wanted either his Deputy Secretary, Colonel H. L. (later General the Lord) Ismay, or Colonel H. R. (later General Sir Henry) Pownall, to take over, and he gained the support of the C.O.S., who, in Chatfield's words, wanted 'a

Secretary who speaks our language' – that is a serving officer, and not a Treasury official. In the event no one man succeeded Hankey, for Chamberlain appointed Bridges as Secretary of the Cabinet and Ismay as Secretary of the C.I.D. Nevertheless Pownall noted in his diary: 'what has happened is that in this battle Fisher won and Hankey lost. His last big fight!'[47]

The C.I.D. organisation itself is best seen not as a corporate body, but rather as a forum for interdepartmental discussion. No doubt there was some truth in Hankey's claim that 'meeting round a table week after week ministers, staff officers and civil servants got to know one another, to respect one another and to like one another. . . . "*Tout com-prendre, c'est tout pardonner*".'[48] Yet in Fisher's case the process failed to induce any respect for the C.O.S. apart from Chatfield. Fisher's view, in 1939, was that 'since Hugh Trenchard, we have had no Chief of the Air Staff (except in name). . . . And so with the Army – since George Milne, there has been no Chief of Staff who could think.'[49] Rather than rely upon those whom he considered to be these men's unworthy successors Fisher continued to consult Lord Trenchard on all military matters.[50]

Fisher seems to have had some grounds for doubting whether the C.O.S. Sub-Committee was an effective body for co-ordinating defence policy as a whole before 1939. Hankey told Chatfield in June 1938 that that Sub-Committee was 'the main plank in the system I devised to prepare the way for my departure', but later he admitted that after Inskip's appointment the C.O.S. had 'seized the opportunity of a minister unbiased by previous experience of their controversies to re-open some of the most difficult'.[51] Inskip himself apparently thought that any attempt to make the C.O.S. divide a fixed sum for future defence expenditure between their departments would lead only to each one fighting for his own department.[52] There certainly seems to have been a tendency on the part of the C.O.S. to add up the different departments' requirements rather than to establish priorities on an interdepartmental basis, and Hopkins found it 'odd that three vastly different services with vastly different functions should always require roughly identical finance'.[53] Fisher would have liked to have established himself as a member of the C.O.S. Committee, but the Permanent Secretary of the Treasury was never admitted as a member.[54] Fisher did, however, sit with the C.O.S. and Hankey and Sir Robert Vansit-tart, the Permanent Under-Secretary of the Foreign Office, on the *ad hoc* D.R.C. which drew up the 'defence deficiency' programme of 1934 and the rearmament programme of 1935 for consideration by ministers – and the Chancellor of the Exchequer was always a member of important ministerial committees.

Below the C.I.D. and other committees dealing with defence policy as a whole there were many sub-committees dealing with particular problems, such as the defence of the United Kingdom or the defence of India. These sub-committees in turn set up their own sub-committees to consider technical problems. In general, Bridges or some other Treasury official would attend meetings of the main sub-committee, but not those of the technical sub-committees.* Even so, participation in the sub-committees' work provided extensive information on defence, and indeed military members took the opportunity to educate Treasury officials.

The Treasury had in any case to be informed of developments before expenditure could be incurred, but the C.I.D. organisation helped the Treasury to keep in touch at all stages. For example, within a month of Mr. (later Sir) Robert Watson-Watt's submission to the Air Ministry of his historic paper showing the possibilities of radar, in February 1935, Fisher, Hopkins, Barlow and Bridges knew as much about radar's possibilities as any member of the Air Staff. In order for the research to go ahead the Air Ministry had to approach the Treasury for sanction to spend £10,000 which had not been included in the annual Estimates, and the object of the research was explained to Bridges. He reported to his seniors that:

> I shall be happy to pass on orally such parts of the explanation as I was capable of understanding, but I should be sorry to have to write them down. I gather that ... the line of research indicated is certainly worth pursuing.[55]

The Treasury continued to be informed of developments both by further submissions for approval of expenditure and by Fisher's membership of the C.I.D.'s sub-committee on Air Defence Research. It was this sub-committee which recommended in September 1935 that a chain of radar stations be set up to locate aircraft approaching the coast and which in July 1936 noted that the outlook for this aspect of defence was 'very promising'.[56] Fisher was also chairman of an *ad hoc* C.I.D. sub-committee on Air Raid Precautions in the summer of 1937, so that when in December of that year he was in dispute with the Air Staff over the relative advantages of offence and defence in aerial warfare he had had ample opportunity to become acquainted with the subject.

Treasury participation in C.I.D. sub-committees could shade into Treasury control of expenditure. For example, in November 1937 Bridges took advantage of his membership of the Home Defence Committee to remind planners of the need for economy, and suggested that a report by the committee's Sub-committee on the Protection of Points of Importance Against Air Attack should be held over until it was possible to have a complete picture of all requirements. The Committee's minutes record that 'there was some discussion' whether the recom-

* See Appendix II for Treasury participation in C.I.D. sub-committees.

mendations of the sub-committee 'were not too liberal . . . taking into consideration the enormous demands on the Treasury'. Ismay later recalled how, in the Home Defence Committee's work, 'economy had become so ingrained on us that we asked for no increases which could not be justified in the greatest detail'.[57]

The most important C.I.D. sub-committees from the point of view of Treasury control, however, were those grouped together under the Principal Supply Officers Committee.* The P.S.O.C. had been set up by the C.I.D. in 1924 so to co-ordinate the supply arrangements of the three defence services that in a future war the competition and delays which had marked 1914 would be avoided. The P.S.O.C. itself was a high policy body, meeting infrequently. The work of allocating industrial capacity between the defence departments was done in its own sub-committees, according to hypotheses of service requirements approved by the Cabinet. There were seven of these Supply sub-committees, each dealing with a specific field of related weapons or of strategic goods such as machine tools or gauges, and their work was co-ordinated by a Supply Board.

The P.S.O. organisation included members of the Board of Trade and the defence departments, but not until 1936 did the Supply Board include a representative of the Treasury. Fisher was long reluctant to endow the P.S.O. organisation with any hint of executive authority, but in April 1935 he told the C.I.D. that the Treasury was now agreeable to the evolution of the P.S.O.C. from a purely advisory to a more executive body, with a full-time chairman and secretary.[58] Two months earlier the annual report of the P.S.O. had suggested that the time might have come when a Treasury representative could be usefully added to the P.S.O.C. Barlow, however, advised Fisher that membership of the Supply Board would be more useful as 'it would enable us to learn more of the real needs and methods of the defence departments'.[59] A year passed before a Treasury representative – Barlow himself – actually attended a meeting of the Supply Board, and it was not until the summer of 1937 that Barlow sat on the P.S.O.C. itself.

Membership of the Supply Board enabled Barlow to reinforce Treasury control of expenditure in that he was able to check that the planning of supply was going ahead according to hypotheses approved by the Cabinet, and not merely by defence departments themselves. In October 1937, for example, Barlow objected to an Air Ministry requirement for aircraft instruments, on the grounds that it was based on a hypothesis which had not yet been submitted to the Cabinet, and when the chairman, Sir Arthur Robinson, remarked that the hypothesis had been approved by the Air Council Barlow said he could not regard this as the last word on the subject.[60]

In conclusion, Treasury participation in the C.I.D. organisation

* Hereafter referred to as P.S.O.C.

served three functions. At the earliest stage of planning Treasury officials could remind defence departments that the resources of the Exchequer were not inexhaustible, and that there was a need to settle priorities. Informed of what plans were afoot Treasury officials could brief the Chancellor, who might persuade his Cabinet colleagues to accept changes in the defence departments' proposals. Finally through the P.S.O. organisation Treasury officials could see that planning was in fact going ahead on the lines approved by the Cabinet. In short, participation in the C.I.D. organisation gave the Treasury the power to inform and be informed, and without such participation it would have been difficult for the Treasury to influence defence policy. As it was, the Treasury's powerful central position enabled its representatives to speak with authority even before the formal processes of Treasury control came into operation.

Treasury Control and the Co-ordination of Defence: (i) *The Purpose of Treasury Control*

The work of the C.I.D. organisation was to lay down what was desirable, but while following the procedure of Treasury control the Treasury and the defence departments had to consider more closely what was possible, and this gave the Treasury an important co-ordinating function. Proposals for expenditure had to be examined to ensure that they were in accordance with defence programmes as approved by the Cabinet; that there would be no duplication or other wasteful aspects, and that contracts would be placed in accordance with procedure approved by the P.A.C. When proposals were submitted to the Treasury important decisions had to be taken regarding the speed with which the various parts of the rearmament programme were to be carried out.

Johnson, in his account of the pre-war machinery for directing defence policy, assumed that the Treasury sought to play off the different departments against each other.[61] But in fact Fisher abhorred those who stirred up interdepartmental rivalry, even when an interdepartmental squabble seemed to play into the Treasury's hands. For example, in 1933–4 the Air Ministry attacked an Admiralty proposal for a new aircraft carrier, arguing that the cost of this vessel must impinge upon the finance available for other services, and that land-based aircraft would be more effective. Instead of joining forces to block the new carrier Fisher castigated the Air Ministry for going too far in interfering with naval strategy, and noted:

> The style and type of letters identify Sir Christopher Bullock [the permanent Secretary of the Air Ministry] with this business; he is a very clever young man, but most argumentative and singularly gifted in rubbing people up the wrong way; he never knows when to stop nor the limits of his own or other people's affairs (I am very disappointed in the absence of any sign of his maturing or mellowing).[62]

To Fisher good interdepartmental relations were more important than detailed costing of proposals. When, in 1937, the question of the transfer of the Fleet Air Arm from the Air Ministry to the Admiralty was reopened, Barlow and Bridges thought it impossible to take a Treasury view until the details of the proposed transfer, and possible concomitant duplication of effort by the two defence departments, had been examined. Fisher, however, asserted that the decision ought to be taken in principle first and that the Air Ministry and the Admiralty should work out the details in the light of that decision, otherwise there would be endless wrangling. He noted with obvious asperity:

> The controversy . . . is a canker in the proper relationship of these two military Services, and, had the present Chief of Air Staff (Ellington) been anything more than a routine officer he would have recognised that the Navy have a case. . . . (A) good relationship between the two Services is a national interest and generosity of attitude is . . . a greater contribution than petty parochialism.[63]

Although Fisher had earlier held the view that the Air Ministry should control the Fleet Air Arm, he now gave his support to its transfer to the Admiralty. Fisher's philosophy of Treasury control was far above the counting of candle ends. He believed that Treasury criticism of proposals for expenditure had a constructive role to play by ensuring that essentials received full priority. As Permanent Secretary he encouraged a new relationship between the Treasury and spending departments whereby the former would become the latter's 'candid friend' rather than the traditional 'abominable no-man'.[64]

Fisher had seen in 1919 that in order to be able to play this new role, the Treasury would need officials with a wider vision than those who had entered the department straight from university. He suspended direct entry into the Treasury, and instead hand-picked men who had proved themselves in other departments, so that, by the 'Thirties, all the principals and assistant principals in 5D and 8D had experience outside the Treasury. Despite tensions engendered by years of retrenchment a newly-retired Deputy Secretary of the Admiralty could write in 1933 that Fisher had promoted 'team work throughout the Civil Service . . . with conspicuous success'.[65]

It would be quite wrong, however, to suppose that the Treasury's co-ordinating role was appreciated by everyone. The delays imposed by Treasury control could be galling to a minister anxious to get ahead with his own work. For example, Duff Cooper, when Secretary of State for War, was bitterly resentful of the time taken to consider his proposals for improving Army recruiting by increasing payments for overseas service, improving service conditions and improving soldiers' prospects on leaving the service by giving them preferential treatment at Ministry of Labour industrial training centres. Duff Cooper wanted a decision by Christmas 1936, but Chamberlain insisted that the

proposals should not be circulated to the Cabinet until their implications had been worked out by the Treasury and all the departments
which might be affected. It was traditionally the Chancellor's right to
hold up Cabinet consideration, except in the most urgent cases, of
proposals involving expenditure until the Treasury had had time to
examine the proposals. In the case in point the Treasury officials found
that the War Office's proposals for overseas service would have placed
a heavier burden on India than the Indian Government was willing
to bear, while those on industrial training were unacceptable to the
Ministry of Labour. Interdepartmental discussions were held under
Rae's chairmanship to resolve these difficulties, and despite Duff
Cooper's attempts to force the pace of decision-making – attempts which
created friction between him and Chamberlain – only some of the
War Office's proposals were approved, and then not until January
1937.[66]

Duff Cooper was no more patient regarding the Treasury's work on
supply. While he was First Lord the Admiralty asserted that only ship-
borne anti-aircraft guns could defend merchantmen from air attack,
and proposed an extensive programme for guns and fitments so that
merchantmen could be armed in time of war. Rowan, the Treasury
official who examined the programme, suggested that the Air Ministry
might examine the possibility of defensive aircraft as an alternative – a
suggestion which was not unreasonable at a time of acute shortage of
anti-aircraft guns for the defence of British cities, but a suggestion
which was bound to be seen in the Admiralty as a delaying tactic.[67]
Shortly afterwards, in October 1938 when Duff Cooper had resigned
from the Government, the one-time Secretary of State for War and
First Lord wrote a revealing article on Treasury control – more revealing than perhaps he intended. He noted that service officers 'know very
well what they want' when they put forward proposals for expenditure:

> But when they are faced by the Treasury expert, with his first-class
> brain and long training in negotiation, who first seeks to prove that
> what is alleged to be wanted is not wanted at all, and, as his second line
> of defence, suggests a dozen ways in which it could be more cheaply
> obtained, then the serving officers, though they may stick to their guns,
> in every sense of the word, are bound to take time in finding answers
> to questions that had never occurred to them. So weeks are lost, and
> sometimes months, and men who are longing to get on with the work
> begin to despair.[68]

It is difficult not to sympathise with frustration felt in defence
departments, but surely, in any system of defence where there are three
independent services, there is a need for an independent 'Devil's
advocate' to make officers think about 'questions that had never
occurred to them' while planning within their own department. Duff
Cooper's thesis was that while Treasury control was 'an admirable
system' in normal times, the need in 1938 was for speed in decision, if

necessary at the expense of paying a higher price for supplies than would be justifiable normally. But failure to settle priorities in advance could also lead to delays, since, quite apart from finance, industrial labour and raw materials were not unlimited.

For example, after Munich the Admiralty was understandably anxious to obtain Treasury sanction for increased expenditure on underground storage of oil fuel reserves – to secure them from air attack – but Gilbert was able to advise the Chancellor that the probable effect of such expenditure would be to slow down the construction of protected storage of petrol – a much more dangerous substance if bombed. By 1939, despite planning by the P.S.O. organisation, interdepartmental competition for scarce supply factors, including building labour, was such that Chatfield, by then Minister for the Co-ordination of Defence, joined with the Treasury in advocating the need to co-ordinate defence programmes from the point of view of labour supply and industrial capacity if delays were to be avoided, and a Cabinet committee was set up in July to consider the problem.[69]

The creation of a Ministry of Supply the following month brought no ready-made solution to interdepartmental competition. Mr. Harold Macmillan, who was at that Ministry in 1940, recalls how then there was a 'great battle of priorities. . . . Army, Navy, Air Force – each wanted their particular demands marked A1. The result was that everything became Priority 1, and confusion for a time was worse confounded'.[70] It would be rash to assume that laxer Treasury control before the war would have quickened the pace of essential parts of the rearmament programme, for the Treasury made every effort to see that essentials received due priority, and that less important proposals were not allowed to clog the programme.

Why no Ministry of Supply was set up earlier is another question, and broadly the Government's case was that only with wartime powers over industry could such a Ministry prove effective, and, as it could be manned only by taking men from the existing defence departments, the re-organisation required would serve merely to delay the rearmament programme. The peacetime planning body was the C.I.D.'s Supply Board, and the Treasury view in late 1938, as expressed by Barlow, was that 'many of the advocates of a Ministry of Supply have not the least idea of the extent of the work that has already been done in allocation of capacity, settlements of priority, accumulation of raw materials and provision of war potential. A Ministry of Supply now could do no more in peacetime'.[71] Treasury control of expenditure provided not only a check on whether the rearmament programme was going ahead according to plan, but also an opportunity to consider whether proposed additions to the programme were really necessary – and such additions were a constant source of trouble to the Supply Board since they involved revision of its war plans.

Treasury officials were trained to criticise, and to look for the 'thin end of the wedge' whereby approval for one proposal, say for anti-aircraft guns, would commit the Treasury to approval later of expenditure on related, but as yet unmentioned, equipment such as searchlights or rangefinders. Much of this discussion between the Treasury and departments, Bridges admitted, was 'wearisome and frustrating',[72] but it was necessary to state the antithesis of a defence department's case so that priorities would be assigned and the synthesis of a balanced policy could emerge.

The purpose of Treasury control was not, however, simply a matter of making administration more efficient. Fisher intended the Treasury to be an independent influence within the machinery of government. As he told a Treasury Organisation Committee in 1936:

> The object should be to make of the Treasury a 'general staff' with the recognised right to recruit at any grade from other Departments; in this way a 'corps d'élite' might be formed. . . . Such a 'corps d'élite' would be able to carry out the proper functions of the Office which include the forming of independent and constructive views on policy questions, and not merely negative criticism. The Treasury should not attempt to replace the specialist Departments but should not hesitate to concern itself with policy as necessary in exercising the power of the purse. In particular it must concern itself with foreign . . . affairs (which are now-a-days largely economics, finance and armaments).[73]

Treasury Control and Co-ordination of Defence: (ii) The Treasury Inter-Service Committee

Two main administrative problems stood out in settling priorities among new proposals for expenditure. Firstly, there had to be adequate consultation not only between the defence department making a proposal and the Treasury, but also with other departments which might be affected by the proposal. Secondly, such consultation had to be sufficiently swift so as not to retard rearmament. The normal procedure prior to 1936 was for a defence department's new proposals for expenditure to be discussed by that department's finance officers and Treasury officials only, although the Treasury would sound out opinion in other departments when this was thought appropriate, and approval often waited upon lengthy formal interdepartmental correspondence. During 1935–6, however, administrative machinery evolved which enabled representatives of all three defence departments – who might be serving officers as well as civil servants – to meet together with Treasury officials to discuss proposals face to face. This new procedure both expedited decision-taking and improved co-ordination, since implications of one department's proposals for the others could be discussed by those best qualified to do so.

Throughout the period of rearmament the greatest threat to Treasury control came from Cabinet approval of isolated proposals by individual defence departments made without reference to the rearmament programme as a whole, either from the point of view of supply factors or finance, or, indeed, from the point of view of whether the new proposals could be considered part of a balanced defence policy. It was, therefore, important for the Treasury that its officials should have a chance to consider proposals for expenditure before ministers were asked to take a decision. Over the years a convention had grown up whereby except in cases of extreme urgency no memorandum proposing expenditure might be circulated to the Cabinet without having been discussed beforehand with Treasury officials. Bridges' division would ensure that the Chancellor and the Cabinet were briefed not only as to the advantages of a new proposal but also as to the various arguments which might be brought against it. On the whole up to about 1935 the service ministers seem to have approved of this procedure, at least when some department other than their own had new proposals to make. In November 1933, for example, it had been Lord Hailsham, the Secretary of State for War, who had intervened to prevent Cabinet discussion of proposed increases in the Air Force before the Chancellor had considered the defence Estimates as a whole.[74]

New procedure for approval of expenditure emerged without aforethought during the Italo-Abyssinian crisis of 1935–6. A ministerial committee, the Defence Policy and Requirements Sub-Committee of the C.I.D.* was set up in July 1935 with responsibility for closer co-ordination of policy and strategy. It had wide terms of reference, and the fact that it was a C.I.D. sub-committee and that it had the failing Ramsay MacDonald, who had just vacated the premiership, as chairman, does not suggest that the D.P.R.C. was conceived originally as an executive body. But within a month of its inception the D.P.R.C. found itself concentrating on very immediate problems of putting the Empire's defences in the Mediterranean and the Red Sea areas in order, in case Mussolini's intended attack on Abyssinia should lead to a more general conflict. A tendency developed for defence departments to use the D.P.R.C. as the appropriate body not merely to give ministerial decisions as to general policy but also to give approval to specific proposals involving expenditure on emergency measures. The Chancellor of the Exchequer was a member of the D.P.R.C. but when, as sometimes happened, proposals were produced at its meetings 'out of a hat' the Treasury officials were effectively short-circuited, as there was no time for prepared criticism.[75]

To remedy this, a standing interdepartmental committee of Treasury officials and representatives of the defence departments was set up in September 1935 with Hopkins as chairman to deal with expenditure arising from the crisis. Prior criticism by Treasury officials was restored in that the new committee, known as the Treasury Emergency

* Hereafter referred to as the D.P.R.C.

Expenditure Committee,* examined specific proposals for expenditure in the light of general policy laid down by the D.P.R.C. before these proposals went to the D.P.R.C. for ministerial approval. The defence departments benefited from the new procedure since the T.E.E.C., meeting up to three times a week, expedited Treasury sanction of their proposals by avoiding the delays involved in the normal method of official interdepartmental correspondence. The T.E.E.C. itself was no more than an informal forum for carrying out Treasury business and there was no question of the Treasury representatives being outvoted by the other members.[76]

It was a natural step to use the same committees to deal with the rearmament programme as with the emergency expenditure of 1935-6. At an interdepartmental meeting of officials held at the Treasury in February 1936 under Fisher's chairmanship it was decided that the existence of the T.E.E.C. should be regularised under the title of 'Treasury Inter-Service Committee'† by a Treasury minute and Parliament informed of its existence.[77] Like the T.E.E.C. the T.I.S.C. was to consider urgent specific proposals for expenditure, and the T.I.S.C. was to be empowered to authorise such expenditure, formal Treasury sanction following later only by way of confirmation. The T.I.S.C. was also to consider proposals to vary normal contract procedure, and would have the power to approve such contracts which fell within the scope of any general agreement made by a defence department and its suppliers.[78]

The T.I.S.C. was not part of the C.I.D. organisation, indeed it was not until 1939 that copies of T.I.S.C. agenda and minutes began to be sent to the C.I.D. Secretariat. It was not the business of the T.I.S.C. to discuss defence policy. If there was some doubt whether a given proposal was in accordance with policy as decided by the Cabinet the matter would be referred by Treasury officials to the Chancellor, who would raise it with the minister, or ministers, concerned. Treasury officials would, of course, advise the Chancellor as to what line he should take, but the matter would be decided at the ministerial level. The T.I.S.C. existed only as a convenient means of conducting Treasury control. As Hopkins explained at an early meeting, 'the problem before the Treasury was without precedent. It was to devise a form of control which would not interfere with the execution of the [rearmament] programme and would at the same time satisfy Parliament and the P.A.C.'[79] This the T.I.S.C. achieved. Although there were delays in giving sanction for expenditure in cases where a department wished to go beyond what Treasury officials believed to be the authorised programme, or where proposals by one department had been submitted before those of another in the same field were ready,

* Hereafter referred to as the T.E.E.C.
† Hereafter referred to as the T.I.S.C.

most proposals were approved at the first meeting to which they were submitted, and there is no doubt that the net result was acceleration of the rearmament programme as a whole.[80]

Hopkins was chairman of the T.E.E.C. and T.I.S.C., but he was unable to attend all the meetings of the latter (there were 248 between March 1936 and the outbreak of War), and after mid-1936 Barlow usually took the chair. Bridges (after July 1938 Gilbert) was almost always present together with one or more members of his division. The secretary of the T.E.E.C. and of the first two meetings of the T.I.S.C. was Hopkins' private secretary, Mr. E. W. (later Sir Edward) Playfair. Thereafter the secretary was a member of 5D, Compton, or, in Compton's absence, Mr. George Oram. The defence departments were represented for the most part by civilians, such as Directors of Finance or Contracts, but military members might take part. Indeed, by bringing together military men and Treasury officials in committee for the first time, the new procedure created what one of Bridges' assistants has described as an 'ideal Ministry of Defence'. Military men and Treasury officials could educate one another, and Treasury officials learned a lot.[81]

One element inserted by the Treasury in the T.I.S.C. procedure ensured that the Treasury would be kept informed of how expenditure outside the annual Estimates was going, and how much was likely to be incurred in the future. At the first meeting of the T.I.S.C. Hopkins proposed that the committee should receive quarterly returns from the defence departments showing the total value of contracts placed, the amount actually paid to date, and the amount expected to be paid by the end of the current financial year, and the balance with its estimated spread over subsequent years. The departments would be expected to submit explanatory notes where the figures in the returns varied substantially from earlier forecasts. The defence departments were far from keen to undertake to submit such returns, especially since their overworked staffs were also expected to prepare monthly progress reports for the D.P.R.C., but the Treasury insisted upon some financial inspection.[82] The returns to the T.I.S.C. made in December 1936 had considerable significance since it was from the large increases in forecasts of future expenditure contained therein, compared with those of February 1936, that the Treasury realised how far Treasury control was slipping away, and began to advocate financial restraint, or what was called 'rationing' of defence departments' expenditure.

Treasury Control and Co-ordination of Defence: (iii) Rationing of Finance

Part of the *prima facie* case for believing that the Treasury restricted defence expenditure unduly is that it was at the Treasury's suggestion that in February 1938 the Cabinet fixed a 'ration' of £1570 million for the defence departments' expenditure for the quinquennium 1937–41.

It may seem odd that Fisher, who in 1948 described pre-war rearmament as 'ludicrously unsubstantial', should have sought in 1937 to limit
future defence expenditure. But there were sound administrative
reasons – quite apart from economic reasons – in 1937 why the finance
available to defence departments should be rationed.

The Treasury's economic rationale for limiting defence expenditure
is discussed in the next chapter. The point made here is that the
Treasury's attempts to limit defence expenditure were not motivated
solely by careful calculations of what the country could afford, for,
especially when such calculations were made four or five years in
advance, as they had to be in connection with the rearmament programme, no exact figure could be arrived at.[83] The Treasury wanted
fixed limits to each defence department's expenditure because even in
normal times this was the Chancellor of the Exchequer's only really
effective weapon in controlling defence expenditure. While 5D did
examine new proposals on their technical merits this was always, as
Bridges observed, 'difficult terrain for a Treasury attack',[84] because
although the Treasury officials were exceptionally well-informed lay-
men, ultimately only the defence departments themselves had the
professional knowledge to distinguish between which items in their
draft Estimates were essential and which were merely desirable.
Accordingly, in normal times the Chancellor would allocate to each
department a sum rather smaller than it had asked for for the following
year, bringing about what Bridges called the annual 'massacre of the
innocents' as the less important items were squeezed out of the
Estimates.[85] Not unnaturally each defence department over the years
had become adept at including in its draft Estimates items which were
desirable but not essential. Even so, at least in the years immediately
preceding 1936, the Treasury seems to have been content with the way
that the departments played the game in the annual pre-Budget
'battle'.[86]

So long as Budgets had to be balanced by taxation defence departments were effectively 'rationed' to what the Chancellor could find for
them out of taxation once the political requirements of civil expenditure had been met. From 1919 strong political pressure for retrenchment in government expenditure had meant that the Chancellor could
actually require a reduction in defence expenditure each year down to
1932, and it was only gradually that fears arising out of the financial
crisis in the immediate past were overborne by fears about a war in the
immediate future. Strict budgeting meant that each year each department could spend only its funds as they had been voted by Parliament,
and new proposals had to wait for another year, to take their chance
along with recurrent expenditure in the 'massacre of the innocents'.
Supplementary Estimates which would have enabled these projects
to be brought forward into the current financial year were strongly

disapproved by Treasury, Cabinet and Parliament alike. It was the relaxation of this strict system of annual Estimates that began the weakening of Treasury control.

The adoption in 1934 of a five-year programme to make up deficiencies in the defence services did not in itself mean any major departure from normal methods of financial control, since the Chancellor of the Exchequer was not required to commit himself in advance to finding either the total finance required or the sums allocated in the programme to the different departments in each year.[87] At the same time, once the deficiencies in the nation's defences had been recognised by the Cabinet, it was harder for the Treasury to refuse Supplementary Estimates, especially where public and government concern about the deficiencies was acute, as in the case of the Air Force, and by May 1935 the Treasury was willing to let the Air Ministry go ahead with the placing of additional contracts in advance of a Supplementary Estimate being submitted to Parliament.

With the adoption by the Cabinet in February 1936 of the five-year rearmament programme the Treasury agreed to a relaxation in the procedure for the annual Estimates. Financial control was to be an ongoing process, and although departments were still to allocate sums annually to Votes, the Treasury would now sanction items individually where it was desired to expedite them, rather than withhold sanction until the whole Vote had been approved, as hitherto. To encourage civilian engineering firms to enter the armaments field contracts were to be placed on a long-term basis, extending beyond a single financial year, and, to accommodate the ongoing nature of the programme, expenditure was to be incurred in advance of parliamentary approval, and Supplementary Estimates were to become the norm.[88]

The defence departments were not slow to exploit their new freedom, for although the rearmament programme agreed to by the Cabinet in February 1936 contained forecasts of expenditure by each department over the next five years, the departments were not bound by their own forecasts, and the departmental programmes themselves were provisional and liable to be modified as military technique advanced or the situation abroad changed. Whereas the cost of the rearmament programme, excluding naval construction, had been estimated at £245 million in February 1936, eleven months later the departments' revised forecasts totalled £426 million.[89] While the rise could be explained partly in terms of rising prices it was also due to acceleration in the original programme and 'to some considerable extent', Bridges thought, to additions to the programme, often made necessary by new inventions which it was impossible to leave unused.[90]

It was, Bridges believed, impossible in the long run for the Treasury to refuse to sanction expenditure for projects which defence experts declared to be necessary, except on the ground that the money could not be found. Moreover although annual Estimates continued to be prepared to maintain what he called the 'bare decencies' of Parliamentary control, the fact that the departments were allowed to enter into contracts extending beyond the financial year meant that the money required in any particular year was determined largely by progress made with orders placed the previous year, and the fixing of annual totals by the Chancellor became almost meaningless.[91] If production were behind schedule a larger part of the cost than had been intended fell on the next financial year, but if production were ahead of schedule additional finance had to be provided in the first year of the contract, while it was difficult to refuse further orders for the second year if the alternative was that productive capacity would be idle.

In January 1937 Hopkins advised Chamberlain that Treasury control was slipping away, and could be resumed only by naming an aggregate sum of expenditure for each department, which might not be exceeded over the next five years. As Hopkins himself noted later, the proposal to 'ration' defence expenditure, which led to the review of defence policy by Inskip and to major changes in defence policy, had an exclusively financial origin. Treasury officials realised that a necessary concomitant of financial 'rationing' was that the rearmament programme itself should be re-investigated so that priority would be given to those items which on strategic grounds should be completed first, but 'rationing' itself was seen as a means of re-establishing Treasury control of expenditure rather than of influencing the direction of defence policy.[92]

This is not to say that once Inskip's review was put afoot Treasury officials, Fisher in particular, did not try to influence the outcome with strategic arguments. But 'rationing' itself, as Bridges insisted, was not a new principle. Limiting expenditure over five years was an attempt at re-establishing the degree of financial control which the Treasury had exercised when there had been fixed annual Estimates. Fisher declared that the alternative to 'rationing' was for the Government to announce to the House of Commons that Treasury control had been suspended, since it would be dishonest to maintain a 'mere pretence' of Treasury control.[93] As the maintenance of a form of Treasury control was one of the Government's chief defences against criticism that it was allowing the manufacturers of armaments to make excessive profits the Cabinet was not likely to agree to such an announcement.

It would be wrong to assume that for the Treasury the figure of £1500 million, suggested in Inskip's Interim Report in December 1937 as the sum within which total defence expenditure over the five years to April 1942 should be brought, was an absolute limit. The Cabinet was left with the option of increasing taxation if it was felt that the immediate international situation should be judged so serious as to necessitate expenditure above that figure.[94] Hopkins himself did not believe that the Cabinet in accepting Inskip's Interim Report really thought that defence expenditure could be brought within the £1500 million limit, even although the defence departments were to recost their programmes according to the strategic priorities set out in that report. Hopkins felt that something more than £1500 million could be found, although he had deferred to Phillips' opinion in settling on that figure, and it was probably not too difficult for Hopkins to suggest to Inskip in February 1938 that a higher global figure be adopted in the minister's Second Report so as to avoid delay in fixing the individual departments' 'rations'. 'Rationing' was essentially a bargaining counter to ensure that the defence departments would have to shed some of the lower-priority items in their rearmament programmes, and between themselves, the Treasury officials admitted the possibility of upward revision at a later date of the figure of £1570 million adopted in February 1938 by the Cabinet as the limit for the defence departments' expenditure over the five financial years 1937-41.[95]

In the event only the War Office and the Admiralty were subjected to any kind of rationing. Alarm about the growing strength of the Luftwaffe led the Cabinet to agree in April 1938 to the Air Ministry ordering as many aircraft as it was believed British industry could produce by April 1940, and financial rationing was ignored. An Air Council Committee on Supply was set up with Bridges as a member, Bridges having full financial authority to approve proposals for expenditure which he considered to be clearly justified under the programme. During the first three months of its existence very large sums – totalling about £70 million between 29 April and 30 June – were approved as incidental in the course of working out the most effective means of enabling individual firms to maximise output.[96]

Even in the cases of the War Office and the Admiralty the limitations of industrial capacity rather than of finance applied. Inskip, unable to reconcile in his Second Report even the new figure of £1570 million with the re-costed defence programmes which, with probable additions, he thought might cost up to £2000 million, had tried to evade the dilemma by suggesting that the defence departments should 'press forward resolutely' in 1938 and 1939 up to the limits of what could be spent without interfering with normal trade. This proviso, he had thought, would keep annual expenditure at about the level of the 1938 Estimates.[97] But the C.O.S. rebelled against the 'doctrine of non-interference' with civil trade which the Cabinet had adopted along with the rearmament programme in 1936, and in March 1938, only a month after the Cabinet had accepted Inskip's recommendation, the Cabinet decided to end the policy of 'non-interference' and to ask industry to give full priority to rearmament work. The defence departments did indeed 'press forward resolutely' with the placing of contracts, and by June 1938 Hopkins felt that defence expenditure had 'slipped its leash once more and [rationing] is for the moment almost lost to view.[98]'

On the other hand, since the Cabinet had agreed in June 1937 not to approve further major additions to the rearmament programme until after the review of defence policy had been completed, the attempt at fixing a 'ration' had imposed a braking effect on the growth of the defence departments' programmes for almost a year. This, rather than the figures of £1500 million or £1570 million for the quinquennium from 1937, is what mattered. There was no question of financial limits being dictated by the Treasury – individual departments' rations were negotiated, with Inskip acting as the honest broker. Nor was there any delay in placing contracts which could be carried out in the financial year 1937, although there was some delay in placing contracts for future years.[99]

The anguished protests of defence departments recorded in various minutes and memoranda relating to rationing of finance need not always be taken at face value. For example, Duff Cooper, recalling negotiations on the Admiralty's ration in the summer of 1938, wrote in his memoirs:

> My interview with the Chancellor was satisfactory. . . . I expected he would try to beat me down to accepting a round sum of £400 million for the next three years. My people thought they could just do with £405 million, but I succeeded in getting £410 million. The Controller and the others were very pleased.[100]

Moreover the allocation of the ration of finance between the different years of the programme, Hopkins noted, was understood to be 'more or less fluid', so that departments were free to accelerate their programmes, and thus bring forward expenditure from later to earlier years. From the crisis summer of 1938 the policy of rationing was really in suspense, and all the Treasury could do was to urge departments to concentrate on essentials.[101] Barlow thought in January 1939 that it was 'worth clinging to the shadow [of rationing] that remains', since Sir Frederick Bovenschen, the War Office's Deputy Under-Secretary, had said that he found it helpful in securing some consideration of priorities by military members of that department. The Admiralty, on the other hand, Barlow thought, had 'never taken [rationing] seriously'.[102] In fact, the Admiralty's records show that in July 1938 Duff Cooper took the policy seriously enough to have all Admiralty departments and branches circulated with financial guidelines designed to enable the Admiralty to keep within its ration. The original Admiralty and War Office Estimates for 1939 were still related to rationing of finance, the Admiralty obtaining only £1 million more than the £148 million agreed on by Inskip and Duff Cooper in July 1938 as the appropriate sum for 1939.[103]

The crisis months of early 1939, however, saw an almost complete break-down of financial restraint. The Cabinet sanctioned a series of major additions to the authorised programme, so that the February forecast of £580 million for all defence expenditure in the financial year 1939 had to be re-estimated at £630 million in April and £750 million by July.[104] By May 1939 Fisher thought that the Treasury was 'being progressively put out of action' by decisions taken by the Cabinet on an *ad hoc* basis without consulting Treasury officials.[105] But down to early 1939 Treasury control could exercise a braking effect on the defence departments. The fact that Supplementary Estimates could be obtained did not negate completely the value of annual Estimates. Additions to the latter had to be submitted to the T.I.S.C., and as The First Sea Lord, Sir Roger Backhouse, commented in December 1938 regarding delays in providing air raid shelters at Portsmouth:

> Anything connected with money which is not in the Estimates presents great difficulty, as proposals have to be what is called 'co-ordinated' by some Committee or another. It is a marvellous way of putting things off and drives one to despair.[106]

Treasury Control and Co-ordination of Defence: (iv) Finance, Contract Procedure and Profits

The Treasury was only part, albeit the key part, of an elaborate system of public finance, which aimed at efficient and economical administration. Briefly, within each defence department there were supply officers responsible for providing whatever the department required; finance officers who had to examine critically proposals for expenditure, and to defend those which they sanctioned, and contracts officers, whose duty it was to see that supplies were bought on the most favourable terms. In the words of an official historian: 'since attention had to be paid to the views of so many bodies and persons, ranging from the P.A.C. to the finance officers of departments, the whole system was inevitably accompanied by caution and delay'.[107] Departmental finance branches had to be satisfied about the probable cost and practicability of proposals before submitting them to the Treasury. Once Treasury sanction had been obtained finance branches continued to watch expenditure to ensure that as far as possible it was kept within the limits of the approved estimate, and even a proposed purchase designed to implement the authorised rearmament programme might be refused if finance officers in the department in question were not satisfied that the purchase was necessary to supply the needs of the force concerned, and that money was available within the Vote to cover the expenditure involved. Finance branches exercised close control over expenditure right up to the outbreak of war, and when, as sometimes happened, finance officers failed to prevent excessive expenditure on a particular contract, there was strong Parliamentary criticism.

Thus although Fisher instructed Bridges to cut all corners and to urge and chivvy defence departments to quicker spending, defence departments' own finance branches remained a possible source of delay. Fisher himself was partly responsible for this since defence departments' finance branches were as formidable as they were in the 'Thirties because of the policy of decentralising financial control which he had carried out in the 'Twenties. Under the post-1920 system the permanent civilian head of a defence department became that department's Accounting Officer, directly responsible to the ministerial head for control of expenditure, with the status of a full member of the department's Council or Board. Fisher, moreover, seems to have been determined to maintain the authority of departmental finance officers during the rearmament programme.[108]

The influence of finance officers varied from department to department. Lord Eustace Percy, who was in the Cabinet in 1935–6, remarked that the system of indirect Treasury control within departments worked well enough in the Admiralty and Air Ministry, 'but in the War Office ... long tradition had built up its civilian finance officers in time of peace into a crippling *imperium in imperio* intent upon checking every initiative of the professional soldiers'. Pownall, in 1939, when he was a member of the Army Council, complained of military members having:

> to fight our way not only in the Treasury (who on the whole are pretty reasonable and quick) but also to fight our way past our own Finance to get to the Treasury. We have to break down their opposition to *asking* for money. It's mostly the system, but of course it is also the personalities who have been ... brought up in the system.[109]

Quite apart from tradition and attitudes of individuals the War Office system peculiarly favoured an *imperium in imperio* for finance officers. Defence ministries were divided into divisions each dealing with particular kinds of supplies – for example guns or victuals – and in the case of the Admiralty and Air Ministry each of these supply divisions was responsible for its own finance, and finance officers were close colleagues of the supply and contracts officers over whose work they exercised financial control. The War Office, however, had a separate Finance Department, and consequently its finance officers were more removed from supply and contracts officers. Any system designed to maintain the standards set by the P.A.C. was bound to impose some delay on military men anxious for orders to be placed, but the War Office system does seem to have created more frustration than others. At all events Treasury officials could rest assured that, left to their own devices, War Office finance officers in particular would not countenance extravagance.

One aspect of Treasury control which was important for co-ordination of defence was control over contract procedure. This was a shared responsibility between the Treasury and each defence department's

Director of Contracts. The division of responsibility was, broadly, that the Treasury laid down general principles governing the form and the placing of defence contracts, while the individual contracting departments negotiated and administered the contracts, ensuring that each contract conformed to approved principles and that the financial terms were the best that could be made. It had long been laid down by the P.A.C. that Treasury approval was required for all contracts for new buildings or where there was no competitive tendering, and as late as May 1938 the Treasury felt obliged to ask the Admiralty not to place non-competitive contracts on a 'cost plus percentage' basis without Treasury approval, even in so unimportant a case as the purchase of a trawler for conversion to a depot ship. This request, however, seems to have been no more than a sop to the P.A.C. which, Bridges said, had been 'fulminating' about such contracts, since Treasury opinion was that it was impossible for the Treasury to control effectively the cost of individual ships even where the cost exceeded the Admiralty's estimate, for an excess could usually be put down to alterations in design or to the rising cost of materials.[110]

In February 1936 the D.P.R.C. had accepted the advice of the industrialist Lord Weir that 'the word of the man responsible for supply must carry', this being interpreted to mean that any necessary authority from the Treasury to go ahead with placing a contract was to be forthcoming promptly, without waiting for the settling of every detail.[111] On the other hand, a complete collapse of Treasury supervision of contracts could have led to chaotic competition for scarce industrial resources, with each defence department seeking to put its suppliers at an advantage by offering more favourable contract terms than those of other departments. The absence of closed annual Estimates might make the defence departments less concerned about expense than about output, and this possibility was made all the more acute by the decision of the Cabinet in February 1936 to expand the capacity of British industry to produce armaments, both to speed the rearmament programme and to create a reserve of industrial capacity for use in war. Civil firms were to be encouraged to enter the armaments field by the placing of non-, or barely, competitive 'educational' orders, and one of the first tasks of the T.I.S.C. was set to up a sub-committee to consider contract procedure for the creation of what was known as the 'shadow' armaments industry.

Finance, contract and supply officers from the defence departments pooled their collective wisdom with that of Barlow and Bridges under the chairmanship of Robinson, chairman of the Supply Board, after whom the sub-committee was named. It was this Robinson Committee which recommended that when completely new factories were set up the Government should pay the entire cost, thereby acquiring ownership and ensuring that the 'war potential' so created could be maintained once the rearmament programme was complete and production fell.[112] The defence departments were instructed to make arrangements with private firms to operate the factories for a fee, and it was only in exceptional cases that the Treasury sanctioned capital grants to private industry to accelerate production. Treasury approval was required for all contract proposals which involved the creation of a factory or capital assistance, and Treasury officials regarded this control at the production stage as a means of offsetting the loosening of financial control through the annual Estimates.[113]

It is not to be supposed that the Treasury officials were unaware of the need to build up Britain's arms industry, or that they put cost accounting before national security. Fisher spoke out in the D.P.R.C. in January 1936 against alienating industrialists by introducing statutory powers to compel firms to open their books to inspection as a check on prices. In the Robinson Committee Barlow and Bridges spoke of the need for safeguards against excessive profits, but rather than insist on lengthy negotiations with industry, or risk discouraging civil firms from taking on defence contracts, the two Treasury representatives accepted a method of fixing profits which they believed would almost certainly result in profiteering by some firms. The Treasury view was that the only way to prevent excessive profits and to encourage firms to use their resources efficiently was to calculate the permissible level of profit as a fixed percentage of a firm's capital assets directly employed on the contract, but it was agreed that profits on the initial contracts at least should be calculated as a percentage of a firm's total costs, including labour – a procedure hardly conducive to encouraging increased productivity.[114]

There was undoubtedly a delay of some weeks in the placing of some of the first rearmament contracts while contract procedure was being worked out. But Hopkins believed that contracts could be approved the more speedily thereafter if standard forms and procedures could be agreed upon at the outset, for the more varied the form of contracts the more time would be lost while the T.I.S.C. considered the possible implications of individual contracts so far as the establishment of new precedents was concerned.[115] Contract procedure on rearmament contracts was not dictated by the Treasury, but was worked out interdepartmentally in the T.I.S.C. after the most urgent principles had been dealt with by the Robinson Committee, which reported on 18 March 1936. Routine, as opposed to rearmament, contracts were co-ordinated not by the T.I.S.C. but by a sub-committee of the C.I.D., the Contracts Co-ordinating Committee. For example, this committee, made up of defence departments' Directors of Contracts and a representative of the Treasury, reduced interdepartmental competition, and thereby kept down prices, through the joint purchase of such items as blankets, medical supplies and coal.

The ideal of completely uniform contract procedure did not prove to be practicable. Each of the defence departments had the responsibility of conducting its own negotiations with its suppliers, who, like the aircraft manufacturers or the Machine Tool Trades Association, might be organised into powerful cartels capable of insisting upon terms which would not cramp unduly their opportunities for making profits. Certainly the Machine Tools Association's non-co-operative attitude to the checking of prices by defence departments led the Select Committee on the Estimates to conclude that there was *prima facie* evidence of excessive profits.[116] Where one industry dealt primarily with one department – the aircraft industry is a case in point considered below – the terms reached by that industry and that department might differ from terms offered by other departments to their suppliers.

There was also a difference between the Admiralty and Air Ministry form of contract on the one hand, and the War Office form of contract on the other, arising out of differences in the organisation of the departments. Chamberlain suggested in March 1936 that the Admiralty and Air Ministry form of contract, whereby fixing a price was left as late as possible, was preferable to the War Office form of contract, whereby a maximum price was fixed at the outset, subject to reduction if costing examination showed the price to be excessive. Hopkins, however, had to advise Chamberlain that the War Office would be unable to change over effectively without large alterations in its organisation. The Admiralty and Air Ministry, he explained, had a system of technical cost accounting carried out by engineers and other experts, primarily designed to see that contractors adopted the cheapest processes and to instruct them in how to do so. The War Office, on the other hand, had a staff of ordinary cost accountants whose business was simply to estimate in advance what the cost of an item would be given the processes which a firm intended to employ. The War Office was clearly at a disadvantage when dealing with new firms, and Fisher urged that all changes in the War Office's organisation necessary for getting its job done be carried out. It was Fisher who chaired the C.I.D. sub-committee which recommended changes in the War Office's organisation in 1936 to this end, including the establishment of the new post of Director-General of Munitions Production, a post filled, most unusually, by a naval officer, Engineer Vice-Admiral Sir Harold Brown, previously Engineer-in-Chief of the Navy.[117]

The T.I.S.C.'s role was to consider contract principles, not individual contracts. The T.I.S.C. enabled representatives of the Treasury and the defence departments to examine new agreements made by one of the departments which might set a precedent for future agreements by the other departments with their suppliers. For example, in the summer of 1937 the Admiralty negotiated an agreement with firms supplying it with armour that payments made to them to enable them to increase their productive capacity would include an agreed percentage of 'profit', this sum to be calculated on the actual cost of the work done in increasing productive capacity. It was the representatives of the Air Ministry and the War Office on the T.I.S.C. who pointed out that the case differed from that of 'shadow' factories in that the extensions to the firms' plants would belong to the firms, not to the Government, and that firms should not expect to make 'profit' while increasing their own assets. Barlow agreed with the Air Ministry and War Office representatives that the armour firms' claims were inadmissible in principle, but that in the case of one firm which had agreed to do the work under the impression that it would be allowed the additional sum to the actual cost of the work done, payment should be made provided that it was made clear that there would be no such payments in future.[118]

Precedents accepted by the T.I.S.C. were carefully collected by the Treasury Officers of Accounts, two officials already well versed in rulings by the P.A.C. When in doubt an official in 5D could apply to the Treasury Officers of Accounts for advice on whether any new proposal was in accordance with approved contract procedure. The procedure for agreeing to a proposal was, first, for agreement to be reached within the defence department in question between its supply, contract and finance officers. Then there would be oral discussion between a finance officer and a member of the Treasury's 5D, and only then, if agreement could not be reached, or if it was desired to have interdepartmental discussion, would the matter go to the T.I.S.C. Where the Treasury Officers of Accounts could advise that the proposal was not in accordance with established procedure the official in 5D would warn the defence department accordingly.

This advice from the Treasury could strengthen the hand of finance officers within a defence department. For example, in the summer of 1938 a Yorkshire firm engaged in making tanks found itself threatened with bankruptcy, and applied to the War Office for advances to give it working capital. Advances, known as progress payments, calculated as a percentage of the cost of work done on a contract, were common practice, but established procedure required that they could be made only after the contracting department's officials had inspected the firm's books, and the work done. This inspection usually took some weeks, and the Yorkshire firm wanted the progress payments to be made more quickly, before the War Office officials had completed their inspection. The finance side of the War Office found itself pressed by the Director-General of Munitions Production to agree, but on application to the Treasury received a ruling from the Treasury Officers of Accounts that it would be irregular for the War Office to act, in effect, as the firm's banker by supplying it with finance on this basis.

Further negotiation led to the firm being able to raise commercial bank credit on the condition that the War Office made progress payments of 90 per cent of the work done instead of 80 per cent hitherto, a variation in contract to which the Treasury agreed reluctantly rather than see the firm go out of business, with consequent loss of industrial capacity for the War Office programme. The result seems to have been that the firm continued a hand-to-mouth existence for want of working capital until August 1939, when officials of the newly-created Ministry of Supply threatened to take the matter to ministerial level unless the Treasury would allow provisional progress payments before inspection of books or work done. It was a mark of Treasury control weakening before the threat of war that on that occasion the Treasury officials gave in without a fight.[119]

The promise in the Defence White Paper of 1936 that Treasury control would be maintained was not altogether carried out so far as prevention of profiteering was concerned. The 1938 P.A.C. had mis-givings over the Admiralty's arrangements for financial criticism and control, and the Committee's report led to an internal Admiralty enquiry. This concluded that the Admiralty's system was 'well adapted to its purpose', but required 'tuning', and more staff on the finance side. Yet the Admiralty's contract and finance officers had fewest problems, since the vast bulk of that department's suppliers were experienced firms, with a long record of Admiralty contracts behind them, and the Admiralty also had its own dockyards to set a standard for costing purposes.[120]

The War Office, on the other hand, had to deal with more inexperien-ced suppliers than either the Admiralty or the Air Ministry, since its regular suppliers, unlike shipbuilders or aircraft manufacturers, had lacked civil outlets for their products during the years of retrenchment. As noted above, the War Office's organisation, at least until 1936, was ill suited to deal with inexperienced suppliers, yet the department was the most successful in avoiding P.A.C. criticism. The War Office persuaded almost all its main contractors to open their books to its cost accountants but the main contractors laughed at a suggestion that sub-contractors' books should be open to the main contractor as a further check on profiteering. The question of sub-contractors' prices remained a vexed one for all departments, and in the summer of 1939 Hopkins was receiving information of an allegedly growing practice of collusion between some main contractors and some sub-contractors whereby the former entered in their books the standard price for a sub-contractor's product, while the latter in fact charged a reduced rate for bulk orders, the difference being paid into a separate account.[121]

Most controversy, however, was centred upon Air Ministry contracts. Prior to 1939 the aircraft manufacturers refused Air Ministry cost accountants access to trading accounts. A formula for costing Air Ministry contracts, known as the McLintock Agreement, was negotiated in May 1936 by the Secretary of State for Air, Lord Swinton, and the industry, but as early as October 1937 Sir Donald Banks, the Air Ministry's Permanent Secretary, was 'concerned' about the way in which the agreement was working out. The principle upon which the Ministry worked – a principle which Swinton claimed to have devised himself – was that for the first batch of a given order a firm received certified expenditure plus a fixed profit. On the basis of the first batch the firm and the Air Ministry would then estimate what future production costs were likely to be, and a 'target' price would be negotiated which allowed for basic cost plus a fixed profit. Firms were to be encouraged to reduce cost below the target price by offering them one-tenth of the difference. Banks' experience, however, was that delays occurred in fixing prices, resulting in firms in effect being paid expenses plus an element of profit (without risk, or much incentive to reduce costs). Rightly or wrongly he suspected that some firms were 'playing for time' in negotiations with this end in view.[122]

It was not until February 1939 that investigations by the Treasury and the Air Ministry led the Treasury to the conclusion that there was good reason for believing that the terms of the McLintock Agreement made it inevitable that profits should be excessive. Although the McLintock Agreement was to have covered the whole period up to 1942 and had no provision for termination or variation, it was reviewed and modified by the Air Ministry and the aircraft industry between March and July 1939, the move to reduce the manufacturers' profits being strongly urged by members of all three parties in the House of Commons. Aircraft contracts were a matter for the Secretary of State for Air, but the whole affair exposed the weakness of Treasury control so far as the prevention of profiteering was concerned.[123] As early as December 1936 a Treasury Officer of Accounts had pointed out to Bridges that there was no committee or body of experts engaged as a whole-time occupation in investigating and checking the extent of profits. Responsibility was fragmented between the different departments' Directors of Contracts and of Supply, and different types of accounting systems were in use. Bridges observed that the defence departments had given only lip service to the Robinson Committee's conclusion that the best method of assessing profits was with reference to the capital actually used on a contract, and not with reference to turnover, and suggested to Barlow that the matter should be taken up with the defence departments.[124] In fairness to the defence departments it must be said that it was far from easy to recruit in the time available staff with the qualifications necessary to carry out the Robinson Committee's recommendations.

The Treasury and the contract departments officials were at a disadvantage in that they lacked the special knowledge and experience of an inspector of taxes, or even the knowledge of some of the Government's critics who wrote in the *Economist* or the *Statist*. Accordingly Barlow appealed to the Inland Revenue for assistance, but the Inland Revenue officials felt that their statutory obligation to taxpayers who gave them information in confidence meant that the departmental Treasury could be given only aggregate figures which would show the trend of aircraft firms' profits in 1937 without identifying individual firms. These aggregate figures were not received by Barlow until December 1938, and when available they showed up the Air Ministry badly. The Air Ministry's suppliers were receiving almost twice as much return on capital as the War Office's suppliers, whose profits were calculated as a percentage of capital employed on contracts. As Barlow pointed out this did not mean that much more than £2 or £3 million was being made a year in excessive profits, but it did mean that the aircraft manufacturers' costs were too high and that the Air Ministry was not getting value for money.[125] The responsibility for this lay firmly with the Air Ministry's Contracts Department, whose officials, in common with those in the contracts departments of the other defence departments, were so anxious that supply should not be interrupted by fastidious financial safeguards that information given to them in confidence by firms was denied to the Comptroller and Auditor General, of whose intentions, Bridges thought, contracts departments were 'intensely suspicious'.[126]

The T.I.S.C. procedure of interdepartmental discussion failed then to bring about uniformity in contract procedure. Variations arose out of the different departments' suppliers' demands, and out of differing departmental organisations – and the effect seems to have been to put the War Office at a disadvantage. The War Office had the highest proportion of inexperienced suppliers, and yet was the least able to advise these suppliers on new production methods. The War Office's fastidious financial safeguards do seem to have prevented high profits on its contracts, but this very fact meant that its suppliers were at a disadvantage with regard to finance capital compared with the Air Ministry's suppliers. Aircraft firms could find more finance capital both out of higher profits and out of new issues on the Stock Exchange, where new investment was attracted by their profits.[127] There is not the slightest evidence that this situation was deliberately engineered by the Treasury, but, as will be seen in Chapter V, the relative laxness in Treasury control over Air Ministry spending was an effective means of giving Air Force expansion the highest priority.

Fisher's Personal Influence

Having reviewed the Treasury's influence as a department, it is possible to see the significance of Fisher's influence as the man who was Britain's senior civil servant from 1919 to 1939, and one who was close to Chamberlain at a critical time. Fisher's appointment in 1919 as official Head of the Civil Service as well as Permanent Secretary of the Treasury was criticised then and later for giving the Treasury too much influence over other departments. A Treasury minute of 1919 had given him the last word in advising the Prime Minister on the appointment of official heads of departments (the permanent civilian heads in the case of defence departments), their deputies and their chief establishment officers. This power was said by Hankey, and others, to give rise to 'lurking doubt' in the minds of civil servants as to the effect that fighting too hard for their departments against the Treasury might have on their careers.[128] Fisher's own defence of his position – that 'executive authority is vested solely in H.M. Government, and officials, however high in rank, exercise no executive authority *of their own* [sic]'[129] – was constitutionally correct, although perhaps not entirely convincing, since any Prime Minister would be bound to give great weight to Fisher's advice on senior appointments. On the other hand, it is known that Fisher encouraged 'lively and vigorous discussion' between departments,[130] and this suggests that subservience to the Treasury was not a means to winning Fisher's favour. At the same time, as in the example of Bullock, the Secretary of the Air Ministry, quoted above, a civil servant who pushed his department's case to the extent of creating bad feelings between departments was likely to offend Fisher's sense of teamwork.

Bullock also provides an example of Fisher's authority within the Civil Service. Bullock was dismissed from the Civil Service in 1936 following an enquiry set up by Fisher into an approach made by Bullock with a view to obtaining a position with Imperial Airways. Bullock had had reason to brood over his future for some time by 1936. Aged only 45 then, and ambitious, his future prospects in the Civil Service seemed dimmed after an incident in December 1934. Lord Londonderry, the Secretary of State for Air, believed at that time that Bullock was engaged in 'unwarrantable activities' against him – the activities being unspecified, but involving a challenge to Londonderry's definition of the constitutional position of civil aviation. Fisher intervened, and, having discussed the matter with Baldwin, demanded that 'Bullock will promise that in future he will . . . act with loyalty to his Ministers', and that he 'will understand that any deviation from loyalty . . . will be met by summary dismissal'. Bullock was duly cautioned by Baldwin and Londonderry.[131]

Bullock had had hopes of succeeding either Fisher or Hankey, and by his own account had had 'frank talks' with both, only to be discouraged by them. At some point in 1935 he discussed the idea of his leaving the Civil Service for finance or commerce with Fisher, and, according to Bullock, Fisher 'expressed himself in favour' with the idea. In the same year Bullock approached Sir Eric Geddes, chairman of Imperial Airways, to sound out the possibility of succeeding him one day.[132] Fisher considered the latter an approach improper at a time when negotiations were in progress between the Air Ministry and Imperial Airways for an important contract. This opinion was confirmed by a Board of Enquiry, of which Hopkins was a member, and before which Fisher was a witness. The findings of the Board were considered by Baldwin, Chamberlain and the Secretary of State for Air, Swinton, and in August 1936 Bullock was dismissed.[133] Bullock believed that 'petty spites and personal animosities' had played their part in the affair, but even once out of the Civil Service he took the view that:

> I simply can't afford to antagonise (e.g.) Warren Fisher further, until I have consolidated my worldly position – he could by virtue of his office block me in so many directions if he chose. No Chairman or Board wants to be otherwise than on good terms with the powers that be![134]

It seems to have been all too easy to antagonise Fisher. Even Bridges, who was not likely to overstate the case, admitted that Fisher was 'rather impatient' and 'given to quick enthusiasms, both for people and for causes'. Moreover, Fisher offended by his 'habit of talking in an unguarded way about what he regarded as the demerits of those – quite a large number – whom he held in no high repute', and there was 'bitterness' over his appointment as official Head of the Civil Service.[135]

Bullock's case might suggest that Fisher dominated civil servants in defence departments, and if so this would be important. Members of the armed forces usually served within a ministry for only three years at a time, whereas Bullock had been at the Air Ministry for seventeen years, five of them as official civilian head, at the time of his dismissal. That in turn was a short period compared with Sir Oswyn Murray, the Permanent Secretary of the Admiralty, who retired in 1936 after thirty-nine years at the Admiralty, nineteen of them as official civilian head, or Sir Herbert Creedy, the Permanent Under-Secretary of the War Office, who retired in 1939 after thirty-eight years at the War Office, fifteen of them as official civilian head. Such experienced men often came to exercise a 'great if intangible influence'[136] in a department. There are no real grounds, however, for assuming that men of the standing of Creedy and Murray went about in fear of Fisher. One may reasonably take the attitude of Banks, Bullock's successor at the Air Ministry, as the test, and the Air Ministry's records show that in 1938 Banks was advising the Air Staff on how best to gain Treasury approval for their proposals. The method consisted of 'seeking sanction for additional expenditure as necessary, and not asking for too much at one go', even if this meant not disclosing the total cost of a scheme in advance.[137] Since the Treasury always preferred to judge proposals in the light of the ultimate total cost, and since Treasury officials spent a good deal of time trying to discover possible future financial implications of any given proposal, this advice by Banks hardly suggests that he was acting as an outpost of the Treasury.

It would be wrong to suggest that Fisher's position as official Head of the Civil Service was unimportant, as no doubt it strengthened the hands of Treasury officials in their day-to-day dealings with civil servants in defence departments, but it would be easy to exaggerate its importance. Moreover, Fisher's personal powers of patronage were a diminishing asset by the later 'Thirties as he was due to retire in September 1939.

Fisher, like any other civil servant, had to exercise influence, if at all, through ministers, and Watt has asserted that Fisher developed a relationship with Chamberlain while the latter was Chancellor, and that 'in view of what is known of Chamberlain's use of advice from those he trusted it may be assumed that Fisher retained considerable influence over him as a result'.[138] As already noted Chamberlain was the minister who made the most important contribution to the formation of defence policy, so that if Fisher was able to influence Chamberlain, he (Fisher) would also be able to influence defence policy. There is, however, a methodological difficulty in assessing a civil servant's influence on his minister. It is possible to note instances where Chamberlain disagreed with Fisher's advice – though such instances were rare before late 1938 – but one cannot assume, without falling into the *post hoc, ergo propter hoc* fallacy, that where Chamberlain and Fisher were agreed the former was being 'influenced' by the latter. Chamberlain had a mind of his own. What one can do is to trace the personal relationship between the two men – for it was not static – and this suggests a chronology of when Chamberlain was more, or less, likely to listen to Fisher.

Chamberlain had been Chancellor briefly in 1923–4, but it seems to have been during his long tenure from 1931 to 1937 that the relationship described by Watt developed. Watt had to *assume* that the relationship continued thereafter because his main informant, Fergusson, left the Treasury in 1936 when he ceased to be Chamberlain's Principal Private Secretary.[139] But Fisher's personality was sufficiently volatile to make any such assumption unsafe. Hankey, indeed, seems to have suggested to at least one subordinate in the C.I.D. Secretariat early in 1934 that Fisher was 'rather mad', having 'some mysterious nerve disorder' which affected his judgement, and Hankey later told Baldwin as much.[140] Fisher had been on sick leave in 1933, and he may well have overworked himself. Sir James Grigg, who knew Fisher well, has been quoted as saying that in his earlier days Fisher had been 'the greatest public servant of the century', and that those who saw him only when he was about to retire had not seen him 'in his prime'.[141] When one takes into account the strain of work and anxiety which Fisher and others bore during his last six years as Permanent Secretary it is easy to see how tensions may have developed.

Nevertheless, relations between Chamberlain and Fisher seem to have been easy as late as July 1938, when Chamberlain invited Fisher and his wife, together with Wilson and his wife, and members of the Prime Minister's Office, to an informal weekend at Chequers. Moreover, the tone of Fisher's private correspondence with Chamberlain was extremely warm, as for example a brief note to Chamberlain in 1936:

> Neville Dear – I did enjoy getting a little note from you – it gives such a cosy feeling. Bless you.
>   That's a truly delightful paper about Bullock, isn't it? But there's no escape from the consequences,
>   With fond love,
>   Warren[142]

So far as rearmament is concerned, according to Fisher, it was in September 1933 that on his return 'from a long illness, during which [he] had leisure to observe the contemporary rise of Hitler' that the Permanent Secretary urged a review of Britain's defences, and Chamberlain and the Cabinet agreed to the setting up of the D.R.C. in November of the same year. Subsequent to that Committee's report Fisher had several talks with Chamberlain, who persuaded the Cabinet in the summer of 1934 to halve the Army's proposals for re-equipment and to increase the Air Force's expansion programme.[143] Thereafter Fisher and Chamberlain questioned and chivvied those responsible for defence, with a view to settling priorities and to speeding the execution of the most important parts of the rearmament programme. As will be seen in Chapter IV it was only at the very end of 1938 that the views of Fisher and Chamberlain on defence policy began to diverge, although both were still agreed on the necessity of rearmament. But by that time the two men had already fallen out over the policy of appeasement.

Fisher has been accused of being a supporter of appeasement,[144] and certainly down to September 1938 he had not opposed Chamberlain's foreign policy. But Fisher was passionately opposed to the form appeasement took at the time of Munich.[145] The Government hoped rearmament would deter aggression while appeasement removed the causes of war, and during the crisis summer of 1938 he supported the Government's lead in urging a solution to the problem of Czechoslovakia's German-speaking minority. But in doing so Fisher assumed that any solution would be on 'the basis of the geographical Czechoslovakia we have known for the last 20 years'. Then on 15 September Chamberlain flew to Berchtesgaden, accompanied only by Wilson and a senior Foreign Office official, and returned to London the next day to consult the Cabinet, having given Hitler the impression that Britain would not fight for Czechoslovakia. In Fisher's subsequent view Chamberlain had 'sold the Fort', and he made a written protest on 17 September.

Fisher told Chamberlain that:

> Germany now demands the dis-integration of [Czechoslovakia], that is to say a reversal of the policy underlying all our efforts hitherto. . . .
>
> In our unwearying efforts in the cause of peace we have secured the approval of the world and surely it is vital not to jeopardise that – and to become *particeps criminis* with the Germans – by even appearing to surrender to force.

Fisher thought that any plebiscite imposed on the Czechs must be a real one, 'in contrast to the farcical one engineered in the case of Austria'. For Fisher the conditions for a real plebiscite included prior demobilisation by the Germans; the presence in the disputed areas of an 'international neutral police force'; a breathing space for the inhabitants to 'cool off their hysteria', and the plebiscite itself to be arranged and conducted by 'neutral elements'.[146] These were hardly the terms secured at the Munich Conference later the same month, and Fisher's subsequent talk of Britain's 'moral responsibility', coming at a time when Chamberlain admitted to his sister Hilda that he was 'nearer . . . to a nervous break down than I have ever been in my life', led to a rift between the two men. Fisher also found he could no longer work in amity with Wilson.[147]

By early 1939 Fisher realised he no longer enjoyed Chamberlain's confidence. Fisher ceased to attend the C.I.D. after 9 February, leaving it to Hopkins or Barlow to represent him, and, although Hopkins – and Hore-Belisha – continued to consult Fisher, there seems to have been no contact between Chamberlain and Fisher while major policy issues were being discussed at the end of March.[148] Although he was not due to retire until September 1939 Fisher decided to go on extended leave, so as to allow his designated successor, Wilson, to take over. He wrote to Chamberlain and Wilson on 15 May what he described as his 'swan song', criticising the present conduct of government business whereby, he said:

> The idea appears to be that nothing should be thought out, in advance or at any time, that panic conclusions should be reached without preparation or knowledge, and that the fait accompli, thus scientifically arrived at, should be presented to those who can provide experience, knowledge and practical advice.[149]

In particular he criticised 'an indefinite multiplication' of inadequately-briefed Cabinet committees, and claimed that ' "let not the left hand know what the right hand doeth" is the up-to-date rule of business'. This criticism was no doubt aimed at Chamberlain, who prided himself as an efficient man of business. Calling for proper interdepartmental examination of issues at the official and service level before they went to Cabinet committee, Fisher told Wilson, in words also intended for Chamberlain, that: 'I sincerely hope that, as you are fortunate enough to enjoy the Prime Minister's confidence, you may be more successful in this vital matter than I have been'.[150]

On 20 May Wilson took over Fisher's duties as Permanent Secretary of the Treasury and official Head of the Civil Service, while continuing to act as Chamberlain's confidential adviser. May 20 also saw Fisher writing in terms which hint at his emotions at this time, to Ismay:

> Pug Dear – bless you for your letter. For anything I may be worth, you can count on me. . . . And *please* let this be au revoir, *not* farewell, with love, Warren.[151]

Thereafter Fisher devoted himself to working for Civil Defence. He was regional commissioner for the North-Western Region, with head-quarters at Manchester, until May 1940, and in September 1940 he was appointed a special commissioner in the London region to co-ordinate the work of restoring roads and public utility services. This was a strange contrast to Hankey, who was brought back from retirement in 1939 to be a minister without portfolio in the War Cabinet. Fisher had little respect for Chamberlain's War Cabinet, the members of which he considered to be 'as a whole, nothing more than a set of inexperienced mediocrities', characterised by 'general incompetence'.[152] Fisher's attitude to ministers was eventually to lead to his dismissal, in 1942, by the Minister for Home Security, Mr. Herbert Morrison, after Fisher had publicly criticised Morrison's treatment of one of Fisher's former Civil Defence colleagues at Manchester.[153]

The final years of Fisher's career illustrate the growing strain and tensions in government circles as the crises of the 'Thirties grew worse. Fisher was not alone in feeling stress as a result of a lagging rearmament programme and a failing foreign policy. Men faced baffling problems in the political, economic and military spheres, as will become apparent below. In the circumstances it is easy to understand Chamberlain's preference for Wilson, whom Vansittart described as 'wise, calm and serene',[154] rather than the temperamental Fisher. Wilson came to act as a shield against Fisher's more outspoken comments. On 1 October 1938 Fisher prepared a memorandum for Chamberlain calling for a 'thorough reform of the Air Staff and ruthless selection to secure the right men', but Wilson secured Fisher's agreement to keep back the memorandum until Chamberlain's return from leave on the 18th, by which time the Secretary of State for Air had been able to prepare a memorandum counter-attacking Fisher by condemning the Treasury's alleged restrictions on Air Force expansion.[155]

Fisher was dedicated to one aim from 1933, to make Britain secure, and, in Grigg's words, he 'devoted himself to persuading, in season and out of season, his political masters to rearm'. An examination of the mass of Treasury files of the period shows, however, the Grigg was wrong in believing that this concern for rearmament led Fisher to take 'less and less interest in his proper Treasury functions'[156] – at least before 1939. Rearmament, and its cost, dominated all the major questions facing the Treasury from 1935. While carrying out his normal functions as Permanent Secretary and official Head of the Civil Service Fisher also aroused Whitehall to the country's danger with more effect than critics of the Government realised at the time. There were, of course, other warning voices, but Britain was fortunate in having an official head of the Treasury who was determined to expedite, and not to retard, rearmament.

Summary

In the absence of a Ministry of Defence the Treasury's functions must in any case have given it a key role in co-ordinating defence, both as regards formulation and execution of policy. Its representatives participated in the work of the C.I.D., including the important P.S.O. organisation, and Treasury control of expenditure could be used to hinder, or not to hinder, individual items in the rearmament programme. Since Treasury officials lacked the technical knowledge of members of defence departments, the preferred method of exercising Treasury control was to set overall financial limits within which defence departments themselves must decide priorities, but Treasury officials, with their first-class, logical minds, were formidable enough critics to force defence departments to think out proposals thoroughly.

The Treasury's influence over rearmament was increased by the facts that down to May 1937 its ministerial head, Chamberlain, was the most active minister in the National Government, and that its official head, Fisher, was also head of the Civil Service. Chamberlain and Fisher sought to shape defence policy according to how they interpreted the country's needs, and down to the autumn of 1938 they worked in harmony. It is best to see Chamberlain and Fisher as a team, of which other important members included Hopkins (for finance and the day-to-day running of the department) and Bridges (for detailed supervision of defence programmes). By the end of 1938, however, Treasury influence on rearmament was weakening, for personal and other reasons. The aforementioned team had been broken up with the departure of Bridges to the Cabinet Office and the ending of Chamberlain's and Fisher's harmonious relationship. At the same time Treasury control of expenditure was weakening in face of the increasing danger of war.

III

The Treasury's Influence on the Financial Limits to Rearmament

This chapter deals with the question of why the Treasury, despite Chamberlain's and Fisher's advocacy of defence preparedness, sought to limit defence expenditure. In considering the influence of the Treasury in this respect one has to bear in mind that, although the Treasury was the central department of finance, there were other advisers on government economic policy, notably the Bank of England and some government departments, especially the Board of Trade and the Ministry of Labour. At the highest level links between the Bank and the Treasury were very informal – the Governor, Norman, would call at the Treasury almost every evening to discuss matters with Hopkins, Phillips and Leith-Ross – while Norman saw himself as 'the bridge' between the City and Whitehall.[1] In addition to traditional sources of financial wisdom there was also, as already noted, the E.A.C.'s Committee on Economic Information, on which Phillips and Leith-Ross sat with economists and financial experts. The most active non-official members were the economists J. M. Keynes and Hubert Henderson, and Sir Alfred Lewis of the National Provincial Bank, although Keynes was absent from meetings, through illness, for much of 1937–8. Economists, City men and civil servants also met in the more informal atmosphere of the Tuesday Club, which was run by Keynes and Mr. Reginald McKenna, chairman of the Midland Bank, in the hope of 'educating' civil servants.[2]

Although years of high unemployment had led many men to question traditional financial wisdom in the Nineteen-Thirties, Keynesian economics had yet to establish itself as a new orthodoxy. Keynes was still working out his *General Theory* during 1932–5, and when he published it in 1936 he wrote:

> This book is chiefly addressed to my fellow economists. . . . At this stage of the argument the general public, though welcome at the debate, are only eavesdroppers at an attempt by an economist to bring to an issue the deep divergences of opinion between fellow economists which have for the time being almost destroyed the practical influence of economic theory . . .[3]

Publication of the book by no means brought controversy among economists to an end. Henderson, for example, commented:

> Mr. Keynes . . . invites the world to throw upon the scrap-heap a large part of the orthodox theory in which I still believe, to discard the methods of analysis which I intend to continue to employ, and to substitute a new theoretical system of his own which in my opinion asserts what is false and denies what is true, and is likely to cause an immense amount of confusion.[4]

When professional colleagues on the E.A.C. Committee on Economic Information could disagree so fundamentally, it is not surprising that Treasury officials, who were not economists, did not immediately grasp the new economic theory and make it the basis for public policy. Keynes did correspond with Hawtrey while writing the *General Theory*, but in the end felt, with good reason, that he had not succeeded completely in conveying what he was driving at.[5] Hopkins and Phillips were prepared to rethink the theoretical basis of financial policy in the light of new economic ideas, but the Treasury's conversion to Keynesian economics was still incomplete when war broke out.[6] Moreover, Treasury officials seem to have felt that academic economists alone were unlikely to provide answers to practical problems of government. A proposal in May 1939 to establish an 'Economic General Staff' found favour with Fisher and Hopkins, but even then Hopkins observed that this should not be made up of 'a lot of economists operating *in vacuo*', while Fisher commented: 'What is *not* wanted is a panel of economists and doctrinaires'. What was established in July 1939, after discussion between Wilson, Hopkins and the economist Lord Stamp, was a committee under the last named which combined the theory of economists and the practical experience of civil servants, with instructions to survey Britain's war plans in the economic and financial spheres.[7] Treasury officials, then, were willing to work with economists, but the intellectual apparatus of Keynesian economics had yet to establish itself. The same was true of the statistical apparatus, for it was not until 1940 that the official statistics of National Income and Expenditure, upon which so much of government planning has come to be based, were first compiled.

There was good reason why Treasury officials should be slow to abandon traditional concepts and methods. As men responsible for advising on public policy they were concerned with political economy rather than economic theory, and had to take into account the views not only of economists but also of men who bore responsibility or risk for actions in the real world – bankers and businessmen, both British and foreign, most of whom held to traditional economic beliefs. Leith-Ross once complained that 'Keynes, with all his brilliance, appears frequently to misunderstand the psychology of the markets'.[8] Whether or not that was true, the Treasury seems to have continued to regard the Bank of England as being the better judge of the possible effects of proposed policies on business confidence. The views of the taxpayer were also important; as were the likely reactions of foreign powers to any measures in the sphere of international trade.

Chamberlain had little time for what he called the 'fantastic notions' of critics who called for the abandonment of orthodox finance. 'That was all very well for people without responsibility for what might follow', he remarked in October 1933, but a government must be sure that 'the new experiments were really likely to succeed before they ventured upon them.'[9] It was still an axiom of conventional public finance that in peacetime government expenditure should not exceed revenue, and a balanced Budget was taken as a sign of financial stability. Accordingly balancing the Budget was Chamberlain's first priority on becoming Chancellor in November 1931, for he hoped thereby to recreate business confidence and the will to invest after the shocks which the financial community had sustained that year. Paradoxically, one of the greatest shocks of 1931 – the reluctant abandonment of the Gold Standard in September – made possible one half of his policy, which was to make 'cheap money' available for investment. From 1932 to the eve of war in 1939 Bank Rate was held down to 2 per cent, or less than half the average rate during the period from 1925 to 1931, when the Gold Standard had been maintained partly by attracting foreign funds to London with high interest rates. On the other hand, business-men would not invest at low interest rates if they were lacking in confidence – hence the stress placed by Chamberlain on 'sound finance'.

The general picture of economic recovery in Britain, as given by the *Economist* index of business activity, was one of strong and continuous recovery in 1933, but much less so in 1934, and the upswing was resumed only in 1935, which saw the beginning of a two-year period of very rapid recovery. From the middle of 1937 the economy ceased to expand, with a sharp recession following in 1938. Rearmament stimulated an increasing amount of activity, especially in 1938-9, and by the summer of 1939 the level of business activity was as high as it had been at any time since 1932 – but there was another disquieting aspect to the economic situation.

With the exception of 1919 and the year of the General Strike (1926), Britain had never had an adverse current balance of payments in peacetime before 1931. Traditionally Britain imported more goods than she exported, but this crude trade gap was more than balanced by 'invisible exports', chiefly associated with the City of London's position as a centre of world finance, and by income from overseas investments. For generations Britain had been accustomed to a favour-able balance of payments, by which means she could invest overseas in peace, and finance coalitions in war, although in 1914–18 Britain had had to borrow on a very large scale in the United States. In 1931, however, Britain's current balance of payments deficit was over £100 million, and although this figure was halved in 1932, and almost exact equilibrium achieved in 1933, an adverse balance reappeared in 1934. A substantial rise in exports saw a favourable balance re-emerge in 1935, but the following year the position was reversed, with exports stagnant and imports rising rapidly, and from 1937 onwards the current balance of payments was once more substantially adverse, and was indeed somewhat worse than in 1932. Britain's gold reserves continued to increase in 1936–7, on account of an inflow of 'hot money', but such gold could not be relied upon, and, indeed, Britain's gold reserves declined dramatically in 1938 and 1939.[10]

When from the end of 1936 Treasury officials began to talk of Britain's economic strength 'slipping away', essentially what they were talking about was the adverse current balance of payments, and its effects on the country's international purchasing power represented by its gold and foreign exchange reserves, overseas investments, and ability to raise international credit. As Fisher explained to the D.R.C. in January 1934, raw materials and food were available in the United Kingdom only in:

> negligible quantities and therefore have to be secured from other countries who will not, of course, give us them, and, when our international purchasing power is exhausted, will not continue indefinite credits to us.[11]

The triumph after 1940 of Keynesian economic thought, and memories of mass unemployment in the 'Thirties, have led to a common assumption that the Government of the day, and the Treasury in particular, were prisoners of outworn and misleading economic doctrines, which prevented full use being made of the nation's resources for rearmament. Accordingly criticism of the National Government's defence policy has been made in the light of the deteriorating international situation of the 'Thirties, and much less attention has been paid, with reference to rearmament or foreign policy, to the unprecedented balance of payments situation with which the National Government was confronted. Yet the extent to which Britain could rearm was limited by the quantity of raw materials which she could purchase from abroad, for it was calculated that some 25 to 30 per cent of the cost of armaments produced in British factories represented the price of imported raw materials. A substantial part of Britain's rearmament – the E.A.C. Committee on Economic Information estimated that part as one-sixth of the total cost – had to be paid for by exporting goods and services, or by running down her gold reserves and overseas investments, or by borrowing abroad.[12] It is with the balance of payments, and its effects on confidence in the financial community and on Britain's international purchasing power, chiefly in mind that the Treasury's attitude to the financial limits to rearmament must be considered.

The Balance of Risk

Defence policy involves balancing risks, and at any given moment those responsible for defence policy must be prepared to strike a balance in two different ways. Firstly, it must be decided what proportion of the country's productive resources should be devoted to armaments, which constitute an insurance but which in themselves are non-productive. This decision must be made in the light both of military risks facing the country and of possible effects of defence expenditure on the economy which will be called upon to produce and support the armaments decided upon. Secondly, it must be decided how to allocate the available resources between the various military risks. What follows deals with the first of these balances of risk, and the question of the Treasury's influence on grand strategy is left to the next chapter. The three variables in this chapter are the related problems of domestic inflation and Britain's balance of payments position, together with the problem of predicting if and when war would come.

The best starting point for an explanation of the Treasury's conception of the financial and economic limits to rearmament is Inskip's Interim Report of December 1937, part of which, drafted by Bridges, contained what Simon called 'a classic statement of the elements that make up our strength for national defence'.[13] Through the Report the Treasury pointed out to the Cabinet that although the problem of deciding what defence programmes could be afforded was considered in terms of money, the country's resources lay not in the quantity of paper pounds that could be printed, but in its skilled manpower and productive capacity, its ability to maintain credit and the general balance of its trade. Britain's reliance on imported foodstuffs and raw materials meant that the country's credit was closely bound up with its ability to pay for these imports through its export trade.

The sums available for defence expenditure were related to what could be made available from taxation, or 'exceptionally' from the proceeds of loans, but:

> The amount of money which we can borrow without inflation is mainly dependent upon two factors: the savings of the country as a whole which are available for investment, and the maintenance of confidence in our financial stability. But these savings would be reduced and confidence would at once be weakened by any substantial disturbance of the general balance of trade. While if we were to raise sums in excess of the sums available in the market, the result would be inflation; i.e. a general rise in prices which would have an immediate effect upon our export trade.[14]

The Treasury held that the maintenance both of government credit and of a general balance of trade was vital in peace and war. According to the Chiefs of Staff themselves, there was no hope of Britain overpowering Germany in a short war, but Germany was not so well placed as Britain and France with their command of the sea, and access to the world's resources, to face a long war.[15] The Treasury argued that if Britain was to emerge victorious from a long war she must enter such a war with enough financial and economic strength to enable her to make the fullest use of overseas resources. Seen in this light, the Treasury claimed, the maintenance of economic stability was as necessary as the maintenance of armed forces, and could 'properly be regarded as a fourth arm of defence'. On the other hand, if Germany and other countries were to detect signs of strain in Britain, they would no longer be deterred by the prospect of a long war, and it was up to the Cabinet to strike a proper balance between military and economic power.

It will be noted that the emphasis in Inskip's report was on deterrence, which involved defence forces which could be maintained indefinitely, rather than preparation for war at any specific date. The Treasury's views on defence policy were determined largely by what the Treasury saw as the economic and financial limits to rearmament, but the degree to which the Treasury was prepared to advise risking the economy was in turn based on a changing conception, or possibly misconception, of the international situation. Put briefly, the basic Treasury assumptions were that the maintenance of peace between the British Empire on the one hand, and Germany, Japan and Italy on the other, was possible; that this objective required deterrence of aggression through rearmament as well as diplomacy, but that Britain's armed forces should not be enlarged beyond a level at which her economy could maintain them. The underlying fear was that rearmament might precipitate a balance of trade crisis followed by a financial crash on the scale of 1931, weakening Britain's position in the world just when an appearance of strength was necessary to deter the dictators, and it was only by degrees that fears arising from the experience of 1931 were overborne by fears of impending German aggression.

The task of the Treasury, and the defence departments, would have been much simpler if it had been known that war would break out in September 1939. Then the possibility of national bankruptcy at some later date would have been seen in a different perspective. As it was, it seemed to Treasury officials that Britain might exhaust herself through defensive preparations even before war broke out. As Hopkins observed of an ambitious three-year programme formulated by the Air Ministry after Munich:

> The difficulty from the Treasury point of view is that we cannot say whether we shall be able to afford it. Indeed, we think we shall probably not be able to without bringing down the general economy of this country and thus presenting Hitler with precisely that kind of peaceful victory which would be most gratifying to him.[16]

As late as two months before the outbreak of war the Cabinet seems to have been uncertain if and when Hitler would provide a *casus belli* sufficient to unite democratic Britain and her Commonwealth. Chamberlain and his Foreign Secretary, Lord Halifax, both expressed hopes in July 1939 that the Danzig crisis would blow over if Britain presented a firm front.[17] In earlier years the uncertainty had been greater, and down to 1935, at least, the danger from Germany was not seen as an immediate one. Vansittart noted in April 1934 how 'opinions must necessarily vary and depart into the realms of prophecy in estimating the period [before Germany's] expansionist phase'. Prophecies from experts about German armed preparedness were not always helpful: for example, in April 1935 the Air Ministry advised a Cabinet committee that for technical reasons the *Luftwaffe* would not be ready for war until 1942.[18]

In this uncertainty the Treasury had to try to strike a balance between financing armaments now and maintaining sufficient economic strength to finance a war later. Simon summed up the dilemma well in March 1938, after the *Anschluss* had brought the possibility of war much nearer:

> At the present moment we are in the position of runner in a race who wants to reserve his spurt for the right time, but does not know where the finishing tape is. The danger is that we might knock our finance to pieces prematurely.[19]

It was this need to maintain the capability of producing and maintaining defence services in the future as much as reluctance to court unpopularity that lay behind the Government's decision at the beginning of 1936 not to allow the rearmament programme then agreed upon to interfere with normal civil trade and industry. As Chamberlain noted in November of that year:

> I do not believe that [war] is imminent. By careful diplomacy I believe we can stave it off, perhaps indefinitely, but if we were now to follow Winston [Churchill]'s advice and sacrifice our commerce to the manufacturers of arms we should inflict a certain injury upon our trade from which it would take generations to recover, we should destroy the [business] confidence which now happily exists, and we should cripple the revenue.[20]

In retrospect it may well seem to have been an illusion to hope for peace with Hitler's Germany, but if it was an illusion, it was one widely shared outside the Treasury Chambers, and there was no necessary connection between hoping for peace and unwillingness to rearm. There was no more outspoken an advocate of rearmament than Churchill, yet as late as August 1937 he could still publish an essay posing the question whether or not Hitler might yet go down in history as the man who brought Germany back, 'serene, helpful and strong to the forefront of the European family circle'.[21]

Economists may assume 'perfect knowledge', and historians have hindsight, but Treasury officials advising on the balance of risk between military and economic weakness had to do so in face of an uncertain and unpredictable future. The Treasury's attempts to limit defence expenditure are only explicable if seen in their historical context. Apart from uncertainty as to where the balance of risk lay, estimates of the money available for defence varied with the fortunes of the economy, public opinion (and therefore the willingness of the taxpayer to contribute to his own defence) and with the ability of the Government to raise loans. The balance between military and economic priorities moved from a position in 1932, when defence expenditure was entirely subordinated to the economic situation, to the summer of 1939, when priority for defence was such that the Treasury had to advise the Government that quasi-wartime controls over the economy would be required to maintain current defence expenditure after the autumn of that year.

Defence within a Balanced Budget

Part of the *prima facie* case for believing that the Treasury restricted defence departments' finance unduly rests on Chamberlain's opposition in 1932 and 1934 to any immediate large-scale increase in their expenditure. The rise in the Defence Estimates in the two years after the C.I.D. recommended cancellation of the Ten Year Rule was marginal, but it is as well to remember that the occasion for cancellation of the Ten Year Rule was not German rearmament – although covert rearmament was known to be going on in the Weimar Republic – but the crisis in the Far East involving Japan's occupation of Manchuria in 1931, and attack on Shanghai in January 1932. The Treasury did not dispute the C.O.S.'s recommendation in February 1932 that the rule be cancelled, but contented itself with pointing out the weakness of Britain's financial and economic position. Since the country was still in the throes of the crisis which the National Government had been called into being to solve, the Cabinet was little inclined to dispute Chamberlain's opinion that the risk of destroying the country's financial stability was greater than the risks of military unpreparedness. At the time everything was being done to reduce the Budget deficit, and the Cabinet readily agreed that the end of the Ten Year Rule must not be taken to justify an expansion of defence expenditure without regard to the financial and economic position. The Chancellor of the Exchequer was not blind to the military dangers, however, and he said that the question of military preparedness must be raised again when the financial position had improved – he seems to have expected that the defence estimates would rise from £103 million in 1932 to £115 million in 1935. Meanwhile officials within the Treasury were agreed that work on the naval base at Singapore must be allowed to go ahead, even although every effort was being made to pare defence expenditure to the bone.[22]

By the time the D.R.C. met in November 1933 future defence expenditure could be considered against the background of a prospective balanced Budget, and a gradually increasing yield from taxation with economic recovery. Economic recovery was still far from complete, however, and Fisher told the D.R.C. that it was hoped to provide industry with a 'psychological stimulus' in the form of a reduction in what were then considered the high rates of taxation set as an emergency measure during the crisis of 1931. To allow this, it would be better, he said, for additional defence expenditure to be incurred only slowly at first, proceeding on an ascending scale.[23] With Germany rearming, but not as yet rearmed, there still seemed time for Britain to put her house in order, and a balanced Budget and encouragement of civil trade and industry continued to have priority over the needs of the armed forces. The use of defence expenditure to speed economic recovery does not seem to have been favoured in Whitehall outside the Admiralty. The Admiralty in February 1934 urged unemployment in the shipyards as a reason for expediting naval construction, but with its finance restricted within a balanced Budget the Admiralty itself was unwilling to place orders in areas of high unemployment if this meant accepting tenders much above the lowest.[24]

The first D.R.C. Report, which Fisher signed together with Hankey, Vansittart and the C.O.S. in February 1934, put the cost of making up the 'worst deficiencies' in the armed forces at £93 million – a sum which even Hankey, the D.R.C.'s chairman, thought to be 'staggering', although the cost was to be spread over more than five years.[25] Clearly Hankey was not surprised when the Cabinet cut the D.R.C. figure to £77 million. Nor, apparently, was Fisher, who wrote in July 1934 to Sir Ernle Chatfield, the First Sea Lord, that:

> the political reactions of our own people are necessarily a matter of which politicians alone can be the interpreters; their views . . . are that our public is not as yet sufficiently apprised of the reality of our dangers to be ready to swallow at one gulp the financial results of the recommendations that we made.[26]

The political and financial reasoning with which Chamberlain convinced the Cabinet in the summer of 1934 were closely interlinked. The National Government was pledged to restore the pay cuts made in the crisis of 1931 and to restore the pre-1931 rate of Income Tax when the crisis was over, and such steps might provide the desired psychological simulus to trade and industry. These proposed Budgetary concessions would cost the Exchequer £27 million in 1934 and £40 million in a full financial year, or far more than what the D.R.C.

programme would cost. Nevertheless the Cabinet preferred Budgetary concessions to the full D.R.C. programme, and in this ministers seem to have been swayed by electoral considerations. Mr. J. H. Thomas drew attention to the 'peculiar circumstances' in which the National Government had come to power, which, he thought, might lead to a big swing away from it at the next election.[27] No minister took seriously a suggestion by Chatfield that more money could be found for defence within a balanced Budget if civil expenditure were reduced. Indeed, so far was defence from enjoying priority in ministerial minds between February and July 1934 – that is while ministers were considering the D.R.C. Report – that during these months over £24 million were allocated in subsidies to miscellaneous causes, including a new Cunard liner, meat, milk and beet sugar, the last accounting for over £5 million in 1934 alone.[28] The option of not attempting to meet the entire cost of defence out of revenue, and of resorting to a defence loan, was aired in ministerial circles in June 1934, but only to be rejected by Chamberlain in doctrinaire terms as 'the broad road which led to destruction', a view supported by Mr. Walter Runciman, the President of the Board of Trade.[29]

It is clear that the D.R.C. Report had not been altogether successful in arousing apprehension in the Cabinet. The Secretary of State for Foreign Affairs, Simon, was inclined to the view that Hitler's outlook was not threatening to Britain, while Mr. Samuel Hoare, who was later to succeed Simon, doubted whether the German menace was quite so acute as the Report seemed to assume. Hoare, in his memoirs, frankly admitted that up to the time of the Abyssinian crisis he shared the general feeling of complacency in the country, and paid tribute to the 'crusading fervour' of Fisher and Vansittart in campaigning for strengthening Britain's defences. Baldwin at the time seems to have found Fisher's crusading fervour rather tiresome, and according to G. M. Young, when Young remarked in 1935 to Baldwin, by then Prime Minister, that the Permanent Secretary of the Treasury seemed much concerned about Britain's defences, Baldwin snapped: 'better be minding his own business'.[30]

Fisher's manner rather than his message may have been what provoked Baldwin's attitude, for, according to Vansittart, Baldwin did not approve of 'passion',[31] and Fisher was nothing if not passionate on matters touching Germany and rearmament. As early as January 1934 Fisher had felt the need for a white paper to make the public aware of the danger confronting the nation, and to prepare public opinion for increased taxation, and in the winter of 1934-5, along with other officials, he suggested to MacDonald and Baldwin that the time for such a white paper had come. The final draft of what became the White Paper on Defence in March 1935 was produced by MacDonald, Baldwin, Chamberlain and Hankey, and proved much too mild for

Fisher's taste. Writing on behalf of other officials as well as himself he told Baldwin:

> We are so convinced (a) of the reality of the danger of war, (b) of the profound ignorance of our own people, (c) of the degree to which they have been misled by so-called pacifist propaganda, that we feel that if any document is to serve a useful purpose, it must be downright in its expression and avoid all half-hearted or unconvincing phraseology. The chief trend of the Cabinet variations [on the first draft] is to weaken the warning which I have always imagined it is common ground that our public badly needs.[32]

Baldwin, the most powerful man in the Cabinet although not yet Prime Minister, did not respond to Fisher's plea to reconsider the draft. The need to educate public opinion had to be balanced, in the mind of the leader of the Conservative Party, with the need to win an election. By his own account, given in private to a deputation comprising Sir Austen Chamberlain, Churchill and the Marquess of Salisbury, in July 1936, Baldwin had not thought it practical politics in 1934, in view of prevalent pacifist opinions, for a democracy to start rearming freely. He had felt strongly in 1934 the need to win an election as soon as possible so as to have a free hand with rearmament, but the Central Office of the Conservative Party had wanted any election delayed until 1936.[33] In the event Baldwin did not secure his electoral mandate for rearmament until November 1935, and even then much was made of his promise to a meeting of the International Peace Society in London that there would be 'no great armaments'.[34]

This failure to give the taxpayer timely warning of the sacrifices that might be required of the nation was no fault of the Treasury. From mid-1934 Chamberlain spoke frequently in public, at least for a Chancellor of the Exchequer, of the need to fill gaps in the country's defences, and in October 1935, just before the General Election, he quoted Adam Smith's dictum that 'defence is better than opulence' at the Conservative Party Conference. In planning the election campaign Chamberlain had urged Baldwin to meet pacifism squarely by taking 'the bold course of actually appealing to the country on a defence programme', but it was apparently not in Baldwin's nature to be bold.[35]

In the years 1932-4, then, the Treasury and the Cabinet were united in the belief that economic recovery must have priority over defence expenditure, and that orthodox public finance, and tax concessions, were appropriate means to create business confidence. Even Fisher, who showed himself to be a good deal more apprehensive about the danger from Germany than most ministers, looked to economic recovery to produce an expanding revenue for the defence expenditure which he knew would be necessary in future. Given his economic beliefs, this was a reasonable attitude in the period when defence requirements were being considered, for in the first half of 1934 German rearmament had not yet passed the blueprint stage, and it was not until the autumn of that year that the German Army began to equip with weapons prohibited by the Treaty of Versailles.[36]

On the other hand, Fisher's hopes that gradually increasing defence expenditure could be met out of rising revenue received a blow from Baldwin's refusal to be outspoken about the country's danger. Fisher understood the nature of the Nazi régime, and he wanted the taxpayer psychologically prepared to meet the coming German challenge. Given ministers' electoral considerations both with regard to tax and pay concessions and to the rearmament issue itself, it would seem to be unjust to ascribe to the influence of the Treasury alone the cuts made in the level of expenditure proposed by the D.R.C. Even the Treasury's objection to a defence loan in June 1934 was shared by the Board of Trade. When circumstances changed, as they did in 1935, when the extent of German military expenditure became apparent, Fisher seems to have been the first high official in Whitehall to suggest a departure from orthodox finance so that Britain's rearmament might be on an appropriate scale.

The Decision to Borrow for Defence

Roskill has claimed that, regarding 1936–7, 'the Treasury was still markedly reluctant to borrow for defence, and to accept the arguments put forward by Keynes early in 1937 that to borrow £400 million during the next five years was within the nation's capacity'.[37] This version of the decision to borrow to finance rearmament has gained some currency, so much so that Lord Kahn, who knew Keynes, has quoted Roskill, with reference to the Defence Loans Bill of February 1937, as saying that 'the Treasury was still markedly unwilling to accept the arguments put forward by Keynes'.[38] This picture of Treasury opposition to Keynes and the idea of borrowing for defence in 1937 is not, however, upheld by the Treasury papers quoted by Roskill in his footnotes.

According to Roskill a file from the Chancellor of the Exchequer's Office shows that:

> In February 1937, the month when Keynes expressed publicly his views on borrowing for defence . . . Treasury officials admitted that borrowing might be possible, but considered any attempt to assess the sum which could be borrowed 'too problematical'.[39]

The file in question shows that by the time Keynes first 'expressed publicly his views' the Defence Loans Bill of February 1937 had been worked out, and the figure of £400 million as the maximum sum to be borrowed over the next five years announced to Parliament. The file also contains a newspaper cutting of a speech by Keynes to the National

Mutual Life Association Society on 24 February 1937, with comments
on the speech by Hopkins and Phillips which show an attitude to
Keynes and to borrowing quite different from that implied by Roskill,
and which also suggest that the figure of £400 million was reached by
the Treasury unaided by Keynes. Phillips wrote that Keynes:

> makes the point that borrowing £400 million over five years is well
> within our capacity and that it is in the power of the Chancellor to get
> his money without producing conditions of inflation. He puts [the
> savings of the country] as being something like £400 million a year. . . .
> This is all to the good and what we have said.[40]

Hopkins observed that:

> Keynes' figure of £400 million is the sum he regards as being saved by
> *the main* sources of savings, but it is not comprehensive; if he took account
> also of repayments of foreign loans, growth of life insurance, the savings
> of wealthy individuals and many other items, he would very likely put
> the total at £500 million. But we cannot ourselves give a figure; it is too
> problematical.[41]

It was the annual savings of the country, not the sum which could
be borrowed, which the Treasury felt to be 'too problematical'. There
is another error contained in Roskill's work – Treasury officials
accepted the need to borrow for defence in 1935, not in 1937 when the
Defence Loans Bill was presented to Parliament.

As noted above, the Cabinet rejected the idea of a defence loan in
June 1934, and although the idea was put forward by Sir Roger Keyes
in the House of Commons the following month, the Cabinet does not
seem to have felt that support for the idea warranted further consideration on their part.[42] As yet most supporters of a Keynesian solution to
the country's difficulties had civil expenditure in mind. Chamberlain
began to waver in his defence of financial orthodoxy in January 1935,
when Mr. Lloyd George, long a critic of the Government's economic
policy, advocated 'a great Prosperity Loan'. The former Prime
Minister's scheme was to finance industrial and agricultural activity
from a government-controlled fund to cure unemployment, and there
was sufficient public support for the idea for Chamberlain to contemplate some form of capital expenditure with borrowed money. The
Chancellor asked Hopkins to consider whether the principle of loan
expenditure might not be applied to parts of the defence programme,
notably the creation of reserves of industrial plant, to be used for
armaments production in the event of war. Hopkins replied in the
negative, explaining that, according to the accepted principles of
public finance, such expenditure would be 'capital' only if it were
designed ultimately to produce a revenue which would pay off both
principal and interest on the loan – investment in a public telephone
system being cited as an example. Idle war reserve factories did not,
in Hopkins' opinion, come into this category.[43]

About the end of January 1935, however, Fisher received intelligence reports of German state borrowing. He wrote to Sir Eric Phipps, the ambassador in Berlin, of having:

> heard from two distinct sources a disquieting report that Germany is increasing her internal floating debt secretly as a means of finding money for accelerated rearmament (as well as for subsidising exports).[44]

According to the first report Germany's internal floating debt was increasing at one milliard marks a month – the equivalent of £80 million or £50 million, according to whether one used the official rate of exchange or the old gold par of exchange, but, Hopkins thought, rather nearer the latter figure if thought of in terms of goods and services. According to the second report Germany's internal floating debt had already been secretly increased by nine and a half milliard marks of which five to six were said to have been spent on rearmament. Phipps' investigations in Berlin confirmed the broad outlines of these reports, but Phipps thought that the figures were 'in all probability exaggerated', and commented:

> Further I do not think that it is possible for this rate of commitment to be continued much longer without risking a budget crash.[45]

Hopkins agreed that 'the figures appear to be incredibly high', but noted:

> At the same time the experience of Italy ... shows that very large amounts can be raised over a period of years by Government guarantees to private undertakings without substantial damage to the Budget being for the moment openly revealed. The expenditure is no doubt mainly internal, so that the exchange is not directly affected, though ultimately such methods must, of course, assist to make the devaluation of the mark inevitable.[46]

Fisher brought the matter to the attention of the Prime Minister, MacDonald, and Baldwin as well as Chamberlain, and by April 1935, when emergency measures to increase the Air Force's expansion programme were under consideration, it is clear that there was a move within the Treasury to depart from the accepted canons of finance for defence. After talking to Fisher, Fergusson, Chamberlain's Principal Private Secretary, wrote to the Chancellor in connection with Air Force expansion:

> If the increases are to be emergency measures, and in as far as the expenditure is for aerodromes etc., is there sufficient justification, on the ground that the expenditure would be abnormally large and concentrated in an abnormal degree in one or two years, for the cost to be spread over a period of say five or 10 years by loan? This is no doubt a very heterodox suggestion, but obviously there is a point when the argument which is valid as regards normal capital expenditure ceases to be conclusive.[47]

Fisher realised that a decision on so great a departure from peace-time precedent could not be expected from ministers at short notice, but he did suggest, and ministers agreed, in July 1935 that the defence departments should be authorised to examine defence requirements on the assumption that a defence loan would be forthcoming.[48] Chamberlain asked Bridges for an estimate of how much the defence departments would require, and was told that £108 million over and above the then estimated 1935 level of defence expenditure (£130 million), or a total of about £500 million, would have to be spent in the next three financial years if the D.R.C. programme of 1934 was to be complete by January 1939. This was the figure which Chamberlain had in mind when he noted in his diary on 2 August that an extra £120 million might have to be spent in the 'next four or five years'.[49] In the event, prompted by Fisher and Hankey in the D.R.C., the defence departments asked in November 1935 for about £417 million over and above the original 1935 Estimates (£124 million), or a total of £1038 million, to be spent over five years.[50] This total, for what Hankey called a 'policy of perfection', was trimmed by £22 million by ministers in the D.P.R.C. in February 1936, but so far was Chamberlain from placing financial restrictions on rearmament at that date that ministers decided to accelerate the defence departments' programme – that is to spend more money than suggested by the D.R.C. – in 1936-8.[51]

Meanwhile, within the Treasury, Hopkins was reviewing the idea of a defence loan from the point of view of public finance. He wrote to Chamberlain in October 1935:

> We should delude ourselves if we looked upon the expenditure facing us as capital in nature.

– on which Fisher commented: 'I should have thought this something of an overstatement'. Hopkins' memorandum continued:

> We shall in fact be engaged both in paying for stores, equipment, etc., which should have been provided out of past revenue, in making the preliminary outlay for bringing up the size of the forces to a new standard (especially the Air Force), and in paying the current cost of that new standard. But however the expenditure may be divided into these categories, it is most of it ephemeral and all of it unproductive of any money return, and therefore all of it in nature revenue expenditure. So far as I can see the only ground for borrowing – though it may be a sufficient one – is that the expenditure places the Exchequer seriously in deficit *when the country is taxed to full capacity*, and the measure of the reasonable borrowing is provided by the amount of the deficit. It would be unfortunate if the country began to think of a Defence Loan as a comfortable Lloyd-Georgian device for securing not only larger forces but also lower estimates, Budget surpluses and diminishing taxation.[52]

Fisher subsequently accepted that armament expenditure was not 'capital in nature' and although he was a strong advocate of a defence loan, he described deficit financing as a 'rake's progress', and expressed caution at the 'mischievous nonsense preached by distinguished econo-mists'. At the same time he did not believe that the taxpayer, still ignorant of the country's danger, would be willing to provide all the funds necessary for rearmament, and, therefore, it was expedient politically that money should be borrowed.[53] The Treasury, then, was very far from thinking in modern 'Keynesian' terms when it accepted the need to meet defence expenditure out of borrowing. A balanced Budget was still regarded as normal and desirable. To under-stand the doubts felt by the Treasury concerning borrowing for defence one has to bear in mind the experience of 1914–19, when about 64 per cent of total government expenditure had been met by borrowing, and the National Debt had increased from £650 million (on 31 March 1914) to £7832 million on 31 March 1920. Prices had risen sharply during the war, bringing about social unrest and industrial disturbance, and so much short-term government debt had come to be held by the public, especially the banks, when peace came that there had been an inflationary boom, fed by bank credit. At the same time the Budget had been saddled with an unprecedented problem of debt servicing. Orthodox opinion inclined to the view that in 1914–19 too much had been raised by loan and too little by taxation, and it was the experience of that period which the Treasury was bound to have in mind while considering the financing of rearmament.[54]

In 1935–9 the Treasury seems to have been determined to avoid borrowing from commercial banks in such a way as would expand the latter's liquid assets and, potentially, bank credit to the public. By the Nineteen-Thirties the Treasury had begun to think of expenditure rather less in terms of the prospect of spending so much public money, and rather more in terms of employment of resources, and the financing of rearmament down to 1939 seems to have been guided by a desire to secure the use of industrial resources for rearmament. A note on inflation by Phillips in April 1939 gives a clue to Treasury thinking:

> Up to a certain high point the Government can borrow savings sub-scribed out of investors' incomes which would otherwise have been applied to meet the capital outlay of private enterprise. The lender, by foregoing the use of his own income, not only releases purchasing power but releases also productive capacity which the borrower can then take up. . . . It is when the Government either cannot, or will not, raise enough money through this channel and resorts to . . . borrowing from banks that inflation occurs. That latter course is what we shall avoid. We have already borrowed over £200 million for rearmament and the investments of the clearing banks are slightly *lower* than in 1936.[55]

Whether or not expansion of bank credit would be inflationary depended upon whether labour and industrial capacity were available to meet demand, but, as will be seen below, it was by no means certain that the labour and industrial capacity required for rearmament were immediately available at the time borrowing for defence was being considered in 1935-7. It should be stressed, however, that for Treasury officials, as for most contemporaries, inflation was a 'bad thing'. The Treasury's experience of 1914-18 had been that inflation had evil social effects, and created difficulties in the collection of revenue and in the allocation of resources. Hawtrey in particular was outspoken in advocating what he called 'a monetary policy of stabilisation of the purchasing power or wealth-value of the money unit'.[56]

Treasury officials distinguished between 'genuine savings' of the public, and the purchase of long- or medium-term government bonds by firms or commercial institutions with idle balances, who thereby lent to the Government, at higher interest rates than they could otherwise safely obtain, money which would not otherwise have been spent. This, together with the advantages to the Treasury and to the depressed areas of low interest rates, accounts for the modest interest rate – $2\frac{1}{2}$ per cent – offered on the first issue of Defence Loan in 1937. As Phillips observed in December 1936:

> All the big industrial companies have large deposits, for which they would cheerfully substitute a Government loan of 3 per cent or upwards on which they could borrow from their banks in future.

The Treasury seems to have hoped that $2\frac{1}{2}$ per cent would mean that the money for the Defence Loan would come 'as far as possible from the genuine savings of private people'.[57]

The problem of funding new debt by making fresh issues of gilt-edged stock had been much reduced by the successful conversion in 1932 of the large block of 5 per cent War Loan to a $3\frac{1}{2}$ per cent basis, so that whereas in 1931 the amount required for annual interest on the National Debt had been £282 million, in 1935 it stood at £210 million. Even so, Britain's *per capita* burden of National Debt was the greatest in the world, mainly because British governments since 1918 had eschewed inflationary policies, and as late as 1936 the interest paid on the National Debt exceeded the total defence Estimates.[58]

Hopkins, while not wishing to impede rearmament, clearly wished to put off the hour of borrowing for defence until the possibilities of taxation had been exhausted. Writing in October 1935 of the 1936 Budget, he told Fisher and Chamberlain:

> Much depends on figures not yet known, but if it be possible I think there is much to be said for presenting next March Estimates which can be met without a deficit inside an optimistically constructed Budget. These Estimates could be accompanied by a statement that Supplementary Estimates would almost certainly be necessary; and the introduction of the Supplementary Estimates might be the occasion for the commencement of borrowing.[59]

To maintain public confidence in the financial system, and to meet the constitutional requirement that defence expenditure should be voted in advance year by year by Parliament, Hopkins suggested that the Budget for each defence department should take the form:

Votes for fighting services	£x
less sum authorised to be borrowed	£y

$$\text{Net} \quad £x-y$$

It would be 'of the essence', he told Chamberlain and Fisher, that £x—y should always greatly exceed the 1935 defence Estimates, or, in other words, that the amount raised from taxation should be increased. Even so, as Phillips observed later, this form was only a 'pretence at producing a balanced Budget'.[60]

At first Hopkins and Phillips assumed that there would be no Defence Loan as such, but that borrowing for defence would be met by Treasury Bills, funded occasionally by 4 per cent Consols. As it happened the revenue was so buoyant in 1936 that all that the defence departments could spend in that financial year (since new armaments factories had yet to be completed) was met out of taxation. At the end of 1936, however, Hopkins was advised by Phillips that world prices were rising, and that within two years interest rates would also rise. Bank Rate, Phillips believed, might have to be doubled in 1938 to 4 per cent, and the Government should borrow while cheap money lasted. 'We had better contemplate a fairly large long-term loan, £100 million or £150 million, early next year', Phillips wrote.[61]

These figures represented possible borrowing in 1937, not a maximum for the whole period of the rearmament programme. As we have seen, Hopkins believed that the amount to be borrowed should be determined by the difference between what was necessary for defence, and what could be found out of revenue 'when the country was taxed to full capacity'. In February 1936 the Cabinet had approved a D.R.C. programme which envisaged total defence expenditure in the five financial years 1936–40 of about £1016 million. By December 1936, however, the defence departments' returns to the T.I.S.C. showed that the many additions to the D.R.C. programme authorised in that year would mean that that total would be far exceeded, and Hopkins observed that:

It is not at present possible to determine what will be the peak year of defence expenditure: that must depend on circumstances which cannot at present be foreseen, and upon decisions to be taken in future years. It would be prudent, however, to contemplate that the total expenditure on defence over the next five years may well be of the order of £1500 million to £1600 million.[62]

Some idea of what such a figure meant at the time can be obtained from the fact that total central government revenue for the financial year 1936 was £797 million, of which £186 million was spent on defence.[63] In June 1937 the Treasury was to give the Cabinet a figure of £1100 million as the sum available for defence out of anticipated revenue in the quinquennium 1937–41, at prevailing rates of taxation,[64] and it seems likely that the figure of £400 million given to Parliament on 17 February 1937 as the maximum sum to be borrowed, as and when needed, for defence over the quinquennium simply represented the difference between estimated revenue and expenditure.

The figure of £400 million had already been decided upon when Hopkins wrote to Fisher on 4 February 1937 that:

> [the Defence Loans] Bill is extremely important and quite unprecedented in this country. Although public opinion is prepared for borrowing on a considerable scale, I imagine the £400 million will create a great stir. (What immediate effect it will have on Government credit I find it very difficult to judge, but the Chancellor will, I understand, sound the Governor [of the Bank of England] today.[65]

The next day Mr. John Woods, Chamberlain's Principal Private Secretary, reported to Hopkins that:

> The Governor thought that the figure would be a shock and that it would have a depressing effect on our credit. He was not prepared to measure the effect. He remained quite calm on the subject.[66]

It was necessary to include an upper limit in the Bill to reassure the financial public that the Government was not embarking on a policy of unlimited deficit financing, and, as a further reassurance, Hopkins persuaded the defence departments that their annual Votes should bear interest on the debt they were incurring, and also, from April 1942, a sinking fund to pay off the principal over thirty years. Hopkins thought that the Government's claim that rearmament was 'capital expenditure' to make up exceptional deficiencies in the country's defences was a thin pretext for borrowing to meet what was in fact recurrent expenditure. But, he felt, at least the form of the 1937 Defence Loans Bill would show that borrowing was according to a definite plan with a promise of redemption, unlike the 'hand-to-mouth' borrowing on behalf of the Unemployment Assistance Board, which had done so much to discredit the Labour Government in financial circles in 1931. Hopkins noted that:

> In financial quarters throughout the world (where perhaps more than anywhere else the credit of a nation is made or marred) borrowing for a current purpose which merely provides for men in idleness is regarded as one of the worst forms of borrowing, but borrowing for armaments . . . is regarded as unfortunate, no doubt, but still respectable; and of course the history of the last few years has reinforced the latter attitude by many precedents.[67]

However modest the sum of £400 million in the Defence Loans Bill of 1937 may seem in retrospect, the fact remains that at the time the proposed borrowing powers were widely criticised not for being too small, but for being too extensive. The *Economist* in March 1936 had frankly denounced the idea of borrowing for defence as 'unsound finance' and when the Defence Loans Bill was presented to Parliament on 17 February 1937 the Labour Opposition was able to quote one of the Government's own economic advisers, Henderson, as saying that to meet government expenditure out of loans instead of taxes would be to risk credit inflation. The Labour spokesman on economic matters, Mr. F. W. Pethick-Lawrence, pointed out that prices were already rising, and predicted that the pumping of new purchasing power into the economy on the proposed scale would lead to a boom followed by a slump.[68]

This was not Hopkins' view. He told Chamberlain on 23 February:

Few authorities . . . would put our net national income at less than £4000 million a year, and it is rapidly increasing. . . . This expenditure of £1500 million on defence in five years, tremendous as that sum . . . undoubtedly is, cannot be represented as likely to overstrain our economy. Moreover, of this expenditure not more than £400 million will be borrowed. . . . It is pure nonsense to say that we cannot borrow £80 million a year without causing inflation. It is a mere fraction of our annual savings.[69]

Hopkins and Phillips were glad of Keynes' support when in his speech of 24 February he told members of the National Mutual Life Association that he felt 'no doubt that the sums which the Chancellor of the Exchequer proposes to borrow are well within our capacity', especially since, as Keynes himself said, the effect of the Defence Loans Bill on the gilt-edged market had been 'severe'. But as Phillips noted: 'This is . . . what we have said'. Treasury officials and the Governor of the Bank of England were quite calm on the subject of borrowing £400 million for defence over five years, while being concerned, as Keynes himself was, to reassure the financial public that the measure would not lead to inflation.[70] The picture of a reluctant Treasury being prodded by Keynes into borrowing for defence in 1937 is completely misleading. Borrowing for defence was proposed by Fisher, and accepted as inevitable by Hopkins, in 1935, as a measure which was necessary, although not in itself desirable. There remains the possibility that Hopkins and his advisers imposed too narrow a limit on borrowing, but, as will be seen below, there seems to have been a surprising amount of agreement between the Treasury and Keynes in 1937 even on the figure of £400 million as the limit of borrowing for the quinquennium 1937–41.

The Rationale for Rationing: (i) Trade and Industry

If Hopkins thought in February 1937 that expenditure of £1500 million on defence over five years was not 'likely to overstrain our economy', and that it was 'pure nonsense' to say that £400 million of that sum could not be borrowed, why did the Treasury insist later that same year that the defence departments' programmes be worked out anew on the basis that the figure of £1500 million would be a maximum? Part of the explanation has been given already, in Chapter II: rationing of defence expenditure was a device to reassert Treasury control at a time when departments were constantly proposing additions to the rearmament programme which had been adopted by the Cabinet in February 1936. The Treasury wished in 1937 to persuade ministers and departments to 'determine priorities', and to persuade the Cabinet that 'new projects of major importance should be postponed' while defence policy was being reviewed in relation to the nation's resources.[71] Once this had been done, by Inskip in the autumn of 1937, Hopkins was prepared to relax the figure of £1500 million to £1570 million, or something even higher, depending upon the Cabinet's view of the need for higher taxation in the light of the international situation. The Treasury's motives, then, were partly administrative.

Nevertheless, there was an economic and financial rationale to the Treasury's action. It will be recalled that in 1937 war was not yet an immediate prospect, and the aim of rearmament, and the maintenance of Britain's financial and economic strength, was to deter aggression while the causes of war were removed by diplomatic means. Accordingly, it was assumed in the Treasury that the rearmament programme as a whole should not grow so large as to aim at defence services which could not be maintained without weakening the economy.

Yet by the end of 1936 there were clear signs that rising rearmament expenditure was accompanied by rising prices and a current balance of payments deficit. On 31 December Phillips drew attention to the fact that the Board of Trade index of wholesale prices had risen over 3 per cent on the previous four weeks,[72] and Leith-Ross, in a Cabinet Paper prepared the same month at the request of the President of the Board of Trade, warned that rearmament, coupled with increased domestic civil demand, was already diverting industrial activity away from export markets, so that a balance of payments deficit was in prospect. Leith-Ross warned:

We must at all costs avoid getting involved in the vicious spiral of increased prices, increased wages, increased costs and increased depreciation of currency. . . .[73]

Price increases were not necessarily to be deplored, for they were to be expected in a period of economic recovery, and would stimulate investment by heightening expectations of profit. What mattered was that British prices should not rise faster than those of foreign competitors. Chamberlain shared his advisers' concern, and wrote in April

1937 of his fear of 'a sharp steepening of costs due to wage increases, leading to the loss of our export trade, a feverish and artificial boom followed by a disastrous slump, and finally the defeat of the Government'. Fisher noted in June, just before rationing was suggested in Cabinet, that 'we are . . . in danger of undermining ourselves before the Boche feels it desirable to move', and Bridges commented upon Inskip's report in December that 'we simply cannot afford another 1931'.[74]

It may seem odd that the Treasury should have been concerned about inflationary effects of rearmament at a time of high unemployment, but it was a concern shared by Keynes in the spring of 1937. The view expressed by Keynes in March of that year, in an article entitled 'Borrowing For Defence: Is It Inflation?', was that:

> The Chancellor's loan expenditure [of £80 million a year] *need* not be inflationary. But unless care is taken it may be rather near the limit. This is particularly so in the near future. It is in the next year or 18 months that congestion is most likely to occur. For ordinary investment is still proceeding under the impetus of the recent years of recovery. . . .
>
> The number of insured persons who are still unemployed is, indeed, as high as $12\frac{1}{2}$ per cent. But . . . we cannot regard even half of those unemployed insured persons as being available to satisfy home demand. For we have to subtract the unemployables, those seasonally unemployed etc., and those who cannot readily be employed except in producing for export [e.g. textile workers].
>
> Thus it is not plain sailing. If we suppose the full rate of Government spending to begin immediately, without any improvement in the export industries or any reduction in other activities, unsupported by organised overtime, by careful planning and an interval for the planning to take effect, there is a risk of what might fairly be called inflation. . . .[75]

Keynes' article suggests that, according to the best economic advice available at the time, greater and more rapid rearmament than in fact took place involved the risk of inflation in 1936 and 1937. The risk was also implied in the reports of the E.A.C.'s Committee on Economic Information which, for example, told the Government in February 1936 – that is before the rearmament programme had begun – that the steel industry's output in 1935 had been its highest ever to date, and that the industry was approaching its full capacity to produce.[76] Keynes went so far as to suggest, in January 1937, that the Chancellor should 'meet the main part of the cost of armaments out of taxation, raising taxes', since 'just as it was advisable for the Government to incur debt during the slump, so for the same reasons, it is now advisable that they should incline to the opposite policy'.[77]

Britain's army of unemployed could not readily be used for rearmament work. During the long years of depression the number of apprenticeships had been reduced, while new industrial processes had rendered obsolete the skills of some of those men who had served their time. Time was needed for training, or retraining. Ministers considering the rearmament programme in the D.P.R.C. early in 1936 were told by Lord Weir, the industrialist who acted as their adviser, that the lack of highly skilled labour was the worst bottleneck in industry.[78] The bottleneck could be eased by putting semi-skilled men on work normally done by skilled men – if the trade unions would agree. But even during 1914–18 the government had not dared to impose industrial conscription, and the unions' experience of 'dilution' then, followed by unemployment and attempts to reduce wages in peace, did not make mutual trust between Government, employers and labour easy. The Cabinet expected in 1936 that employment arising out of rearmament would be temporary, and that therefore it would be difficult to enlist the support of the trade unions, who were expected by Mr. Ernest Brown, the Minister of Labour, to be 'suspicious and obstinate'.[79]

How far individual trade unions were suspicious and obstinate in their dealings with employers is uncertain, but it may be noted that as early as the autumn of 1936 some Trades Union Congress leaders, notably Sir Walter Citrine, were thoroughly alarmed at events in Abyssinia and Spain, and invited the Government to rely on their wholehearted collaboration in rearmament. The following September the T.U.C. adopted by an overwhelming majority a National Council of Labour statement committing a future Labour government not to reverse the policy of rearmament until international relations had improved. Members of the National Government, on the other hand, seem to have feared close collaboration with the unions, believing that the latter's price for such collaboration might be a less flexible stance in foreign policy. As late as March 1938, after Hitler had occupied Austria, Inskip, the minister most responsible for the industrial aspects of rearmament, argued against the further expansion of the Air Force on the grounds that such expansion would require an approach to the trade unions, with a view to 'dilution', and such an approach was likely to be badly received.

> The sort of difficulty he anticipated from the trade unions was that they would make conditions: for example, they might demand that the Government undertake the use of arms in support of Czecho-Slovakia, or insist on the question being dealt with by the League of Nations.[80]

At that late date, despite Inskip's doubts, the Prime Minister invited the General Council of the T.U.C. to meet him, but found that organised labour was deeply suspicious that employers were trying to exploit the situation for their own advantage. Undoubtedly trade union standards were much relaxed, but the process seems to have had some way to go at the beginning of 1938.[81]

At all events, the reality which Treasury officials had to take into account in 1936 and 1937 was that, according to the Ministry of

Labour, there was a tendency in the South-East of England, even before the rearmament programme had begun, for employers who could not obtain skilled labour from elsewhere to raise wages in competition with each other. The Ministry suggested that wherever possible defence contracts should be placed in the Special Areas, where the country's reserves of skilled labour were to be found, and from 1936 one finds Chamberlain, at the ministerial level, and Barlow, at the official level, urging defence departments to place orders where there was unemployed labour, and steps were taken to encourage tenders from firms in those areas which had not been contractors to defence departments hitherto.[82] It would be difficult, however, to say to what extent the fact that most new armament factories were built well away from the Midlands and South of England was a result of Treasury influence – the fact that the Midlands and South would be the areas most exposed to German bombing did much to enforce a 'regional policy' on employment.

On the other hand no effort was made to control industrial activity so as to prevent civil trade competing with rearmament work. Ministers were told by Lord Weir in January 1936 that the rearmament programme could not be carried out in five years, as recommended by the D.R.C., without affecting exports – unless quasi-wartime controls were imposed on industry, as in Germany. Yet not one minister in the D.P.R.C., which included Baldwin, Mr. Anthony Eden, the Foreign Secretary, and the three service ministers, as well as Chamberlain, was disposed to disagree with Weir's belief that such controls would be impossible politically in Britain, and the Cabinet agreed that rearmament was not to interfere with normal civil trade.[83] Naturally the Treasury supported this principle, but it was the policy of the Government as a whole, and when in 1937 Swinton tried to have the policy changed, he found that the Prime Minister (Chamberlain) and the Board of Trade were the most strenuous opponents of any peacetime direction of industry.[84] The whole ethos of the National Government inhibited any consideration of taking powers to prevent firms engaged in civil work from competing with rearmament work. In the words of a Government statement in March 1936:

> For the Government in a competitive country like Great Britain, which depends on the profits of industry . . . , to put difficulties in the way of industrial enterprise is to place on its shoulders a great responsibility. The course of wisdom and truth is that the Government must at all costs avoid compulsion. . . .[85]

One form of labour shortage which had a particularly detrimental effect on rearmament was that of building labour, since for want of it armament factories, barracks and other works were delayed. The Ministry of Labour warned in the summer of 1936 that unless there was a decline in speculative housebuilding the shortage of building labour could be expected to be serious for at least eighteen months. By 1936 there had been a consumer boom for two years and a total of 530,000 private houses had been built in 1934 and 1935, compared with less than 200,000 in 1932 and 1933. At the end of 1936 Leith-Ross, in an analysis of the causes of the reappearance of a deficit in the current balance of payments, assigned only a small part of the blame to rearmament, and pointed to other significant factors, including the increased demand for imported manufactured timber caused by the continuous development of building activity.[86] Nothing, however, was done by the Government to bring about a decline in house-building, principally, it would seem, because ministers feared what Inskip called 'the political reactions' to such a step.[87]

With the benefit of hindsight, Phillips in June 1940 could describe the failure to put the country's productive capacity on a war basis in 1936 as 'an initial error', the large rearmament orders producing nothing for a year or more while industrial bottlenecks sprang up on every side.[88] As it happened the consequences of a radical departure from the policy of non-interference with civil trade were considered by the Treasury and the Board of Trade following a suggestion by Churchill in July 1936 that 20 to 30 per cent of the value of the country's industrial production should be devoted to munitions. The Board of Trade estimated that such a policy might enable a seven-fold increase on the 1936 level of expenditure on warlike stores, but warned that such a change would be impossible without restrictions on the production of goods either for the home market or for export, implying 'a much reduced standard of living or a heavy adverse balance of payments'. The Treasury officials' view at the time was that extensive restrictions on the home market would arouse so much resistance as to undermine public support for rearmament. Moreover, they noted, export markets, once lost, would be very difficult to recover even in the long term, while in the short term the effect would be to weaken the country's financial strength which 'at present is our decisive advantage' vis-à-vis Germany.[89]

Moreover, the threat from Germany was not seen as an exclusively military one. At the end of 1936 Leith-Ross warned that with German exports in 1935 at only 54 per cent by volume of their 1929 level, compared with 75 per cent in the case of Britain, serious trade competition could be expected in the markets for engineering and other industries most likely to be affected by rearmament.[90] The Department of Overseas Trade could offer no suggestions in 1936 on how to combat unorthodox methods used by Germany to increase her exports, apart from trying to obtain the co-operation of German government departments in advance of discussions between representatives of British and German business organisations. Waley's comment was that 'It does not seem to me that any action to protect our exports can usefully be taken (apart from cartel arrangements): it is part of the wider problem of getting Germany out of her lunatic asylum into the fresh air'.[91] The imposition of exchange controls, or other direct government intervention in organising overseas trade, was repugnant to Whitehall officials, who, with their liberal economic views, tended to associate controls with dictatorship. Whitehall officials held to the traditional conception of Britain's role in the international economy, and as late as the end of 1938, when sterling was under severe pressure, Waley noted that the adoption by Britain of exchange controls on the scale of those in Germany would be 'a serious blow at international trade, which is a vital interest to us'.[92]

The loss of overseas markets in 1914–18 had had grave repercussions on Britain's staple export industries, and in the early and mid-'Thirties British exports were still losing ground in some traditional markets, owing to severe Japanese competition, the effect of which could only be increased if the pace of rearmament raised the level of British prices. The actual diversion of production to rearmament also raised problems in the case of Britain's more successful export industries, and in February 1936 Wilson and Fisher, through Inskip, arranged for a quota of the machine tool industry's output to be reserved for exports, the balance of rearmament requirements being met from imports until domestic production could be expanded. Even before the end of 1936, however, Treasury officials believed British firms were slackening in their efforts to obtain export contracts, since rearmament offered an easier and more lucrative field, and in December 1936 the President of the Board of Trade, Runciman, felt constrained to give businessmen a public warning that the high level of orders owing to the defence programme must be considered temporary, and that they should not allow their export trade to be lost.[93]

There was no easy escape from the constraints of industrial capacity and the need to maintain Britain's competitiveness in world markets. The effects of domestic inflation on export prices could be offset only if the exchange rate of sterling in relation to foreign currencies was allowed to fall, but the experience of depreciation of sterling after September 1931 had been that while British exports benefited briefly, other countries were provoked to devalue their currencies or to raise tariffs, and the general effect of economic nationalism had been to reduce the total volume of world trade. Such a reduction was not in Britain's interests, as a trading nation, and in September 1936 Britain entered a tripartite agreement with the United States and France to maintain the greatest possible equilibrium in exchange rates, with a view to encouraging international trade. In any case depreciation of sterling would lead to higher prices for essential imports, while once key industries such as steel and machine tools were fully committed to the rearmament programme, it would be difficult for many exporters to respond to the stimulus of a lower exchange rate, and the effect of any considerable depreciation would be simply to drain the country of its gold and foreign exchange reserves. Broadly speaking this is what happened, even with wartime controls over foreign exchange and domestic consumption, after depreciation in August 1939 raised the sterling price of imports from America by about 20 per cent.[94]

In any case American neutrality legislation meant that Britain would have to rely more on her own industrial resources than in 1914–18, even if her ability to purchase abroad had not been reduced by the running down of her financial reserves in that war. Failure after 1933 to make any repayments on War Debts to the United States meant that, under American neutrality legislation, Britain could raise neither public nor private loans in the United States, and, in the event of war, she could buy arms only on a dollars-draining 'cash and carry' basis. Fisher in July 1937 had thought that the question of settlement of the War Debts might, with advantage, be reopened, and he wrote to Simon that 'final settlement in about 18 months from now of, say, £150 million (transferred in gold) might well have an incalculable value in its influence on Middle West opinion as against a future when we were in a European mess'. Hopkins, however, advised the Chancellor that there was no prospect for the time being of negotiations for a settlement being successful, as it would be impossible to reconcile British public opinion to what would be acceptable terms to the Americans – that is the re-institution of payments on a scale similar to those made before regular repayments had been discontinued in 1931. Simon, after consulting Chamberlain, accepted Hopkins' opinion, and Fisher had no option but to acquiesce.[95]

It was the potential effects of unlimited rearmament on Britain's economic competitiveness – and, therefore, ultimately on her military strength – which provided the main rationale for the rationing of defence expenditure. As early as October 1936 Bridges, commenting on the constant additions being made by departments to their programmes, noted:

> Clearly it is desirable, if practical, to increase the measure of insurance provided by our defences, and to provide against being caught short on some vital item. But it is essential to remember that there are physical limits to what can be provided in a limited period. If the defence departments all try to force the pace at once there will be a jam.[96]

This jam, Bridges noted would lead to a rise in wages and costs of raw materials, affecting both the rearmament programme and exports. Confirmation for this view came in the following month when the defence departments' supply officers reported that there was not sufficient skilled labour available to maintain all of the projected defence forces in war. Bridges observed:

We must face the fact that the full programmes at present being planned by all three Services may be beyond the resources of our industrial organisation.[97]

The need to work out priorities in the defence departments' programme so that the programme as a whole did not weaken the economy provided the background to Treasury officials' calculations as to what finance was available for defence. It is to these calculations that we now turn.

The Rationale for Rationing: (ii) Finance

By 1937 it was apparent that the defence programmes were getting ahead of manpower and productive capacity. At the same time the 1937 Budget ran into difficulties of a nature which suggested that the business community was not yet ready to make sacrifices for national defence. This last Budget by Chamberlain contained an unprecedented tax, euphemistically described as National Defence Contribution, or N.D.C., on business profits. The tax was to be graduated according to the growth of profits, and Chamberlain believed it would help prevent unrest outside the business community, when the inevitable big profits and rise in the cost of living accompanying rearmament provoked accusations of profiteering. The City and business organisations, however, were shocked at what seemed a socialist measure: Stock Exchange values slumped, and discontent in the Conservative party was such that Chamberlain felt that he had 'risked the premiership'. In the end he and his successor, Simon, had to come to terms with the business community, and a straight 5 per cent tax on profits was substituted for a graduated scale.[98]

The slump in confidence on the Stock Exchange aroused by the N.D.C. scare had unfortunate repercussions on government borrowing. An issue of £100 million of 2½ per cent National Defence Bonds in April 1937 was a complete fiasco so far as subscriptions from the general public were concerned, and £86½ million had to be taken up by the Issue Department of the Bank of England – a then secret procedure for underwriting government loans. By way of comparison the Issue Department had had to take up only £60 million of a £100 million issue of 2¾ per cent Funding Loan in November 1936. The bonds taken up by the Issue Department had to be peddled out to the public as and when possible – at a discount as it proved – and by the end of 1937 it seemed clear the Government would be forced to increase its reliance on Treasury Bills for future borrowing. A decline in public confidence in gilt-edged values was to be avoided because between 1940 and 1945 large blocks of government bonds would fall due to be repaid or converted into new issues, and if these conversions had to be made at a discount the Government's cheap money policy would be threatened at a time when a slump in industrial activity was expected following the end of rearmament work.[99]

Treasury officials advised not only that the rate of rearmament should not be such as to weaken the economy, but also that the size of the defence forces ultimately to be created should not be such as could not be maintained permanently. Defence loan expenditure was seen as a temporary expedient, to be followed by a return to a balanced Budget after the completion of the rearmament programme, which was planned for the end of the financial year 1941. At first glance the Budgetary position after 1941 may seem an obscure worry for the Treasury in 1937. But given that rearmament was to involve capital expenditure over a limited period, and that the Government's policy was to secure peace and not to make war, the Treasury's foresight was reasonable. Similar foresight was being exercised in Germany by General Fromm, head of the Organisation Department of the German Army High Command, who, in 1936, had realised that the cost of maintaining the armed forces which Germany was building up would be 'unbearable for any length of time'. Fromm began to wonder whether there was 'a fixed intention to send the armed forces into action at a definite point in time'.[100] Hitler could escape from the economic difficulties of rearmament by going to war at his chosen moment, but the British Government did not wish to plan its rearmament on such a basis.

The essential point in the Treasury's arguments relating to the Budget after 1941 was that there was bound to be some kind of recession then, and that this would reduce revenue at a time when there would be increasing calls on the Exchequer for unemployment relief. N.D.C., being a temporary tax, would have been repealed with the end of the rearmament programme. Not only would the Government's borrowing powers under the 1937 Defence Loans Act have ceased, but repayment of the principal as well as payment of interest on the sum borrowed for defence would have begun – a total charge of perhaps £20 million on the Budget. Hopkins and Phillips also believed that to maintain the Government's credit the provision of a Sinking Fund over and above that £20 million would be necessary, as ten years would have passed since there had been a regular programme to redeem the National Debt as a whole.[101]

According to Admiralty and Air Ministry figures the future normal annual maintenance cost of these two Services, on the basis of their approved programmes, would be £88 million and £75 million respectively, while, the Treasury told the Cabinet in June 1937, it would be 'most unwise to assume' that more than £150 million to £170 million could be found for all three defence departments after the expiry of the Government's borrowing powers in March 1942.[102] Privately Hopkins and Phillips believed that as much as £220 million might be found out of revenue for defence after 1941, if there were no recession, and if there were no Sinking Fund for the National Debt,[103] and no doubt the lower figure was put forward because the main object of the exercise was to force the defence departments to moderate their demands. But Treasury officials genuinely believed that unbalanced Budgets after 1941 were to be avoided, and the Cabinet was warned solemnly that:

> it will be appreciated that there is no surer way to bankruptcy than to allow temporary borrowing for a capital purpose to merge into permanent borrowing for current needs, and that solution must be ruled out at once.

The implications of the contemplated level of defence expenditure after 1941 were spelled out by the Treasury as either 'an intolerable level of taxation or a startling reversal of accepted policy in regard to social expenditure'.[104] The second option was hardly an option at all, as the Cabinet had agreed in March 1936 that rearmament was to be carried out without restriction on social services. That same year had seen the march of the unemployed from Jarrow, and later, in 1938, Simon, rather over-dramatically, was to conjure up for his Cabinet colleagues the spectre of revolution, if the Government should be unable to meet the cost of unemployment assistance in a post-rearmament slump.[105]

As for the first option, taxpayers in the 'Thirties, when the standard rate of Income Tax was much lower than today, do not seem in retrospect to have been near 'an intolerable level of taxation'. But ideas of what was acceptable then were formed by what had gone before. The highest standard rate of Income Tax adopted in 1914–19 had been 6s. in the pound, and the adoption of a 5s. rate in 1931 had been a crisis measure (two years previously the rate had been 4s.). The reduction to 4s. 6d. in 1934 was intended as a sign that the crisis was past. To raise the rate again might be taken as a sign by investors that the country was back on the road to 1931. Accordingly it had been by cautious, threepenny steps, that Chamberlain approached the 5s. level in 1936 and 1937, and a gasp went up from the House of Commons when Simon announced a rate of 5s. 6d. in 1938. Earl Winterton who, before taking office as Chancellor of the Duchy of Lancaster in 1938, was associated with Churchill in advocating faster rearmament, recalled in his memoirs how he (Winterton) was 'stunned' by Simon's War Budget of 1939, when a standard rate of 7s. was imposed. Within the Treasury officials wondered at what point in raising the level of taxation the law of diminishing returns would make itself felt.[106]

Advised by the Treasury, the Cabinet instructed the defence departments to re-estimate their future annual maintenance costs, which they did in the summer of 1937, and these totalled £255 million on the basis of approved programmes, which the departments described as inadequate, and £301 million on the basis of the programmes which the departments wanted. The enormous gap between these figures and the Treasury's Procrustean figures for what could be afforded, compelled Treasury officials to relax their assumptions somewhat by the time

Inskip made his review of defence in the autumn of 1937. The figure of £200 million for annual defence expenditure was now admitted to be possible, but it was stressed that the difference between the yield of taxation in an exceptionally good year and a year of severe depression might exceed £100 million.[107]

It may be asked why the Treasury did not take steps to avoid a post-rearmament depression. In articles in *The Times* in January 1937 on 'How to Avoid a Slump' Keynes noted how rearmament was 'neither permanent nor large enough while it lasts to sustain prosperity of itself', and advocated the establishment of a Board of Public Investment. This board would regulate public investment so as to even out the trade cycle, and, in particular, just as 'three years ago it was important to use public policy to increase investment, it may soon be equally important to retard certain types of investment'.[108]

Within the Treasury Phillips agreed that to try to run both civil and military expenditure at full blast over the next four years would be to create conditions for a great slump, and that civil demand should be postponed as far as was practicable until after rearmament was complete. It was, he observed to Hopkins, too late to postpone the second Cunard liner (the future *Queen Elizabeth*), but some roads and government housing schemes could be done away with, and 'we could tell the Ministry of Health to obstruct local authorities' programmes'. Hopkins thought that, politics apart, the practical difficulties in using public capital expenditure in this way would not be very great, but he anticipated that the political difficulties would certainly be very great.[109] An interdepartmental committee of officials was set up in June 1937 under Phillips to consider civil public expenditure from the point of view of evening out the trade cycle, but by the time it reported in August in favour of postponing some public works schemes a recession was threatening to spread from America to Britain. In such circumstances the problem became one of finding additional public works schemes for 1941 rather than postponing existing ones.[110]

The Treasury did not press the issue of cutting civil public expenditure, for one lesson which it had learned from 1931 was that a radical economy campaign with regard to social expenditure was unlikely to be worth the political upheaval. To Chamberlain's credit, too, no man could have felt more disgust than he that the country's resources should be devoted to armaments rather than to improving the condition of the people. Treasury officials were aware of this, and, for example, Barlow, while casting around for economies, wrote to Hopkins in 1938 that:

> [Public] physical training is a thing on which progress might be slowed down, but it is so dear to the Prime Minister's heart that it might be imprudent to raise it.[111]

The political difficulties of implementing a counter-cyclical public investment policy left the Treasury in 1937 contemplating the problems of balancing the Budget in a post-rearmament slump when unemployment relief might cost £100 million a year. During the 'Thirties the figure for unemployment relief had not fallen below £55 million in any one year, in contrast to a figure of £20 million in 1929. Small wonder the Treasury could not give Inskip exact figures for the amount available for defence out of a balanced Budget in 1942.[112]

In November 1937 Inskip decided that the uncertainties of the Budgetary position after 1941 were such that expenditure on rearmament must depend on what was necessary to make the country secure, and on what could be afforded out of revenue and borrowing in the next four years, and not upon what could be afforded out of revenue after 1941.[113] This decision removed a major part of the Treasury's argument for rationing of defence expenditure, but, as will be seen in the next chapter, the Treasury's arguments had made ministers sufficiently aware of the danger of national bankruptcy as to persuade the Cabinet to decide upon major changes in defence policy in December 1937. Moreover, Inskip accepted the Treasury's argument that financial strength was a 'fourth arm of defence' when he fixed rations of finance for each defence department for the quinquennium 1937–41 within a global figure of £1570 million. Although these rations were not strictly adhered to, the Treasury was able to draw attention to the need for financial restraint by referring to the effects of rearmament on the balance of payments, and, therefore, upon the 'fourth arm of defence'.

The current balance of payments deficit in 1936 had been of modest proportions – £18 million – but in 1937 it was £56 million, or rather more than in 1932, and it was natural to suppose that unlimited expenditure on armaments might raise the deficit to the crisis proportions of 1931 (£104 million), causing a collapse of business confidence and public credit. One bright feature was the continued inflow of foreign gold, which was attracted by Britain's political and economic stability, and which resulted in a rise in Britain's gold and convertible currency reserves from just under £500 million in March 1936 to £825 million in March 1938.[114] The trouble was that a fall in confidence in Britain's stability, financial or otherwise, could just as easily result in an outflow of gold, as happened in 1938–9. Keynes, in an article in January 1937, commented that 'above all it is desirable that we should view with equanimity . . . the prospective worsening of our trade balance. . . . We have today a plethora of gold.'[115] But this was, perhaps, the counsel of perfection. The Treasury had to think in terms of the fears, real and imagined, of businessmen and rentiers.

One way in which domestic demand, and therefore the strain on the balance of payments, could be relieved was to rely more upon taxation, and less upon borrowed money, for rearmament. Accordingly the Treasury's advice contained in Inskip's report of December 1937 was not that defence expenditure in 1937-41 should not exceed £1500 million in any circumstances, but that if, in view of the international situation, a greater sum was required,

> it would probably be found necessary that the excess should be found by an increase in the level of taxation, rather than by increasing the total sum made available for defence from borrowed money.[116]

Hopkins said he had been impressed by some parts of the defence departments' case during the review of defence, and by December he was considering the possibility of raising 'what till recently was thought to be the top level' of taxation. By February 1938 he was advocating 'a solid increase in taxation here and now'.[117] Against this advice to Simon, Fisher commented that he (Fisher) had:

> some difficulty in coming to a conclusion whether we should start up now increasing taxation. Would that discourage the now fortunately favourable prevalent mood in favour of rearmament? Would it affect business psychology and help to bring about a depression? It is anyone's guess ... the world is a lunatic asylum, and unorthodox measures may be unavoidable for a time.[118]

Hopkins, however, successfully argued against an increase in borrowing powers, pointing out to Simon that underspending by the defence departments in 1937 meant that almost £340 million remained of existing borrowing powers for the next four years. The 1938 Budget allowed for £90 million to be borrowed, and for an increase in revenue of £30 million, involving a 6d. increase in the standard rate of Income Tax.[119] The *New Statesman* was hostile to this increase in taxation when it was announced, but support for Simon's Budget came from the *Economist*, the *Manchester Guardian* and *The Times*. Even before the Budget had been presented to Parliament, however, as will be seen below, events abroad suggested that the assumption of a peacetime economy might be invalid.

Moving towards Wartime Finance

Inskip, in his Second Report of February 1938, had advocated rearmament to the fullest extent compatible with a peacetime economy, with a further review of defence before March 1940 'in the light of improvements in the international situation which it is the object of our foreign policy to bring about'.[120] Over the next 18 months, however, the risk of war increased, and a transition occurred whereby instead of rearmament being rationed by finance, financial policy had to be reviewed in the light of the needs of rearmament.

Hitler's occupation of Austria in March 1938 provided the C.O.S. with an opportunity to attack the policy of non-interference with normal civil industry, and on 23 March the Cabinet approved a statement, to be made in Parliament, that 'the Government will henceforward ask that full priority should be given [by industry] to rearmament work'.[121] In fact, for some time a gradually increasing degree of priority had been accorded to defence contracts, to the detriment of exports, but, as Inskip pointed out, the difficulty was to induce firms which were carrying out remunerative civil contracts to release skilled labour for armament work. This, rather than finance, was the heart of the matter, and Brown, the Minister for Labour, warned the defence departments that an attempt to produce all their requirements at a speed greater than labour supply would allow would lead to delays and uncoordinated deliveries, and would thus defeat its own ends.[122]

The problem of acceleration could be solved only by allocating priorities within the rearmament programme or by diverting resources from civilian use, reducing British living standards (which were higher than those in Germany). Defence expenditure by Britain at the German level, Simon advised, would require government powers similar to those of the Nazi government to control wages and enforce loans, if the result were not to be inflation. The Cabinet had agreed in February 1938 to limit the defence departments' expenditure in the quinquennium 1937–41 to £1570 million, and, the Chancellor thought, 'higher defence expenditure could not be reached unless we turned ourselves into a different kind of nation'.[123] The Government of the day was not disposed to increase state control over private income and property, and there was no conscious decision by ministers to move in that direction. Instead ministers drifted with events, and were saved from having to impose quasi-wartime controls in peace by the outbreak of war.

Simon wondered whether the recession which had begun late in 1937, by reducing revenue at a time when defence expenditure was increasing, might not shake the foundations of his Budget. But he was answered by Hopkins that whatever new factories might be laid down, and whatever arrangements might be made for the dilution of labour, industrial factors would still limit the amount of money which the defence departments could spend in 1938. The problem, so far as finance was concerned, lay in the prospects for 1939 and subsequent years, when industry would be geared for arms production, and when there would be far wider limits to what the defence departments might spend. On the other hand, Hopkins told Simon, the *Anschluss* had provided an opportunity of winning over public support for rearmament, and this should make it possible to raise more money by taxation, and possibly by borrowing, than had hitherto seemed possible, without impairing financial stability. Although Hopkins did not say so, much would depend on the country's political leadership to take advantage of this new situation. He added a caveat:

Time is needed for the position to crystallise. As I see it the Budget as now settled is, on the whole, adequate for present needs, and sufficiently forthright for the temper of the people. I doubt if Government credit would at the present time stand up against severe proposals. We should, I suggest, stand upon the [rearmament] programme as settled, and give financial circles time to recover their breath after the political and general alarms to which they are now giving way rather than think of a more rigorous programme. Any less rigorous one is clearly unthinkable.[124]

The Government's domestic credit, so far as the funding of debt incurred for rearmament was concerned, stood up well in the crisis summer of 1938. Simon was able to tell the Cabinet in June that a new issue of Defence Loan had had a very good press, and had been well received.[125] When proposals were made after Munich to increase the Air Force programme, however, Hopkins estimated that if the Air Ministry were given everything it asked for, and the other departments were held to the Inskip ration, £820 million would have to be borrowed in the last three years of the quinquennium to March 1942, allowing for the fact that revenue was falling owing to the recession, and civil expenditure was rising. About £180 million would have been borrowed in 1937 and 1938, so that total borrowing for the quinquennium would come to £1000 million, compared with the £400 million authorised by the Defence Loans Act. The Cabinet was warned that 'it was quite certain that this enormous sum could not be provided out of the savings of the country' – that is to say, Hopkins believed that borrowing on such a scale must tend to be inflationary.[126]

Such an opinion seems to have assumed that Bank Rate would remain low. Why there should not have been a credit squeeze at a later date through raising Bank Rate is not clear, but Keynes and the Treasury seem to have been agreed that dear money was to be avoided. In April 1939 Keynes gave three reasons why 'in no circumstances' the Treasury should offer 'any loans at a higher rate of interest than, say, $2\frac{1}{2}$ per cent'. Constant low interest rates kept down the burden of the National Debt; gave security and stability to financial institutions, and kept down the cost of necessary investment.[127]

Hopkins' opinions as to the inflationary effects of borrowing £820 million over three years may appear at first sight to be unduly alarmist. But his judgement receives support from the view of Mr. Roy (now Sir Roy) Harrod, in 1939, that even with wartime controls on the economy, and on credit in particular, the limit to non-inflationary government borrowing would be between £300 million and £500 million a year – and in 1938 the Treasury could not count on wartime powers. Harrod shared Hopkins' preference for taxation over inflation, noting that 'the idea that the burden [of armaments] can be lessened by resort to inflation is illusory'.[128] Among Cabinet ministers, Mr. Walter Elliot, Minister of Health, faced with the Treasury's arithmetic at the beginning of November 1938, still thought that in the light of Munich it might be necessary to make a supreme effort to achieve air parity, even if it meant borrowing £1000 million. But he appreciated that it might be hard to do this 'without some radical change in the organisation of this country',[129] and as yet neither the mood of the Cabinet nor that of the wealth-controlling parts of the community was prepared for radical steps to enable the state to control the country's resources more fully. On 7 November the Air Ministry was told to scale down its new proposals.

Expansion of the Government's borrowing powers was considered by the Treasury and the Bank of England in December 1938. Leith-Ross thought that increased borrowing for armaments would raise domestic prices, but Phillips commented that the existence of 1,800,000 unemployed – many of them perfectly employable – was a sufficient guarantee against immediate domestic inflation. Hopkins, who expected the figure for the unemployed shortly to pass the two million mark, agreed with Phillips that the situation was quite different from 1936 and 1937, and advised Simon that the existing £400 million borrowing powers could be increased. A figure of a further £400 million was put before Parliament in February 1939, making £800 million in all for the quinquennium 1937–42.[130]

What the recession of 1938 did show was the extent to which the economy, and revenue, were dependent on world trade trends. Phillips noted that while advocates of rearmament were inclined to claim that heavy expenditure on defence must reduce unemployment, and raise revenue, in the years in which the expenditure was incurred, the fact was that in the twelve months to 30 September 1938 £310 million had been spent on defence – £120 million more than in the previous twelve months – and unemployment had *risen* by 450,000. Defence expenditure must create employment, but it was not, Phillips thought, a factor of the first magnitude, and could easily be outweighed by other factors.[131]

Other factors included a decline in export trade, reflecting unfavourable conditions abroad, especially in the United States, and cyclical factors at home, notably a decline in house building. On the supply side, there were shortages of industrial raw materials and of certain categories of skilled labour. Even more ominous for the future was the effect of 'war talk' on business confidence in fields other than armaments. As early as December 1937 *The Times* 'City Notes' had commented on how share prices rose and fell with hopes of a successful appeasement of Europe, and at the beginning of 1938 Wilson had looked to progress in talks with Germany and Italy to revive business confidence.[132] Perhaps ministerial statements in 1938–9 on the international situation might have been more frank had it not been felt necessary to soothe the sensitive nerves of the City of London.

In the circumstances the revenue position for future Budgets seemed uncertain and even discouraging, with a lower return quite possible even with higher rates of taxation. The gold and foreign exchange problem in 1938–9 was even more depressing. The current balance of payments deficit had been £56 million in 1937, and in the autumn of 1938 Phillips expected the figure for that year to be £100 million. An adverse balance had been tolerable, he felt, while foreign confidence in Britain, and lack of confidence in certain Continental countries, had led to an inflow of foreign gold to London, as in 1937. But in the six months between the *Anschluss* and Munich Britain's gold reserves fell from a peak of £800 million to £650 million, and the outflow continued unabated even after the Munich settlement, the latter event quite failing to steady financial nerves. Serious difficulty was experienced in the autumn of 1938 in maintaining the value of the pound, and in the last quarter of the year sterling fell on the open market to a figure of just over 4·60 against the dollar, compared with a top figure of 5·0 earlier in the year. By January 1939 Hopkins, through Simon, was warning the Cabinet that 'it must be said that recent conditions have been painfully reminiscent of those which obtained in this country immediately prior to the financial crisis of 1931'.[133]

When, in the months after Munich, the defence departments demanded fresh additions to their programmes, the Treasury was placed in an awkward position if, as it did, it wanted to maintain the 'fourth arm of defence'. As Hopkins, through Simon, told the Cabinet, there was on the one hand a persistent fear abroad that war was coming, and that Britain might not be ready for it: on the other hand, further anxiety was created by the obvious worsening of Britain's financial position, by the growth of armament expenditure, and the associated heavy increase in the adverse balance of trade. Furthermore, while Phillips and Hopkins were agreed that borrowing for defence was not, for the moment, likely to create domestic inflation, they also agreed it was likely to undermine foreign confidence in the pound.[134] As a result of this dilemma the Treasury's views on defence policy became more and more centred on the need for selective expenditure to put the country's defences in such a state as to make it clear that Britain could survive the opening round of a war, while keeping total expenditure at a level which would not weaken further confidence in Britain's financial stability.

Above all the Treasury sought to persuade ministers not to let themselves be committed publicly to a vast programme of expenditure after March 1940. For if the Government were to make such an announcement, and it was later found that the continued financing of rearmament was destructive of the country's economic and financial strength, the result would be a débâcle, in which defence plans would be seen openly to have been frustrated by financial and economic

factors. Hopkins advised Simon in October 1938 that whatever could
be spent over the next eighteen months to make the country safe from
air attack, and perhaps in some other respects too, should be spent, and
that the Treasury must be prepared, 'by hook or by crook', to borrow
the requisite money. But, Hopkins added, the emphasis should be on
acceleration of the existing programme, and new programmes in which
the bulk of expenditure would come after March 1940 should be resisted
as far as possible.[135]

Despite the lack of a Cabinet decision in 1938 regarding quasi-
wartime measures to finance rearmament, new government powers
were under consideration at the official level. An E.A.C. paper of
31 October 1938 concluded that, given time and new government
powers, peacetime expenditure on armaments could be raised by
between £400 million and £500 million per annum, or more than
enough to meet the defence departments' needs, without inflation. The
paper, drawn up by Mr. P. K. (later Sir Piers) Debenham, a young
Cambridge economist who was assistant secretary to the E.A.C.'s
Committee on Economic Information, assumed that the bulk of the
unemployed could be put to work; that finance could be diverted from
investment for civil purposes to rearmament, and that consumer
expenditure could be reduced. Dividends would have to be limited,
and new issues on the Stock Market controlled, while price controls
would also have to be introduced. Debenham thought the best way to
utilise unemployed labour would be to revive the old export industries,
but he admitted the American slump was setting off world trade trends
which might make this difficult. He also thought there was much to be
said for acquiescing in an adverse current balance of payments while
British industry re-adapted itself to the new conditions, but he had to
admit the danger was that a persistent adverse balance might well
impair confidence in sterling. Exchange controls, he thought, would be
one of the first steps that the Government would have to consider,
and export monopolies and import boards for raw materials might
follow later, together with the measures to control domestic investment and consumption.[136]

Debenham himself was too junior to wield influence on his own
account, but his figures and arguments demanded attention in the
Treasury. His paper was circulated for comment to two economists,
Henderson of the E.A.C., and Mr. Henry Clay, Economic Adviser at
the Bank of England, both of whom agreed with Debenham in almost
every respect, offering only a few detailed comments. Waley, however,
commented that the 'present tendency to believe that all the things
which Germany and Japan are forced to do are the best things for us
to do is a very dangerous one'. Waley felt that exchange controls and
the like would set a trend in international trade which, in the long

term, would be detrimental to Britain's interests, and he preferred allowing the pound to fall in relation to the dollar as a measure to correct the balance of payments. He was inclined to reverse Deben-ham's order of priority, and to take measures to control the domestic economy before tampering with trade. Control of the new issue market would, he thought, be the first thing to be considered in the event of an upturn in the trade cycle, when non-essential industries might compete for capital with essential industries and with govern-ment borrowing. If, later on, rearmament 'not only cures our present deflation but threatens us with indescribable inflation, it seems to me', he wrote to Hawtrey, 'that a policy of high taxation is a much better cure than plans for limiting dividends and controlling prices'.[137]

Treasury officials and E.A.C. economists were agreed that the balance of payments was, in the words of a report in December 1938 by the Committee on Economic Information, 'the key to the whole position'.[138] It was Keynes who contributed most of what was novel in the December report, although the document itself bore the signature of Lord Stamp. Phillips thought the report was 'tough reading', and commented that 'any one member of the Committee could have produced a much clearer and better statement of his views, but, as always happens, an endeavour to reconcile in one draft different shades of opinion has produced a document which . . . in places is hopelessly obscure'.[139] There was general agreement that time had to be bought until British industry had re-adapted itself to the new conditions of demand caused by increased rearmament – there was no suggestion that the Government itself should direct the reorganisation of industry – and that this could be done only by continuing to run a current balance of payments deficit. Unlike Waley, the Committee concluded that a depreciation of sterling would be of little benefit, since currencies based on sterling would follow suit, and exchange controls and other barriers to trade would reduce the effect elsewhere, as after 1931. Instead it was suggested that government control of overseas investment and other steps within the existing financial system would enable Britain to stand an annual balance of payments deficit of £50 million 'for a considerable period'.[140]

At a time when the deficit on the current balance of payments was already in excess of £50 million any suggestions were of consider-able interest to the Treasury. Phillips discussed Keynes' ideas with the Bank of England, and both he and Hopkins recorded disappointment when the authorities at the Bank told them there was little of practical importance in Keynes' suggestions. The Bank opinion was that Keynes underestimated the volume of 'bear' speculation against the pound. On specific points, the Bank pointed out that restrictions on overseas investment had already been introduced; and as for Keynes' suggestion of direct borrowing in Canada, the Bank claimed that Treasury Bills issued there with a U.S. dollar option would find their way on to the London market, where they would be taken up greedily as a hedge against sterling depreciation.[141] It is not clear why the Bank and the Treasury thought that the purchase by British residents of securities issued overseas could not be prevented, but in both institutions there was a reluctance to impose controls which might impair London's reputation as a financial centre.

If the weapons with which the pound could be defended seemed limited, the alternative of allowing sterling to depreciate was not, as the E.A.C. Committee had noted, likely to provide an answer to the balance of payments problem either – unless other countries could be persuaded to let Britain reap the benefits of depreciation. The most important other country was, of course, America. As early as 27 October 1938 Waley had received from the British Embassy in Washington 'very advance warning' that if sterling were to fall much below its present value there would be very strong pressure from the farm bloc in Congress for a corresponding cut in the dollar, as in 1933–4. The American Treasury itself was opposed to dollar devaluation, so long as it was satisfied that the pound was not being driven down deliberately by the British for competitive purposes, but it was believed that Roosevelt might give way to pressure from the farmers, who had an eye on export markets at a time when American domestic prices for farm produce were low.[142]

As sterling continued to fall against the dollar it became necessary to make a grand gesture to convince Americans that everything possible was being done to defend the pound, and in January 1939 it was decided to transfer from the Bank of England to the Government's Exchange Equalisation Account all the gold put into the Bank since the Account had been brought into being by Chamberlain's Finance Act of 1932. This would give the operators of the Exchange Equalisation Account the maximum resources with which to combat bear speculation against the pound.[143] The Account itself was under the ultimate control of the Treasury, but was managed on a day-to-day basis by the Bank of England. The Account had been established to be invested in securities or gold as the Treasury thought best 'for checking undue fluctuations in the exchange value of sterling'. The Bank sold Treasury Bills from the Account when it needed sterling to pay for gold or foreign exchange, and bought Treasury Bills when it acquired sterling by selling gold and foreign exchange. The purpose of balancing transactions in gold and foreign exchange with transactions in Treasury Bills was to insulate the domestic market's supply of cash from the effects of influx and efflux of foreign speculative funds. But from time to time in the period up to 1938 gold had been transferred from the Account into the Bank of England.[144]

In January 1939 the advice to the Treasury from the Governor of the

Bank of England, Norman, was that Bank Rate should be raised to support sterling, but the Treasury was reluctant to take a deflationary step at the time, and Bank Rate was held at 2 per cent. The transfer of gold into the Exchange Equalisation Account did little, however, to check speculation against the pound, and with the fears arising from the German occupation of Czechoslovakia in March, the Account began to lose gold uninterruptedly. By June the gold stock was £300 million down on the £800 million figure of fifteen months before, and the operators of the Account warned Norman that, as Hopkins had feared five months earlier, patriotism was not enough to prevent British as well as foreign capital from leaving the country, and that holding the exchange rate only facilitated withdrawals.[145]

It only remained to be decided at what point the Government was no longer prepared to let the nation's gold reserves be further diminished. That point came on 22 August, when it was announced that further sales of gold and foreign exchange by the Account would be suspended, and that the value of sterling would be left to market forces. At the same time the public was asked to refrain from transferring capital abroad, and to reduce demands for foreign exchange. Two days later Bank Rate was raised to 4 per cent, but formal exchange controls were not introduced until the outbreak of war.

Towards 'Conscription of Wealth'

While currency speculators were pushing the Government towards taking new powers regarding foreign exchange, the Exchange Equalisation Account's operations made possible a delay in interfering with the domestic credit structure, although the proposed level of borrowing for defence continued to grow. Receipts of sterling by the Exchange Equalisation Account as a result of the drain of gold had made it possible to reduce the normal volume of Treasury Bills in the hands of the market by about £150 million by May 1939. The Treasury proposed to meet a large part of loan expenditure incurred in 1939 with those Treasury Bills – but, the Cabinet was warned, this operation could not be repeated in 1940 without inflation, if, as expected, the slack in the economy had been taken up meantime.[146]

This factor, together with a falling return on taxation following the recession of 1938, accounts for the modest nature of Simon's taxation proposals in his last peacetime Budget. Fisher urged in January 1939 that heavier taxation, including a standard rate of Income Tax of 6s. (the highest level reached in the First World War), should be imposed so as to 'introduce a new and more realistic psychology' in the nation.[147] But the architects of the Budget, Hopkins and Phillips, chose to keep the standard rate at 5s. 6d. Of the £630 million forecast in April to be spent on defence in the financial year 1939, well over half (£380 million) was to be borrowed. The increase in the Government's borrowing powers, by £400 million for the period up to March 1942, announced in February 1939, had been a deliberate understatement to prevent too violent a reaction on government credit, and it was fully intended to obtain further authority from Parliament when necessary.[148]

The press, with the significant exception of the *Daily Herald*, made favourable comment on the Government's decision to depend on borrowing. *The Times*' City Editor noted on 22 February that fear of increased taxation had weighed more heavily with the market than fear of heavy borrowing.[149] The Labour Party, however, was critical, pointing out that the effects of inflation would fall most heavily on the poor, while the rich were to be spared taxation which they could well afford. Especially after the Government announced its intention to introduce conscription there were increasing demands from the Left for conscription of wealth as well, so that men conscripted for the armed forces might be properly equipped. The leader of the Opposition, Mr. Clement Attlee, called for 'proof that the wealthy classes of the country are devoted to democracy and to resisting aggression'. Chamberlain had anticipated such a demand, and had already asked the Treasury to investigate 'conscription of wealth' as a corollary of conscription of manpower.[150]

The matter, however, was far from simple as the Treasury wished to wait until a stage of full employment – that is when all labour that could be employed in the short term had been employed – had been reached before introducing quasi-wartime controls over private investment. Such action at an earlier stage, Hopkins thought, would be dangerous, as it would be regarded as a deflationary measure and would be a shock to business confidence.[151] Opinions were divided as to the effects which the increased 1939 defence programmes would have on employment: Keynes was predicting in the spring and early summer that rearmament and conscription combined would shortly absorb most of the unemployed who were capable of being employed on the jobs on offer in 1939; Hawtrey, on the other hand, advised that the assumption that Britain was moving towards full employment was optimistic in view of the set-back to the economy in 1938. Norman confessed that he had never felt so confused and baffled, and did not know which way to turn.[152]

But during the late spring and early summer of 1939 the Treasury had the adoption of quasi-wartime powers in peacetime under consideration. The state of the 'fourth arm of defence' demanded no less. As early as 6 April a Strategic Appreciation Sub-Committee of the C.I.D. was warned by Barlow that the C.O.S. in their planning could not safely assume that the country's financial strength would support a long war. There were, he said, three ways in which Britain could finance purchases abroad: with gold and foreign exchange, of which, for the moment, she held more than in 1914; with foreign securities, of which there were far fewer in British hands than in 1914, and by borrowing. But the first two were threatened by the continuing adverse balance of payments, and it did not seem likely that America would be keen to lend to a nation which had not yet paid off its debts from the last war. Yet without credit Britain could not draw on America's resources on an appreciable scale in war, and already there was cause for anxiety regarding purchases for which dollars were required.[153]

The attitude of America was crucial. Roosevelt's unsuccessful attempt in June 1939 to amend the Neutrality Act left British Foreign Office Intelligence with little hope that the Senate would ever agree to major amendments in time of peace.[154] In the event, the Act enabling Lend Lease was not passed until 18 months after the outbreak of war, after Britain's gold reserves had all but vanished. Until Roosevelt could persuade enough senators to change their minds, Britain's armed forces must depend upon British industry both to produce arms and to produce enough goods for export so as to finance the purchase of raw materials. But, under the existing rules of running the economy, British trade and industry were failing to withstand the strain of rearmament without also running a heavy current balance of payments deficit, thus further reducing the country's reserves of purchasing power.

When, after the German occupation of Czechoslovakia, the Cabinet approved major additions to the rearmament programme, which would produce armed forces of hitherto unprecedented size in peace-time, the time had clearly come to reconsider the existing financial and economic rules. It was estimated by June that, once the rearmament programme was complete, the defence departments would require £450 million annually simply for maintenance, and such a figure, the Treasury believed, was unattainable on anything resembling the 1939 scale of taxation (which was expected to produce only £250 million for defence). But from March 1939 the political atmosphere was ripe for draconian measures. Chamberlain remarked that it was a mockery to call conditions thereafter 'peace'.[155] Once decisions to increase the size of the armed forces had been taken, the economic and financial means had to be found to translate these decisions into reality without inflation.

On 5 July Hopkins appeared before the Cabinet to explain why it was likely that shortly the Government would have to take powers to prohibit new issues on the Stock Exchange; to control companies' dividends and investment of their reserves, and to control building society loans as well as bank advances.[156] The key to the timing of these measures was not to be the outbreak of war – for in July it was not known if and when war would come – but inflationary pressure whenever the economy should reach a stage of full employment. The defence departments were by that date free of financial 'rationing' and it was antici-pated that altogether £750 million would be spent on defence before the end of the financial year, of which £500 million would have to be borrowed. Only £150 million could be raised on Treasury Bills from the Exchange Equalisation Account, and as for the remaining £350 million, Hopkins had told Wilson (who was now Permanent Secretary) and Simon:

> it is quite obvious that the loans required cannot be raised out of savings by ordinary means, and it seems clear that some measure of inflation is pressing us very soon.[157]

Treasury Bills and some slack in the labour supply would enable rearmament to be financed without inflation or resort to extraordinary powers until the late autumn, but thereafter it would no longer be practical to continue to meet what amounted to a war strain with the practices of peace. Simon was already contemplating an autumn Budget, with large increases in taxation, and, as one Treasury official noted ruefully: 'if present trends are not changed, we are heading for a permanent standard rate of Income Tax of 7s. 6d. in the pound'.[158]

Hopkins warned the Cabinet on 5 July that undoubtedly the situation grew more difficult with every month that passed. If war should break out in the near future, Britain would have in its war chest the existing gold stock, less short-term foreign balances which would be removed. But if war occurred, say a year hence, the gold reserves would have been further diminished by the drain owing to the adverse balance of payments, and Britain would be that much less able to finance the long war which the C.O.S. envisaged. The adverse current balance itself would be increased if the production of armaments was further stimulated, so that the more prepared the defence services were, the less able the country would be to support them.[159]

Similar conclusions were being reached in Germany, after Germany's current balance of payments moved into deficit in 1938. By the winter of 1938–9 Hitler faced a pressing choice of slowing down rearmament, curtailing civilian consumption or going to war. Fear of inflation was, if anything, greater in Germany than in Britain, and in November 1938 Goering, who was responsible for the German economy, said:

> There is a tremendous shortage of skilled workers. . . . This cannot be relieved through closing down the factories which produce seemingly unimportant consumer goods. For when the workers can no longer buy consumer goods for their wages . . . that is the beginning of inflation, and that is the beginning of the end.[160]

Hitler did not believe any more than the British Treasury that the 1939 rate of rearmament – broadly similar in Germany and Britain expressed as a percentage of gross national product – could be sustained indefinitely, and on 22 August 1939, the day the British abandoned defence of the pound, he told his commanders-in-chief: 'Our economic situation is such that we can only hold out a few more years. . . . We have no other choice, we must act.'[161]

The British Foreign Office had anticipated such a situation, in January 1939, when Lord Halifax, the Foreign Secretary, had advised the Cabinet that in the course of that year Hitler must either reduce the level of his armaments expenditure, so as to reduce German inflation, or 'explode in some direction', so as to divert the German people from their deteriorating economic position, and by conquest to secure the raw materials which the Reich could no longer obtain through trade. Therefore, while not challenging the Treasury's calculations about Britain's future economic position, he urged that no financial restrictions be placed upon rearmament for what could only by a temporary period of tension, ending either in war or the fall of the Nazi régime.[162] Hopkins saw no reason then or later to believe that the German economy was about to break down, but, as rumours of impending aggression increased, Simon found himself forced to admit in Cabinet by the end of February 1939 that finance was outweighed by other aspects of Britain's situation.[163] This realisation, together with the decline in Fisher's personal influence, accounts for the decline in the Treasury's influence on government policy in 1939.

Summary

How far the Treasury's views on the danger of inflation and an adverse balance of payments – and the possibility of 'another 1931' – made the Government more determined to stand up to Hitler in 1939 is uncertain. But it seemed clear that rearmament on the scale of 1939 could not be sustained indefinitely by either Britain or Germany, and certainly additions to the British rearmament programme after March of that year meant that contemporary British methods of public finance were no longer sufficient. It seems to follow that had Britain rearmed at the 1939 rate in earlier years there must either have been inflation – which Keynes warned was a risk in 1937 – or the Government would have had to impose heavier taxation or greater controls over investment than its supporters would have been prepared to contemplate, except in direst danger.

Inflation was an unattractive alternative. It would have increased balance of payments difficulties; aroused fears in financial and business circles, and exacerbated social tensions by placing the burden of the cost of rearmament upon the less well off. Government borrowing for rearmament was opposed in 1937 by the Labour Party on the grounds that it would be inflationary. The Treasury did not accept that borrowing for defence must be inflationary, but, on the other hand, a balanced Budget continued to be regarded in the Treasury as an ideal. In retrospect, the Treasury seems to have been unduly cautious about borrowing for defence in 1934, but this would not have delayed borrowing for more than about a year, since, even once a decision was taken to borrow in 1935, lack of industrial capacity meant that all defence expenditure could be met out of revenue until 1937. In any case, the real cause of delay down to 1935 seems to have been a lack of awareness in the Cabinet of the country's danger. Greater loan expenditure on rearmament than in fact took place from 1937 would have worsened the balance of payments position.

The alternative to greater borrowing was greater taxation. Phillips noted in 1939 that 'one of the main factors explaining the ability of Germany to spend larger sums on armaments than we do' was the relative product of taxation. Whereas British industrialists insisted on a watering down of N.D.C. to a 5 per cent tax on profits, German industrialists paid a 40 per cent tax on profits, in addition to income tax.[164] Greater sacrifice by the well-off might have encouraged greater and earlier readiness on the part of trade unions to reform industrial practices, so as to 'deskill' jobs and absorb more of the semi-skilled unemployed. Instead British society continued, in Fisher's words:

> to amble along in our old and well-tried and (for the small minority) very comfortable economic paths. Which means ... business ... profiteering out of the occasion of the country's need, and, with this patriotic example before him, the workman ... stimulated to insistence on some improvement of his rather shabby lot in life.[165]

Underlying financial problems there were economic, social and political problems. Treasury officials had to take society – and prevailing economic beliefs – as they found them, and give advice accordingly. Even had society been more ready to substitute guns for butter, the limits set by geography, and Britain's need to earn a living by trade, would have remained. Hitler could escape his balance of payments problems by seizing resources of neighbouring countries, but unless the British Government were prepared to make a pre-emptive strike against Germany, and risk Japanese and Italian intervention, British defence had to be planned on the basis, at least down to 1939, of long-term deterrence. There can be no doubt of the importance of the Treasury's view as to economic and financial limits, at least down to about February 1939. As Chamberlain told the Cabinet after Munich, he had been 'oppressed with the sense that the burden of armaments might break our backs' ever since he had been Chancellor.[166]

IV

The Treasury's Influence on the Formation of Defence Policy

In addition to deciding what proportion of Britain's economic resources should be devoted to defence, the Government had to apportion military resources between various dangers. The Treasury had no professional expertise on strategic questions, but since defence policy must affect what departments would demand from the Exchequer, the Treasury had an interest in strategic debate.

The traditional problems facing British strategists were defence of the United Kingdom; protection of trade routes; protection of the Empire and overseas interests, and prevention of the domination of Europe, and in particular of the Low Countries, by any single power.[1] So long as the Royal Navy could protect Britain, and her trade routes and Empire, the British Army could be used to support European allies. But the effectiveness of British sea power before the twentieth century had been partly due to Britain's position athwart Europe's sea links with the rest of the world, and a new situation developed with the rise of the Japanese Navy as far as could be from the Royal Navy's home bases, but uncomfortably close to important parts of the British Empire. Again, by the Nineteen-Thirties, developments in aircraft meant that the Navy alone could no longer defend Britain, and resources had to be devoted to the creation of an air force and anti-aircraft defences. Inevitably questions arose as to how Britain could best allocate resources between sea, air and land power.

In addition to questions of how military resources should be allocated, there was the question of when Britain's defences should be ready. Since it was assumed that war would come as the result of another power's aggression, questions of preparedness were related partly to estimates of when potential aggressors would be ready for war, and partly to estimates of how long Britain could maintain a given level of preparedness. Government policy was to rearm while maintaining financial stability, so as to deter aggression while diplomacy removed the causes of war.

Apart from strategy and finance, the Cabinet and its advisers took public opinion into account – both popular fear of air attack and revulsion against the prospect of a repetition of the horrors of the Somme and Passchendaele. Leading critics of the Government, like Churchill and

Mr. Leopold Amery, were concerned chiefly with the Air Force, and placed little importance on the Army as late as 1938. The Navy's prestige, on the other hand, was such that a suggestion by Chamberlain in 1934 that the Admiralty's proposed expenditure be cut was resisted by other ministers on the grounds of probable pressure from the Navy League.[2] But while the Treasury took public opinion into account, the department's own arguments were concerned with priorities in allocation of industrial resources, and in the need to maintain financial stability, and it is in terms of its own arguments that the Treasury's influence on defence policy must be traced.

The Position in 1932–3

Historians seem agreed that retrenchment had reduced Britain's defences and armaments industry to a dangerously low level by 1932. But reduction of the services from their 1918 peak had also created new possibilities for reshaping defence policy. Had Britain maintained a higher degree of preparedness it might have proved harder to alter the proportions of finance allocated to the Army and Air Force. A powerful Army in 1932 would have cost more to maintain than was the case, and much of its equipment would have had to be replaced, or would have become obsolescent, by 1939. There might well then have been less finance available for the Air Force, especially as defence policy would have tended to be formed on the basis of existing armed forces, and would probably have involved preparing the Army for the defence of France and Belgium rather than concentrating on the Air Force. If official strategic doctrine under the Ten Year Rule had been 'essentially negative'[3], then at least one result had been something in the nature of *tabula rasa* upon which new policies might be written.

There could not be complete *tabula rasa*, since protection and policing of a world-wide commerce and Empire made demands upon defence services even when it was assumed no major war would occur for ten years. The Treasury view in December 1932 was that expenditure on these everyday problems should be favoured, rather than expenditure related to what an internal Treasury memorandum called 'the contingency of a hypothetical war'. The Navy deployed only cruisers and light patrol forces outside European waters, and, the memorandum pointed out, 'events in the Far East . . . do not suggest that British commercial interests could look after themselves in the absence of [such] forces'. The efficacy of the Navy's presence depended upon the power of the main fleet held in reserve, and no further reductions in naval expenditure seemed possible.

The same was true of War Office expenditure, where home and Mediterranean establishments were understrength on account of the need to detach battalions for Imperial garrison duties. Among the functions of the Army was listed the provision of an expeditionary force capable of operating overseas, but the writer of the memorandum noted that:

> it has been characteristic of all economy 'moves' in the sphere of defence that little attempt has been made to deal with the 'commitment'. Policy has remained substantially unchanged; the means for carrying it out have been reduced almost by rule of thumb.

The Air Ministry alone had increased its annual expenditure in the last decade, and this was due to acceptance of a hypothesis of a war with a first-class power possessing large numbers of aircraft capable of bombing Britain. In addition to what the writer of the memorandum called the Air Force's 'primary function' of providing army co-operation squadrons and policing parts of the Middle East, the Air Force had been building up a Home Defence Force which, despite its name, consisted largely of bomber squadrons designed for a counter-offensive against a Continental power which, 'so far as can be seen', could only be France.[4] Despite Baldwin's notorious 'the bomber will always get through'[5] speech in November 1932, it seems that in December 1932 the Treasury held the expansion of the Home Defence Force in little favour until a more convincing menace appeared.

After the Far East crisis of 1931-2 Treasury officials were agreed that work on the naval base at Singapore must be allowed to go ahead, but Treasury opinion continued to be averse to preparations for a major European war. When in March 1932 the P.S.O.C. raised the question of planning future industrial mobilisation for such a contingency, Fisher approved a suggestion that the Treasury should 'go slow' on such planning and oppose any increase in the P.S.O.'s staff for the purpose. The reasoning behind this was that:

> our problem is not in the least like that of a continental power. . . . Our regular machinery [for] policing the Empire . . . is necessarily costly and it seems doubtful if we should add to our liabilities. As at present laid down policy does not include intensive preparations for war on the continental scale.[6]

Government policy was indeed slow to change after the C.I.D. had recommended dropping the Ten Year Rule in March 1932. Twenty months passed before the C.I.D. set up a sub-committee to survey Britain's defence requirements. It is true that the Cabinet had decreed that total defence expenditure must not rise in 1932, but planning in the C.I.D. need not have been inhibited by that factor alone. Hankey himself blamed the Geneva Disarmament Conference, which lasted from February 1932 to October 1933, for the delay, but, in retrospect, it seems odd that the conference had not been preceded by an inter-departmental enquiry into Britain's minimum defence requirements, for such an enquiry had been suggested by a Treasury official as early as February 1931.[7]

The Emergence of the Triple Threat

Despite Hitler's rise to power there was considerable lack of urgency in government circles when Fisher returned to duty in September 1933. MacDonald had written to Baldwin the previous month that: 'there are some troublesome affairs developing in Iraq, Germany and Ireland . . . [but] there is nothing to worry inordinately about'.[8] Fisher took a somewhat different view and joined Hankey and the C.O.S. in pressing for a review of defence requirements. On 9 November the C.I.D. approved not only the setting up of the D.R.C. but also that the P.S.O.C. should have a 'hypothetical time limit' of five years in which to make plans for industrial mobilisation. The latter decision did not imply preparedness for war in five years, but only that within five years the P.S.O.C. would have completed a *scheme* of industrial mobilisation in connection with munitions. The Treasury in January 1934 refused to accept a claim by the Secretary of State for War, Hailsham, that the C.I.D. decision implied 'the adoption in principle of what is virtually a five year plan of preparation for the defence services'.[9]

Fisher insisted that before any scheme of defence preparedness could be drawn up the D.R.C. should form a clear conception of where the major danger lay. The C.O.S. in their annual review in October 1933 had identified Britain's commitments as defence of her territory and interests in the Far East; her European treaty obligations, and defence of India against Russia, and it was in the light of these commitments that the D.R.C. had been directed by the C.I.D. to prepare a programme for repairing the worst deficiencies in the defence services. Fisher found the Admiralty thought in terms of a war with Japan, while the War Office thought in terms of a war with Germany.[10] No department, apparently, was much concerned with the Russian threat, which disappeared quietly from the D.R.C.'s discussions.

Fisher and Vansittart had little difficulty in persuading the D.R.C. that Germany must be regarded as the ultimate danger, but, as noted in the last chapter, members of the Cabinet were slow to awake to the full implications of a Nazi Germany. Fisher believed failure to recognise where the greatest danger lay might well result in Britain's downfall, and he preached consistently that Britain should concentrate all her strength against Germany. He saw the Far East as Britain's 'Achilles' heel', in that, if for the sake of her interests in China, including Hong Kong, Britain were to commit her resources to a war with Japan, the United Kingdom itself might be attacked and overwhelmed by Germany, for Britain, he believed, could not fight two powerful antagonists on such widely-separated fronts. The argument developed by Fisher in the D.R.C., and supported by Chamberlain in ministerial deliberations on the D.R.C.'s report of 28 February 1934, was that a rearmed Germany could 'knock-out' Britain by air attack, whereas Japan, whatever the damage she might do to Britain's trade and interests, could not do fatal injury to Britain. Moreover, since the most opportune time for Japan to strike would be if Britain became involved in a war with Germany, deterrence of German aggression was the best long-term safeguard in the Far East, and it was against Germany that the bulk of Britain's preparations should be made.[11]

Germany was not yet rearmed and in the breathing space thus allowed, Fisher argued, Britain should 'show a tooth' in the Far East by going ahead with defensive measures which could be made effective in the next few years. Japan would respect strength more than weakness, and if Britain ceased to combine with America at naval conferences in attempting to set a lower limit of naval tonnage for Japan than for Britain or America, Japanese pride would be mollified and the way cleared for a bilateral non-aggression pact between the two Empires. This was no blueprint for weak-kneed appeasement, and indeed in the D.R.C. Fisher successfully urged the Admiralty to advance by a year, to 1938, the date when it was intended that the Singapore naval base should be ready. Chamberlain took it for granted that Britain could not give Japan a free hand in China or the Dutch East Indies, or against Russia.[12]

The Foreign Office had no doubt that a restoration of the Anglo-Japanese Alliance, after which the Treasury hankered, was quite outside the realm of practical politics, if only because of the need not to offend American public opinion (which was hostile to Japan) and of the difficulty in achieving satisfactory commercial relations with Japan.[13] Fisher, who believed that the United States had 'more than once between August 1914 and April 1917 shown a readiness to stab us in the back', argued that 'the very last thing in the world that we can count on is American support', but he had found himself in a minority of one in the D.R.C. when he claimed that good relations with Japan would be more valuable than good relations with America.[14] On the other hand the suggestion by Middlemass that the policy of 'making eyes at Japan' had its roots in the Treasury[15] somewhat distorts the position in Whitehall. Fisher was able to quote in February 1934 a memorandum by Lord Milne, dated 28 October 1932, just before Milne's retiral as C.I.G.S., on the advisability of getting back to friendly relations with Japan, as Germany was the main danger, and Milne's successor, Sir Archibald Montgomery-Massingberd, held that the abrogation of the Anglo-Japanese Alliance in 1922 had been 'insensate folly'. As for differences of opinion between Fisher on the one hand, and Vansittart and Chatfield on the other, this concerned not the desirability of improved relations with Japan, but the importance of not offending America.[16]

With Chamberlain's support, Fisher became a member of the British delegation for the London Naval Conference at the end of 1934. Fisher was careful to create an understanding with Chatfield before the conference, and in June 1934 the First Sea Lord concurred that if Japan would not accept a renewal of the five-to-three ratio in capital ships agreed in 1922, then it would be better to beg to differ without quarrelling rather than to combine with America to insist on the ratio. By October 1934 Chatfield expected the talks with Japan to fail, which they did two months later, when Japan gave notice of her intention not to renew the Washington and London naval treaties after their expiry at the end of 1936.[17] As late as 1937 Fisher was still urging that policy should be to get on terms with Japan, but the 'China Incident' in July of that year confirmed doubts, which had been growing since 1931, about the ability of civilians in Tokyo to control the Japanese armed forces. By December 1937 Bridges was endorsing the Foreign Office's view that Japan's future actions were 'incalculable', a view which Fisher seems to have shared.[18]

Meanwhile, as if the dual danger from Germany and Japan were not enough, there suddenly appeared in 1935 a third potential enemy in the form of Italy. The so-called Stresa 'Front' had hardly been announced in April 1935 when Mussolini's impending aggression against Abyssinia found the British Government caught between its own desire for Italian support in Europe, and the British public's demands for support for Abyssinia and collective security through the League of Nations. Fisher, like almost every official outwith the Foreign Office – and many within the Foreign Office – was opposed to antagonising Italy, through sanctions or otherwise, arguing that the League was powerless, having in 'varying degrees ill-disposed to it Germany, Japan, Italy and the United States of America'.[19]

The possibility of aggression by Italy had been excluded explicitly from the D.R.C.'s purview in 1933–4, and, although *ad hoc* defence measures were taken in the Mediterranean and Red Sea areas during the Italo-Abyssinian emergency of 1935–6, Italy was not immediately included in overall strategic planning. The wrangles within Whitehall over how best to come to terms with Italy have been recorded elsewhere. Suffice to say that within the Treasury the breach in Anglo-Italian relations was not regarded as permanent, and at the end of 1937 Bridges commented that 'in a few years' time the alarms felt about Italy in 1936–7 will seem one of the oddest episodes in our history'.[20] Italy's attitude over Spain and the Middle East had moved the Cabinet sufficiently by July 1937 to endorse a C.I.D. recommendation that 'Italy cannot be considered as a reliable friend' and must be omitted from the list of countries against whom no defence expenditure was to be incurred. But this guideline was interpreted by the Treasury in the light of the belief, expressed by Chamberlain shortly after he became Prime Minister, that while there was little doubt that Italy would join in on Germany's side in war, there was no need to fear attack by Italy if Britain's foreign policy and defence preparations kept peace between herself and Germany.[21] The best military measures to deter Italy, in this view, were those taken to deter Germany.

Britain thus found herself in the period from 1931 confronted successively by Japan, Germany and Italy, until she found herself in a position whereby if she became involved in a war with one of these powers, the other two would probably intervene when it suited them. To make matters worse the powers which might have counterbalanced Britain's potential enemies were undependable, for one reason or another. American isolationism proclaimed itself more loudly than ever through the Neutrality Acts of the mid-'Thirties. Russia, distrusted in any case on account of world Communism, impaired her military efficiency through the purges of her officer corps in 1937-8. France too was rent by internal troubles, and C.I.D. reports on the French Air Force after 1935 were described by Bridges as 'intensely depressing'.[22] The Empire and Commonwealth itself was more a source of liabilities than of immediate military strength. India was in a state of political turmoil, while troubled Palestine absorbed an increasing number of British troops from 1937. The Dominions themselves might represent reserves of military manpower, but they were dependent upon British sea power, to which they contributed little, for their protection.

It is small wonder that in the course of the 'Thirties Whitehall increasingly came to share the view, expressed by Fisher in 1934, that Britain must concentrate on her own defence against Germany, and avoid other commitments. In 1934 Chamberlain toyed with a form of collective security whereby each nation would contribute to an international police force; in 1936 he was the first Cabinet minister to advocate publicly abandonment of sanctions against Italy.[23] In 1934 the Chancellor talked of the possibility of financing Belgium's defences in lieu of sending an expeditionary force; in 1938 Bridges advised Simon that Belgium's requirements for armaments should not be allowed to entail any expense for the taxpayer, directly or indirectly, through the expansion of British 'shadow factories'. By 1938 British industry was fully stretched by rearmament, and the Treasury view, in Fisher's words, was that only 'small packets' of armaments could be 'doled out' to foreign countries to 'keep them sweet'.[24]

The economic strain of rearmament was bound to raise the question of arms limitation pacts, but the Treasury did not seek to retard rearmament on that account after the failure of the Geneva Disarmament Conference in 1933. The whole lesson of that conference, Chamberlain thought, was that 'security came first, and disarmament second'.[25] The signing of the Anglo-German Naval Treaty in 1935 inspired hopes of an air pact, but this proved to be a 'Will-o'-the-Wisp', and in any case the Treasury seems to have seen the possibility of an air pact as a reason to get ahead with Air Force expansion quickly, so as to strengthen Britain's hand in negotiations.[26] In considering the

Treasury's influence on the formation of defence policy nothing can be more certain than that Treasury officials were under no illusions as to the danger posed by Germany, Japan and Italy, whatever hopes may have been harboured in respect of the last two. Deterrence of Germany was seen as the key, but a world-wide Empire and dependence on commerce inhibited total concentration of defence resources against Germany.

Naval Policy, 1934-9

The Treasury's chief concern in naval policy was to ensure that the Admiralty did not use so much industrial capacity that not enough was left for essential parts of other departments' programmes. There were major disagreements between the Admiralty and the Treasury over strategy, and, although the Admiralty went its own way, the Treasury's views are of interest in that they provided the rationale for limiting the Admiralty's finance. After a long-term cruiser replacement programme had been agreed upon in 1933, debate between the departments centred upon the battlefleet. Central to that debate was the question of against whom should Britain prepare. As noted above, the Treasury view was that Britain should concentrate her available resources against Germany; the Admiralty, however, insisted that sea power was indivisible and that the Navy, in addition to commanding home waters, must be capable of defending the Far Eastern Empire and denying the Japanese Navy access to Britain's trade routes.

At the formal level naval policy was discussed in terms of 'standards', or definitions, of what the strength of the fleet should be. The one-power standard adopted in 1925, as restated in 1932, laid down that the Navy should be able to retain in European waters a 'deterrent force', to prevent the strongest European naval power commanding the seas around Britain, until such time as the Navy could take up a defensive stance in the Far East and bring back the units required for home defence. The growth of European navies, however, led to a new standard being proposed by the D.R.C. at the end of 1935. Under this standard the Navy would have been able to send a fleet to Singapore adequate to act on the defensive and to serve as a deterrent, while in all circumstances maintaining in home waters a force able to meet the requirements of war with Germany at the same time. By 1937 this D.R.C. standard was calculated by the Admiralty to require twenty capital ships, instead of the existing strength of fifteen, and in that form it was referred to as the 'New Standard', or a two-power standard.[27]

Under the London Naval Treaty no new capital ship could be laid down before 1937, but as early as 1934 a major interdepartmental battle was raging over the role of the battlefleet. The D.R.C. Report of February 1934 gave a figure of £25 million for the additional cost of naval construction – that is the cost over and above the 1933 rate of replacement – in the quinquennium 1934–8. This was twice the cost of the proposed programme for the Air Force in the same report. Although Fisher signed the report, he made it clear he could not be committed in advance to the D.R.C.'s figure for naval construction.[28] Fisher was far from convinced that the Admiralty recognised where the major danger lay. When he asked Chatfield in January 1934 about Germany's 'pocket battleships', which were designed to attack commerce, Chatfield remarked that new French warships could look after these vessels. Britain's three battlecruisers were her only warships individually capable of outsailing and outgunning a pocket battleship, but, according to Chatfield, the battlecruisers might have to be scrapped and replaced by slower vessels, depending upon what new capital ships were constructed by Japan after 1936. Fisher observed that by then the German, not the Japanese, fleet would present the main danger, and when Chatfield countered by saying that only a two-power standard could overcome the problem, Fisher remarked that it was doubtful if the taxpayer was yet willing to meet the cost – a view shared by the Cabinet. As long as the modernisation and replacement of capital ships were measures designed against the Japanese rather than the German menace – and in 1934 Germany, for practical purposes, had no battle-fleet – Fisher placed these measures in a lower priority than cruisers or destroyers for trade protection, or measures for countering the threat of the German air force. The Navy's role, Fisher believed, should be to defend home waters and Britain's trade routes.[29]

While agreeing with Fisher as to the desirability of an *entente* with Japan, Chatfield refused to let that wish father the thought that a Far Eastern battlefleet could be dispensed with. Whatever could be done to prevent air attacks on Britain would be in vain, Chatfield argued, if the Japanese Navy were left free to interrupt Britain's trade routes.[30] The Treasury tried to meet this criticism by suggesting in June 1934 that the approaches to the Indian Ocean be protected by submarines and light craft based on Singapore. The trade routes themselves would be protected by cruisers. Hankey suspected this proposal reflected Fisher's influence on Chamberlain. Fisher in turn seems to have picked up his ideas on Singapore from Trenchard, who was then advising him on defence questions.[31]

Hankey discreetly added his voice to the protests of the Admiralty that a maritime empire could not be protected by submarines and light craft alone. Chamberlain suggested to the Cabinet committee considering the D.R.C. Report that capital ship replacement be postponed, but this proposal shocked not only Eyres-Monsell, the First Lord, but also MacDonald, Baldwin, Simon and Eden, all of whom were more impressed by the imminence of the Japanese rather than the German menace. At the end of July Chamberlain had to settle for an agreement to differ, whereby the Cabinet endorsed his financial arguments, but questions of naval deficiencies and shipbuilding were left over for subsequent negotiation between the Admiralty and the Treasury later in 1934, and, as it proved, year by year thereafter.[32]

Hankey believed in the summer of 1934 that the German menace would take much more than five years to develop and he urged Baldwin to counteract the influence of Fisher, who, Hankey claimed, had 'never been sound about the Navy', and who, in Hankey's opinion, was not 'a fit man', nor was Fisher's judgement 'at its best'.[33] In fact the Treasury proposals were a good deal less revolutionary than their opponents seemed to suppose. Chamberlain pointed out that a battleship took three and a half years to build, so that even if the Japanese laid down capital ships in the coming year these would not be ready until the latter part of 1939. Until that date the existing British battlefleet would be sufficient to defend the Far East and there need be no abandonment of the Far East. If the situation were to change in the interim there would still be time to change policy, perhaps at the expense of home defence. Meanwhile what the Treasury was proposing was that naval expenditure outlined in the D.R.C. report be spread over a longer period than five years.[34] As it happened Japan did not complete any new battleship until after Pearl Harbour, by which time Britain had three new battleships in service.

It has been said of Chamberlain that he hated battleships because they were expensive, and this may have been true, but Chamberlain told Eyres-Monsell in July 1934 that if the Admiralty were to advise that capital ships would be needed in a war against Germany then he (Chamberlain) would accept that advice.[35] The Admiralty could not so advise in 1934 because Germany had yet to lay down a full-scale capital ship. As for the Anglo-German Naval Treaty of 1935, it was the Admiralty, not the Treasury, which was keen to sign. Chatfield believed that if Germany restricted herself to a fleet 35 per cent the tonnage of Britain's, then sufficient capital ships could be made available from the Home Fleet to deter Japan. Britain might not be able to station as many capital ships in the Far East as Japan had, but Chatfield believed the Royal Navy to be superior in quality, and, therefore, able to accept some inferiority in quantity.[36]

As late as October 1935 the Admiralty was coy about asking the D.R.C. to recommend a two-power standard outright. As it was the function of a C.I.D. sub-committee to make a full statement of requirements, Fisher and Hankey pressed Chatfield to ask for all the ships he needed. Thus invited the Admiralty put in a claim for the D.R.C. standard referred to above, although without yet stating how many capital ships would be required, and while admitting that lack of industrial capacity would prevent such a standard being reached until sometime after 1939. In subsequent ministerial discussion Chamber-

lain warned against setting up a higher standard than could be implemented, since the effect might be to induce other powers to build more
warships than they might otherwise have done. Accordingly in January
1936 the Admiralty was authorised only to work out the programme
necessary to give effect to the proposed standard.[37]

Fisher was not opposed to some increase in naval strength, to enable
a defensive stand to be made in the Far East while Britain was at war in
Europe. But when in April 1937 the Admiralty, in Bridges' words, came
out in favour of a two-power standard 'naked and unashamed', Fisher
insisted that it was impossible to prepare for every eventuality, for then
logically Britain ought to have a three-power standard, to take account
of Italy. The Admiralty's calculations, which did not take Italy into
account, put the annual maintenance cost of the optimum New Standard fleet at £104 million, compared with £88 million for the one-
power standard of the D.R.C. fleet authorised in 1936. Bridges felt the
new Admiralty demands 'really forced the issue of what permanent
standing defence charges we can afford', and as the Treasury at this
time hoped to keep total annual defence costs down to £150 million or
£170 million once rearmament was complete in 1942, the Chancellor
was bound to oppose approval of the New Standard pending a general
review of defence.[38]

Subsequent delay in policy-making did not prevent a commitment
being made at the Imperial Conference in May 1937 that even if
Britain were involved in a war with Germany the Navy would be
capable of acting on the defensive in the Far East until the issue with
Germany had been settled.[39] The New Standard was not dealt with
conclusively during the Inskip Review, Inskip recommending in his
Interim Report of December 1937 that the Admiralty should not incur
expenditure which committed them to a fleet beyond the approved
standard, and that a decision whether to adopt an increased standard
should be deferred.[40] With the waning of his hopes of an understanding
with Japan Fisher himself felt by then that some increase in the
authorised standard might be necessary. Hopkins, however, drew
attention to Cabinet policy, which called for rearmament to create a
maximum deterrent over the next two years, and noted that none of
the major warships proposed to be laid down in 1938 could have much
bearing on what the Japanese might do in 1938–40.[41]

A compromise was hammered out, with Chamberlain and Inskip
acting as brokers between the Admiralty and the Treasury, between
April and July 1938, whereby the Cabinet decided against committing
itself to the New Standard, but did not repudiate it, and a 'ration' for
Admiralty expenditure for 1939–42 was negotiated between the First
Lord, Duff Cooper, and Simon. The figure agreed, £410 million,
exceeded that required for the existing standard, £395 million, but fell
short of the £443 million required for the New Standard.[42] As will be

seen in the next chapter, financial rationing had no effect on the build-ing of major fleet units within existing industrial capacity. The New Standard was once more the subject of C.I.D. and interdepartmental discussion in 1939, but the capital ship programme was still under Treasury review when war broke out.

Meanwhile, in the spring of 1939, a change was taking place in naval policy. Even after Munich the Naval Staff had continued to plan on the basis that the main fleet would proceed to Singapore in the event of a Far Eastern war, but by May 1939 the Naval Staff was emphasising the political impact which an evacuation of the Eastern Mediterranean would have on Greece, Turkey and the Arab world. In the C.I.D. Chatfield, by then Minister for the Co-ordination of Defence, com-mented that a decision would have to be taken when war came which enemy fleet – the German, the Japanese or the Italian – could be knocked out most quickly. The Italian fleet, he thought, seemed the easiest victim. No decision was taken by the Government before the war to abandon the Far East, but in May the Admiralty's Director of Plans recorded that only four capital ships would be available for the Far East if Britain were at war with Germany and Italy, as against seven capital ships if Italy were neutral or eliminated. This order of priorities, he noted, was 'a new departure in policy'.[43]

This change in policy was not directly due to the influence of the Treasury, but represented recognition by the Admiralty of what the Treasury had argued since 1934 – the likelihood that the threat in European waters after 1939 would not permit the despatch of the main fleet to Singapore. The importance of sea power was not underesti-mated, however, either by the Treasury, or the Government, and down to 1938 more money was spent on the Navy than on either the Air Force or Army.[44] What the Treasury sought was balance between priorities. During Inskip's review of defence Fisher showed he shared the view that sea power was essential to enable the resources of the Empire to be mobilised, and economic pressure to be put on Germany. Fisher was just as convinced that sea power should not be sacrificed to air power, as vice versa.[45]

The Admiralty, for its part, recognised the importance of finance, at least by November 1937, when Chatfield and Captain T. S. V. Phillips, then Director of Plans, noted that 'present proposals for expansion of our armed forces are leading us on the direct path to national bankruptcy' and when Chatfield began discreetly to advocate a reduction in the Army's rearmament programme.[46] What follows deals mainly with alternative forms of deterring Germany, but it is important to remember that the financial limits to the Air Force and Army programmes were set by the expensive requirements of the Navy as well as by the Treasury's wish to maintain Britain's economic and financial strength.

Air Deterrence, 1934-6

The inter-war years saw the passing of the age when sea power alone could protect Britain. The First World War had provided a foretaste of what air warfare might mean, and developments in air transport thereafter brought a concomitant increase in the potential of bombers. By 1929 the Treasury official in charge of 5D, Mr. A. P. Waterfield, could write that 'the layman is inclined to believe the next war is likely to be chiefly a war in the air, with the possibility of completely annihilating the enemy at a single blow'.[47] The belief in the possibility of a 'knock-out blow' from the air was to dominate Treasury, and much other, thinking on defence policy in the 'Thirties.

In 1923 Baldwin, then Prime Minister, had stated that Britain must have a 'Home Defence Air Force of sufficient strength adequately to protect us against air attack by the strongest air force within striking distance of this country', and although disarmament talks gave Baldwin a public excuse as late as March 1934 for the non-performance of this pledge, in November 1934 he gave the Government's word 'in no conditions to accept any position of inferiority with regard to whatever air force may be raised in Germany'. But what strength would be sufficient adequately to protect Britain if, as Baldwin had stated in 1932, the bomber would always get through?[48] That the bomber was a decisive weapon was an article of faith with the Air Staff. The Chief of Air Staff, Ellington, went so far as to say in 1935 that Fleet Air Arm, army co-operation, and even fighter squadrons had no place in measuring the relative strength of air forces.[49] The Air Ministry consequently aimed at 'parity' with Germany either in numbers of bombers, or in the weight of bombs which could be dropped, so that Germany would be deterred by the threat of counter-bombing.

Watt has stated, without reference to dates, that Fisher was in 'profound disagreement with the policy of deterrence advocated by the Air Ministry'. But in 1935 Fisher endorsed advice to Chamberlain that the best defence against air attack was 'to make abundantly clear to the Germans that we intend to be able to give at least as good as we get', and Fisher expressed his anxiety that 'nothing should divert our activities and resources from the completion of a fully adequate striking force'.[50] Fisher's support for a bomber deterrent at that time was not surprising, since his chief mentor in defence matters was Trenchard, who certainly believed in the offensive power of aircraft.

Surveying the D.R.C. Report early in 1934, Trenchard advised Fisher that one of the most urgent needs was the creation of a metropolitan air force of 100 squadrons, two-thirds of which would be bombers. During the D.R.C.'s deliberations Fisher had urged greater expansion of the Air Force than the Air Ministry had asked for, but the Air Staff had stressed the technical difficulties of rapid expansion, and Hankey and the C.O.S. had stood firm on the figures of 10 additional Home Defence squadrons (to complete the 52-squadron scheme of 1923), 10 additional overseas squadrons and 20 additional Fleet Air Arm squadrons. It was stated in the D.R.C. Report that to meet 'all eventual requirements' a further 25 squadrons would be necessary, but these were not part of the 'worst deficiencies' to be remedied by 1939.[51] Fisher wanted much greater priority given to air preparations against Germany, and he would have signed a dissenting report asking for the additional 25 squadrons if Vansittart had supported him.[52]

In Fisher's view the order of Britain's strategic priorities should be: first, the Air Force and civil air raid precautions; second, the Army's expeditionary force for service in the Low Countries, and third, the Navy for service in the Far East. He made it his business to see that the Air Force was given due priority when the D.R.C. Report was discussed by ministers, and when in May 1934, after two months' discussion, Chamberlain was invited by his colleagues to review the D.R.C.'s recommendations, Fisher and Chamberlain worked together to produce new proposals.[53] Chamberlain also wanted a strong Air Force to deter Germany, and in June 1934 he submitted to ministers reviewing the D.R.C. Report a paper suggesting that 38 squadrons, instead of the D.R.C.'s 10, should be added to the Home Defence Force, but that no new squadrons should be formed overseas, except for the 3 proposed by the D.R.C. for Singapore, and that Fleet Air Arm requirements should be met by making Home Defence and Fleet Air Arm units interchangeable. In total this amounted to only one more squadron than that recommended by the D.R.C., but it allowed for almost the whole increase to be concentrated against Germany. Although Chamberlain recommended that the Army's and Navy's proposed financial allotments for 1934–9 should be cut drastically, he recommended an increase for the Air Force, proposing £18,200,000 instead of £15,700,000.[54]

Hankey described Chamberlain's proposals as 'panic measures' in that they neglected the Fleet Air Arm and the Far East, and it was probably due to Hankey's influence that the Cabinet committee set up a sub-committee on the Allocation of Air Forces, without any Treasury member, and with Baldwin in the chair. This sub-committee concluded that for technical reasons Fleet Air Arm and Home Defence squadrons could not be interchangeable, and recommended that instead of Chamberlain's 38 interchangeable squadrons there should be 33 for Home Defence and four-and-a-half for the Fleet Air Arm, but otherwise the Treasury principle of locating the Air Force centrally instead of in penny packets around the Empire was observed.[55]

The one major difference of opinion between the Treasury and the Air Staff arose over the question of reserves. The Air Staff demanded that sufficient aircraft should be provided to enable squadrons to maintain their first-line strength despite losses in war, but the Treasury argued that for financial reasons war reserves could not yet be provided.

Hopkins, who conducted the Treasury's case before the sub-committee on the Allocation of Air Forces, played skilfully on the question of obsolescence. Aircraft stowed in reserve in 1934 might well be out of date when war came, and the sub-committee seems not to have been wholly convinced by the counter-arguments of Ellington that types like the Hart biplane would be good for another five years yet, and that 30 squadrons with reserves would be better than 40 without. In any event the sub-committee, and the Cabinet committee, recommended that the bulk of war reserves should be provided only after 1939, and merely rounded up Chamberlain's figure of £18,200,000 for the Air Ministry for 1934-9 to £20 million.[56] Hankey observed privately that new squadrons without war reserves amounted to 'a politicians' window-dressing scheme', but on balance there seems much to be said for concentrating on building up the first-line strength of the Air Force, and with it the number of its pilots, at a time when the machines available for production, like the Hart, would soon be useless except as training machines. This was the policy being pursued at that time by the German Air Force.[57]

One undesirable consequence of interdepartmental differences of opinion was that the Cabinet's approval of the D.R.C. report was not given until the end of July, and, in retrospect, Chamberlain thought that the delays in drawing up and revising the deficiencies programme in 1934 had contributed to the loss of air parity with Germany. Be that as it may, when in November 1934 it was proposed in the Cabinet to accelerate the air expansion scheme so that the bulk of it would be completed by April 1937 instead of April 1939, Chamberlain's first instinct as Chancellor was to object on financial grounds, although he allowed himself to be overruled.[58]

It was not until the spring of 1935, after intelligence had been received of German borrowing for defence, and after Hitler had claimed that the Luftwaffe was already equal to Britain's metropolitan Air Force, that the Treasury became enthusiastic again regarding air expansion. Fisher and Fergusson accused the Air Ministry of complacency regarding the relative productive capacities of the British and German aircraft industries, and the quality of their respective products. Fisher accepted Trenchard's advice that drastic reorganisation of the aircraft industry and immediate expansion of its productive capacity was necessary, and that Lord Weir was the man to supervise this task. The importance of the industrial factor can be seen from the fact that Chamberlain was prepared to give the Air Ministry more money in a Supplementary Estimate than the Air Ministry felt it could spend before the end of the financial year.[59] Weir did undertake to advise the Air Ministry, but, for another three years, aircraft production continued to lag behind orders.

Meanwhile the Air Staff continued to give priority to bombers. The new expansion scheme approved by the Cabinet in May 1935 increased the proportion of bombers to fighters, while a further scheme drawn up in November 1935 added only to the figure for bombers, so far as the metropolitan air force was concerned.[60] The latter scheme, known as Scheme F, became the basis of the Air Force's rearmament in 1936 and 1937, and, prior to the latter year, the Air Staff's counter-offensive strategy was not questioned in the Treasury. In a speech in October 1936 Chamberlain spoke of his 'enthusiasm' for an air force which, when fully developed, would possess 'terrific striking power', and be 'the most formidable deterrent to war that could be devised'.[61]

As for defence against air attack, Fisher's interest down to 1937 centred on Air Raid Precautions.* Subsequently he claimed that although ministers had not been much concerned with A.R.P. before the Munich crisis, he had advanced A.R.P. measures 'by guile'.[62] With regard to measures involving fighter aircraft and anti-aircraft guns, Fisher's only positive contribution down to 1937 seems to have been made in the D.R.C. early in 1934, when he allied himself with Ellington in insisting that the War Office work out its programme for anti-aircraft guns and searchlights on a five-year basis, instead of the eight-year period proposed by the War Office.[63] Even so, both Fisher and Chamberlain down to 1937 seem to have regarded bombers as the most cost-effective form of defence, and in October 1936, for example, Chamberlain wondered aloud in the C.I.D. whether sums being asked for air defence might not be better spent on offensive forces.[64]

The Role of the Army, 1934–6

While Fisher was advised by Trenchard early in 1934 that the creation of a powerful bomber force was one of the most urgent defence needs, the former Chief of Air Staff did not advise neglect of the Army. Indeed, after the D.R.C. drew up its report in February 1934, Trenchard suggested that the Army act, in effect, as an auxiliary to the Air Force. In the first priority of deficiencies to be repaired, along with the Home Defence Air Force and Singapore's defences, he placed provision of anti-aircraft guns and searchlights south of the Wash, and 'the "spearhead" expeditionary force for securing continental air bases'.[65] Trenchard assumed that the Air Force would operate from continental bases, because in 1934 British bombers could hardly reach the Ruhr from home bases.

The War Office itself did not ask for an army on the scale of 1918 – some seventy divisions.[66] Indeed, in D.R.C. discussions in the winter of 1933–4, the C.I.G.S., Montgomery-Massingberd, resisted pressure from Fisher to state the full cost of more than what would be required to equip four infantry divisions and one horsed cavalry division, and a tank brigade, although the C.I.G.S. admitted that four Territorial

* Hereafter referred to as A.R.P.

Army divisions would be required to support these Regular units four months after the outbreak of war. Little or no money was asked for the Territorial Army, the C.I.G.S. said, because the bill for its equipment would be 'enormous'.[67] Pownall, then in the C.I.D. secretariat, thought that if the full bill for equipping both the Regular and Territorial Armies were known, ministers might well declare that the Army was too expensive, and turn to the Air Force, which claimed to be as effective, or more effective, an instrument of defence at much less cost.[68] Be that as it may, the War Office held its peace on plans for the Territorial Army until October 1935, so that until that date debate centred on what could be done with five Regular divisions.

There was some doubt when the Field Force* could be ready for service in Europe. In 1933 a military correspondent of *The Times* had pointed out the dichotomy between Imperial requirements for an Army suited to 'police' work in India or Palestine, and the requirements of modern European warfare for a mechanised Army. Cuttings from *The Times* were filed by Treasury officials, and seem to have been used subsequently to brief Fisher for discussions in the D.R.C.[69] Was the War Office satisfied, Fisher asked in January 1934, with the Cardwell system, whereby colonial garrisons received their drafts from units which in the event of war would form the expeditionary force? The C.I.G.S. apparently was, and he denied any intention of forming a mechanised force designed solely for European operations, and stated that the tanks necessary for a mechanised force were still at the experimental stage. Fisher believed that tanks and mechanisation were necessary concomitants of modern warfare,[70] but, on the C.I.G.S.'s evidence, it seemed that some time must elapse before the War Office could, or would, prepare what Trenchard called a 'spearhead' force, as opposed to a shield of infantry divisions based on the Cardwell system.

Subsequently Fisher argued that air defence, for which the taxpayer would be most willing to pay, should come first, and, once the public mind had been 'introduced to realities':

> We could then proceed to what, in my opinion, is the second priority, and that is the public affirmation that the integrity of the Low Countries is a vital British interest. . . . In hostile hands the Low Countries are a fatally dangerous advance base for air attack on England. . . . The second priority implies the provision of ground forces adequate in number and celerity of expansion for maintaining the integrity of the Low Countries, and by so doing converting them into an advance base for air attack by ourselves on Germany.[71]

On 20 June 1934 Chamberlain, in his recommendations to the Cabinet committee considering the D.R.C. Report, reduced the Army's

---

* The term 'Field Force' was used in the 'Thirties for the Army's divisions which would form an expeditionary force. The term 'Expeditionary Force' seems not to have been used in official documents before 1939, possibly because it evoked memories of 1914.

financial allotment for 1934–9 from £40 million to £19·1 million, but what this meant was not that the Army's deficiencies were not to be repaired, but only that the time taken to do so would be longer than the five years envisaged in the D.R.C. programme. At the time Chamberlain did not believe that Germany would be ready for war in 1939, and, in any case, there was an element of bargaining in his proposals, which, he noted privately, he had pitched 'a little high'.[72]

According to Howard, Chamberlain 'dismissed' the D.R.C.'s arguments that an expeditionary force was necessary.[73] It is true that in a Cabinet committee in May 1934 Chamberlain challenged the need for another 1914-style expeditionary force, but one must remember that he was speaking in committee. Given his belief that it was the proper function of ministers to 'see that strategical problems are fairly and thoroughly worked out by the strategists',[74] it seems probable that in referring questions about the role of an expeditionary force to the C.O.S. he was acting as the 'devil's advocate' rather than voicing his own fixed opinions. The doubts Chamberlain expressed – such as could an expeditionary force reach the Low Countries in time to prevent them being overrun? – were reasonable ones, shared by other ministers. Even the C.O.S. did not claim that Holland could be saved, and as Eyres-Monsell, the First Lord, pointed out, the Germans could attack Britain just as well from Holland as from Belgium. Was not the proper answer to the German air force, Chamberlain asked, an overwhelming R.A.F.? He said he had no objections to rearming the Army if it were to have a useful role.[75]

Chamberlain seems to have been impressed by the argument that possession of Belgian bases would place the R.A.F.'s bombers as close to the Ruhr as German bombers would otherwise have been to London. At any rate his balanced opinion, as given to his ministerial colleagues in June 1934, emphasised that the major danger facing Britain was air attack, and that 'the exclusion of Germany from the Low Countries is essential to our security'. Priority must be given to the Air Force to deter Germany from going to war at all, but, 'should that deterrent fail', Britain's defence would be found partly in an enlarged Air Force, partly in the completion of anti-aircraft defences, and 'finally, in the conversion of the Army into an effectively equipped force capable of operating with allies in holding the Low Countries'.[76] It will be noted that his ideas accorded closely with Fisher's. The Cabinet, no doubt conscious of public support for the Air Force and Navy, and of the lack of such support for the Army, accepted Chamberlain's proposals for the Army, and his figure of £19·1 million for deficiencies in the quinquennium 1934–9 was only rounded up to £20 million.[77]

Some historians have drawn attention to the ideas of Captain Liddell Hart as a possibly important influence on Chamberlain,[78] but there seems to be no evidence of any direct influence on Liddell Hart's part in the first half of 1934. When Liddell Hart sent a copy of his book *Europe in Arms* to Chamberlain in March 1937 the Chancellor wrote to say that he had found Liddell Hart's articles in *The Times* on the role of the Army 'extremely useful and suggestive',[79] but Liddell Hart's articles did not appear in *The Times* before 1935. An article by Liddell Hart was published in the *Daily Telegraph* on 25 June 1934, suggesting that the role of the expeditionary force in opposing an invasion of the Low Countries might be more rapidly carried out by the French, assisted by the R.A.F., and that the Army would then 'not need to be equipped for action on foreign soil in the early stages of a Continental war'.[80] Chamberlain had made his case in Cabinet committee before 25 June, however, and Liddell Hart does not seem to have suggested previously in print that an expeditionary force might be dispensed with altogether in the early stages of a major war. Be that as it may, Hankey had no doubts as late as January 1937 that the principal exponent of the view that the Air Force could replace the Army was Trenchard, and the esteem in which Chamberlain held Trenchard's opinions can be judged from the Chancellor's suggestion to Inskip in December 1936 that the latter invite Trenchard to return from a visit to Africa to advise him on the role of the Army.[81] Liddell Hart, it would seem, was not at this stage the most influential advocate of limiting Britain's land forces in the light of priority for air and sea forces.

Having said that, one must add that Liddell Hart's articles in *The Times* reinforced, and probably clarified, Chamberlain's views at the beginning of 1936. By October 1935 the War Office had produced proposals far greater than those of eighteen months before, adding twelve Territorial divisions to serve as reinforcements for the five Regular divisions already being prepared, as well as providing for additional tank and anti-aircraft units for the latter. Fisher allowed these proposals to go forward unchallenged in the Third D.R.C. Report of the following month, along with proposals for larger Navy and Air Force programmes.[82] In December 1935, however, a report by the P.S.O.C. showed how these proposals would increase the strain of maintaining the services, and in particular the Army, in war, and Bridges wrote to Fisher that it was doubtful if Britain's resources would enable her to make a maximum effort in each of the three services.[83] A month later the Government's most respected industrial adviser, Weir, frankly told ministers that British industry could not meet the demands of all three services within the time stated – five years – without Government controls over industry, which he and ministers believed to be unacceptable in peacetime.[84]

Weir believed the Army was the least effective way of helping allies, and this opinion seems to have been based, at least partly, on Liddell Hart's articles, which Weir had filed in November 1935. At any rate Weir had underlined passages which stated that 'the offensive is [now] as much at an advantage in the air as it is at a disadvantage on land', and that it was worth considering reducing the role of the Army's field units to that of garrisoning the Empire 'with the possible addition of covering the overseas bases of our Expeditionary Air Force'.[85] Whether or not Chamberlain read the articles in question, Liddell Hart's ideas would have reached him through Weir, and it seems significant that the first mention in Pownall's diary of Liddell Hart's influence on ministerial thinking was in January 1936, after Weir had questioned the need for an expeditionary force if a substantial air deterrent were built up. It seems certain that Chamberlain valued Weir's opinion, for he wrote to Weir in December 1936 asking for the latter's views on the relative importance of air and land forces, and Weir repeated his earlier views.[86]

Chamberlain's own opinion in January 1936 was that even with special measures it would take a long time to catch up with German rearmament, and he considered it vitally important to find a deterrent. Eden, newly-appointed Foreign Secretary, agreed that from the point of view of deterrence the Air Force would assume first place. If Britain were to have the air and sea power she needed, and if there were to be no mobilisation of industry, some part of the D.R.C.'s programme had to be left out, and Chamberlain urged, and his Cabinet colleagues agreed, in January 1936 that the twelve Territorial divisions be omitted, pending a final decision in three years, or until such time as the industrial and political situation changed. The Regular Expeditionary Force, however, was to be as complete as possible, with war reserves, within five years.[87]

It has been suggested by Howard that during 1936 Chamberlain 'remained implacably hostile to all idea of involvement on the Continent',[88] but this seems something of an overstatement. Chamberlain spoke publicly in 1936 of rearmament providing a British Army 'trifling in numbers beside the vast conscript armies of the Continent, but equipped with the most modern weapons and mechanical devices that science can give us'.[89] Where Chamberlain seems to have been misunderstood by his critics is that he differentiated more sharply than they have done between the role which a standing army could perform at the outset of a war, and the role of the larger army which, with the assistance of allies, would be required to defeat the German army. Chamberlain concentrated on what could be done in peacetime to deter Germany, and to avoid defeat at the outset of war if deterrence failed. He opposed proposals to build up in peacetime an Army on a scale which, he believed, must impinge upon Britain's air, sea and economic power, but he did not exclude the possibility of enlarging the Army in war. As he told Inskip in May 1937:

Where we may be led in the course of a prolonged war . . . is impossible to forsee. . . . The ultimate role of the Army [is] a thing which we cannot now determine.[90]

In April 1936, after the German occupation of the Rhineland, the Treasury raised no objection to an acceleration of the War Office's programme, so that the Regular Field Force could be ready by 1939, instead of 1941.[91] But while there was some urgency regarding the Army in 1936, there was much greater concern about air defence. British Industrial Intelligence Centre reports suggested that German industry could not equip an army larger than the combined French and Belgian armies much before 1940, but C.I.D. reports on the contemporary strength of the German, and the weakness of the French, air forces provided, as Fisher remarked, 'all the more reason for [having] a strong air force ourselves'.[92]

In September 1936 Ismay, then Deputy Secretary of the C.I.D., prepared a memorandum suggesting that since the Germans would be unlikely to achieve rapid success on land, they might try to prevent a repetition of 1914–18 by 'knocking out' Britain by air attack before large-scale British land forces could be built up. While it was important to prepare an expeditionary force with which to deny the Germans air bases in the Low Countries, Ismay argued, this was only a means to the security of Britain, and not an end in itself. If the Germans could attack Britain without occupying the Low Countries – and the increasing range of aircraft made this possible – then the provision of efficient anti-aircraft defences must have first priority. But the War Office, Ismay noted, seemed to be giving 'even the *ultimate* reinforcement' of an expeditionary force, that is the Territorial Army's field units, 'a higher degree of priority than the *immediate* necessities of Home Defence', that is the Territorial Army's anti-aircraft units. In his memoirs Ismay said this strategic appreciation never got further than Hankey's desk, and, therefore, 'did no harm', but in fact Hankey forwarded Ismay's memorandum to Inskip with the comment that it 'very effectively sets out the case which you and I discussed at our last two meetings', and suggested that Inskip take up the question of War Office priorities at ministerial level.[93]

Once ministers were aware that a choice had to be made whether to devote the country's limited gun-making capacity to field guns or to anti-aircraft guns, large questions of priorities regarding the role of the Army were raised, and by November 1936 ministers in the D.P.R.C., including Chamberlain, were showing a clear preference for anti-aircraft guns.[94] If anti-aircraft guns were given priority, it was doubtful whether much could be done for the Territorial Army's field artillery for some time, because, in common with other aspects of the rearmament programme, plans for anti-aircraft defence were being formulated on an ever-growing scale. The Air Defence of Great Britain* scheme of 1935 would not have been complete until 1950, and would have provided only 136 3-inch guns by 1940. In October 1936 the C.I.D.

* Hereafter referred to as A.D.G.B.

approved plans for 608 heavier guns (3·7-inch and 4·5-inch) as well as 600 barrels for light anti-aircraft guns for use against low-flying aircraft. By February 1937 the Home Defence Sub-Committee of the C.I.D. had drawn up what it called the 'Ideal Scheme', providing for 1264 heavy guns and 1200 light barrels.[95]

Chamberlain was not a man to burke issues. Although the Cabinet had decided eight months earlier to defer a decision on the Territorial Army until possibly 1939, the Chancellor told Inskip in October 1936 both that there must be an early decision on the future of the Army, and what he (Chamberlain) thought that decision should be. Chamberlain took the view on 19 October that five Regular divisions were all that Britain 'could provide for a European war if it came', and that Territorials should be enlisted liable only for service at home for A.D.G.B. work.[96]

Chamberlain put his officials to work on the question, and four days later Fisher drew up a memorandum suggesting that the 17-division Field Force (including 12 Territorial divisions) recommended a year earlier by the D.R.C. should be 'our maximum war standard'. Noting that 'our people ... will never again consent to be conscripted by millions for military service' in Europe, Fisher argued that, even if they were, better use could be made of Britain's economic resources by building up the Air Force. Whereas a Continental power, like Germany, must devote a large proportion of her resources to maintaining an army, Britain's insularity enabled her 'to concentrate to a greater extent on this new arm' which was 'of first-rate, and possibly even decisive importance'. Since 'army demands for munitions ... are proportionately far greater than those of the sea and air', Britain's problem of securing foreign supplies would be reduced by limiting her army, and this, Fisher noted, had 'special significance in view of the isolationist policy of the United States and their ban on munitions exports'.[97]

There remained the question of when a 17-division army should be prepared. Chamberlain wrote to Fisher a month later:

I think we shall find there are two separate questions to consider.
   (1) Should we carry out the D.R.C. plan and prepare to send 17 divisions to the Continent on or within a limited time after the outbreak of a major war?

To which Fisher answered:

As an *ultimate* policy I think yes
(2) [Chamberlain wrote] If the answer is yes, should we use our resources to advance the equipment of the Terriers rather than in expanding or strengthening the Air Force?

To which Fisher answered:

No. Air strength should be an *absolute priority*, accompanied by naval development.[98]

Clearly, then, the Treasury view on the scale and timing of Army preparations depended upon progress being made in building up an Air Force which would deter Germany, and it is necessary to break off from the story of the Field Force to look at air developments in 1937-8.

A New Air Policy, 1937-8

When, in October 1936, Chamberlain opened what proved to be a lengthy debate on the role of the Army, it was still assumed that Britain could build up an air force which would deter German aggression. The Treasury view was that Britain should concentrate her resources on building up a 'striking [air] force', as 'the most formidable deterrent to war that could be devised'. But during 1937 it became apparent that such an air force was beyond the capacity of British industry, at least in the immediate future, and a new air policy had to be formulated so as to make Britain secure against air attack while a diplomatic settlement with Germany was being sought.

As already noted, the defence programmes were reviewed in 1937, at the insistence of the Treasury, with reference to financial limits and to the effects of rearmament upon the economy. While considering future defence policy Inskip took advice from Fisher, Hopkins and Bridges, as well as from Hankey, Robinson, Wilson, Vincent and members of the defence departments.[99] In his Interim Report, accepted by the Cabinet on 22 December 1937, Inskip recommended that 'our first and main effort should be directed . . . to protecting this country against [air] attack',[100] and what follows shows how Treasury support for a policy of air deterrence based on bombers was transformed into strong pressure in favour of priority for fighter aircraft.

There was no hint of change in Treasury opinion when the Secretary of State for Air, Swinton, submitted a new expansion scheme, Scheme H, to Chamberlain in November 1936.[101] The Air Staff believed Germany might have 1700 bombers by 1939, and accordingly Scheme H proposed emergency measures to increase the Air Force's first-line bombers to over 1600 by April 1939, compared with the proposed 1000 by that date under the authorised scheme (Scheme F). First-line fighter strength, however, was to be increased by a mere 50 machines to 476. On receipt of this information Fisher wrote to Swinton, addressing him as 'Dear Tom', saying he was 'relieved that the Air Staff is apparently becoming aware of Germany'. Bridges, on examining Scheme H, remarked he believed it 'would give us a greater degree of security than we should get from corresponding expenditure on the other two Services' – with which Chamberlain agreed.

On 20 January 1937 Chamberlain and Swinton discussed what was meant by air 'parity', to which Baldwin had pledged the Government in 1934. The Air Ministry, in a draft Cabinet paper submitted to the Treasury, had suggested the definition:

(a) A bomber force not inferior to that of Germany.
(b) A fighter force of a strength requisite to meet the *probable* scale of attack [italics added].

But following discussion with Chamberlain Swinton suggested a revised definition:

(i) A defensive force adequate to meet *any anticipated* scale of attack [italics added].
(ii) As (a) above.

Whether or not there was any significance in reversing the order of defensive and offensive elements in the definition of parity, it seems that in January 1937 Chamberlain was more inclined than the Air Staff to stress air defence.

By the time Scheme H was due to be discussed by the C.I.D. in February 1937 the initial welcome afforded by the Treasury to the Air Ministry's proposals had cooled considerably. The reason for this was simply that the existing Scheme F was already in arrears, and there seemed to Bridges, who was briefing Chamberlain, little wisdom in enlarging plans which could not be carried out. In the event, Scheme H was approved only in respect of personnel and aerodromes, and none of its successors, prior to Scheme L of April 1938, was approved by the Treasury or Cabinet. As will be shown in the next chapter, the Treasury had given the Air Ministry all the finance it had asked for, but, because of technical and industrial factors, the Air Ministry found it hard to spend the money. The Air Ministry's progress reports in 1936–7 show how production deliveries of aircraft continually fell below expectations.[102] Bomber deliveries tended to lag even further behind those of fighters, and there seemed little hope of building a bomber force on the scale outlined by the Air Ministry in time to be an effective deterrent to German aggression in the years immediately ahead. One alternative might have been to expedite production by transferring labour and machine tools from civil industry to the aircraft industry, but the Government was not prepared to take the necessary powers.

Even before Inskip began his review of defence policy in October 1937 the Air Ministry had admitted, in response to an enquiry by Chamberlain that month, that Bomber Command would be in no way fit for war at the beginning of 1938.[103] Fortunately, as Bridges observed in a note two days before Inskip's review began, the signs were that the technology of defence in air warfare was catching up on that of offence. The signs to which Bridges referred were those being interpreted by the C.I.D. Sub-Committee on Air Warfare in Spain, from whose reports Hankey the previous month had drawn the inference that the combination of fighters, anti-aircraft guns and searchlights 'might prove very much more effective than we have hitherto assumed'.[104] This reaction at the official level against the tendency to assume that the bomber would always get through may also have been strengthened by the knowledge that radar would eventually make the task of intercepting bombers much easier. The possibilities of radar had been brought to the attention of the Treasury as early as March 1935, and by July 1937 the Air Ministry had been ready to submit proposals to the Treasury for a chain of radar stations at the remarkably cheap cost of one million pounds. Significantly, perhaps, the Air Ministry's note of July 1937 on radar was filed by Treasury officials along with other papers relating to Inskip's review of defence.[105]

The Air Ministry itself, by the autumn of 1937, regarded fighter squadrons in a more favourable light than hitherto. When Inskip opened a discussion on 2 November on the strength of the Air Force Swinton told him that, if parity in bombers were unobtainable for financial reasons, it would be a question whether a façade of first-line bombers without war reserves would be the best deterrent. But, Swinton added, there could be no choice in the case of fighter squadrons. Their scale of operations would be dictated by the enemy from the outset of the war, and these formations must accordingly have sufficient reserves to keep their strength at 100 per cent in sustained operation.[106] In other words, the Air Staff believed that, if economies had to be found, these must be at the expense of bombers, and not fighters. Swinton still felt strongly that Britain should continue to aim at parity in bombers, but Inskip wrote to him two days later arguing that air parity was not so vital as sea power. The Navy must have first call on the finance available, Inskip said, because if the Navy were unable to keep Britain's trade routes open, Britain could not long survive, whereas if the Air Force's bomber strength were inferior to that of Germany, the British people would suffer more than the enemy in war, but the result might not at once be critical.[107]

Meanwhile the C.O.S. were reviewing, independently, Britain's preparedness for war, and on 16 November Bridges noted that the C.O.S. had concluded that the only reason which would be likely to tempt Germany to attack Britain in 1938 would be to gamble on the effect of air attack. Defence against air attack was thus the most pressing of priorities, and on 23 November Hankey prepared a memorandum recommending that the Air Force, the Army's anti-aircraft units and A.R.P. should have first call on finance. The Navy was given second priority, but only because of Britain's relatively favourable position in sea power, and it was made clear that air expansion was not to be at the expense of sea power.[108] This was certainly the view of Fisher who, at Inskip's next meeting dealing with air policy, on 2 December, urged that 'we must frame our policy so as to survive the initial period of a war; thereafter the weight of our naval strength would operate'. Behind Britain's naval strength would be her financial strength, which must not be weakened by pre-war rearmament.[109]

Hankey, at this same meeting, seeking to reconcile the requirements of defence and counter-bombing, suggested that medium bombers could be used to reinforce the home fighter squadrons at the outset of a war, before taking up their offensive role (in 1937 a type like the Blenheim, which later was used as a twin-engined fighter, was rated as a medium bomber). It was agreed that Inskip should discuss this suggestion with Swinton, and Hankey was clearly at the former's elbow in the ensuing strategic discussion. Roskill, indeed, claims that Hankey was the first person in authority to propose that the Air Force's bomber strength might be reduced, and its fighter strength increased.[110] The document cited by Roskill does not, however, support this claim. The document, dated 3 December, is unsigned, but it is clearly prepared by Hankey, and it served as a basis for an *aide-mémoire* sent by Inskip to Swinton on 9 December. Far from suggesting an increase in fighters, Hankey wrote:

> I am not even suggesting an alteration in the ratio between bombers and aircraft [*sic*]. My idea is rather that the numbers of heavy bombers should be reduced. . . . The general suggestion I want to make is that . . . we might substitute a larger proportion of light bombers and medium bombers for our very expensive heavy bombers.[111]

What Hankey was suggesting can, indeed, be seen as a means of *avoiding* an increase in fighters, by utilising multi-purpose machines to reinforce, for a limited period, these purely defensive aircraft. The C.O.S. had reported that German aircraft on the ground would not present very satisfactory targets, and that the use of counter-bombing to reduce the scale of air attack on Britain was '*faute de mieux*'. In the draft *aide-mémoire* Hankey suggested the best strategy would be to concentrate the R.A.F. over British territory, to prevent the Luftwaffe striking a decisive blow, and to inflict as many losses as possible in the air, so as to reduce the German pilots' morale. After that the R.A.F. might adopt a more offensive role, although the smaller bombers would have to operate from French bases.[112]

Fisher supported Hankey's strategic ideas with enthusiasm, as they accorded with the Treasury's principle of maintaining the 'fourth arm of defence' as a deterrent to Germany, while making it clear to the latter that she could not hope to win by a 'knock-out blow'. Even Trenchard, the arch-advocate of the bomber, speaking in the Lords on A.R.P., said on 13 December that 'if we can hold out for the first ten weeks we win' – by which he meant Britain must avoid being beaten by air attack, so as to win time to mobilise the resources of the Empire.[113] The Air Staff denounced the idea of concentrating the R.A.F. over Britain as 'as a surrender of initiative', but Fisher thought that deterrent action should not be regarded as being limited to bombing operations. He noted on 8 December that:

A high concentration of the greater part of our military machines on the destruction of enemy airmen *en route* to and over this country during the first few days would, by impairing their morale, be a very effective deterrent.[114]

In his Interim Report of 15 December Inskip disclaimed any qualification to dictate tactics to the Air Staff, but at the same time recommended that while the full increase in fighter squadrons asked for by the Air Ministry in their latest proposals, Scheme J, should be granted, there should be only 'some increase in the present first-line strength' of bombers. To emphasise the defensive role expected of the Air Force at the outbreak of war provision for bomber reserves was to be reduced in favour of concentrating on creating industrial capacity to produce bombers once war had begun.[115] It will be noticed that Inskip's proposals echoed Swinton's remarks on 2 November about what would be necessary if financial restraint prevented a policy of bomber parity being pursued. Nothing was said in Inskip's Report about Hankey's idea of using medium or light bombers instead of heavy bombers, and it may fairly be said that any changes in Air Ministry policy wrought by the report were the result of the Treasury's financial restrictions rather than any conversion on the Air Staff's part to Hankey's views on tactics or strategy.

Slessor, who headed the Air Staff's Plans Branch in 1937-40, candidly admitted in his memoirs that fighters were not really given priority by the Air Ministry until the autumn of 1938.[116] The Air Ministry's Scheme K, which appeared in February 1938, was still based, Bridges noted, on a hankering after parity in bombers. Bridges advised his superiors that 'the Air Ministry should have all they ask for in the way of fighters (indeed probably rather more than they ask for)', but as for bombers the real need was for consolidation through more rapid construction rather than plans for expansion after 1939. Fisher agreed.[117] The difficulty, as Bridges observed, was in knowing how far civilians were justified in pressing the Air Staff to change its views on the proper proportions between fighters and bombers. The Air Staff had no such doubts. Swinton roundly told the Cabinet that while ministers were entitled to say that not enough money could be found for a given scheme, the Air Staff could not accept that the character of the Air Force should be dictated to them, and it was up to the Air Staff to determine the Air Force's composition.[118] Thus, although between Scheme K of February, and Scheme L of April, 1938, the Air Staff made an adjustment in favour of fighters, increasing the proposed first-line strength from 532 to 608, the proposed first-line strength of bombers remained the same (1360).[119] Swinton carried the day, and the Cabinet decided on 27 April to go for the maximum production of aircraft possible in the next two years, broadly on the basis of Scheme L.

It seems to have required the Munich crisis to bring home to the Air Staff the possible imminence of war, and therefore the need for immediate air defence. At any rate, when, at the height of the crisis, the Air Ministry asked Fisher for Treasury approval for an order for 1000 Hurricane fighters, Fisher gave it at once, with the comment:

> I hope I may infer that the Air Staff are seriously reconsidering the relationship between bombers and fighters from the point of view of this country being the aggressee.[120]

Greater priority for fighters was given in Scheme M, which was proposed by the Air Ministry after Munich. This scheme set a target of 800 fighters in the first line by April 1940 – 200 more than in Scheme L. Even so Scheme L's target of 1360 first-line bombers was retained, albeit not to be attained until 1942, and, moreover, the bombers in Scheme M were to be larger, and more expensive, than those in Scheme L. The heavy bombers in Scheme M were estimated to cost £175 million, as against £45 million for fighters.[121]

Hopkins told Simon on 29 October that an attempt to carry out Scheme M in its entirety would 'probably bring down the general economy of this country', and advised that while financial risks must be taken over the next eighteen months to remedy deficiencies in the country's defences, heavy commitments after 1940 should be avoided.[122] Fisher agreed, and commented that:

> The Air Staff still cling in reality to their will-of-the-wisp of 'parity' – an objective which we cannot attain and don't need. What we do need is to be a sufficiently unattractive hedgehog . . . [so that] the Germans will think many times before they ignore, and still more, attack us.[123]

Fisher saw the 'defensive essential to deter invasion by air' as being the combination of 'anti-aircraft defence and A.R.P., . . . with the necessary strength in fighters'. He had abandoned his earlier views on deterrence by bombers because, as he remarked in July 1938, ' "Parity" in the sense of exact equality with Germany is unobtainable in peace conditions'.[124]

Even after Munich there was, within the Prime Minister's Office at least, still the greatest reluctance to put the aircraft industry on a war footing – the only way in which Wilson, the Government's Chief Industrial Adviser, believed Britain could match German aircraft production. This had been made clear to the Treasury when Wilson wrote to Simon's Principal Private Secretary on 1 November that news of a major mobilisation of industry could not be withheld from Germany, who:

> would feel bound to increase her own capacity. She would, moreover, take it as a signal that we had decided at once to sabotage the Munich Declaration. The Chancellor will remember that we know from Herr Hitler himself that there is a danger that he may feel himself forced to

denounce the [Anglo-German] Naval Treaty, the existence of which is only justifiable, in his view, on the hypothesis that England and Germany do not intend to be at war.[125]

Chamberlain and Wilson still clung to appeasement as well as to rearmament as a means of maintaining peace, indeed they hoped that appeasement could prevent an unending arms race.[126] Chamberlain was still in favour of maintaining the 'fourth arm of defence', and he and Sir Kingsley Wood, the Secretary of State for Air, accepted Hopkins' argument that if Scheme M were revised to concentrate more on fighters and to go slowly on bombers, the strain on the economy would be alleviated. One heavy bomber cost the equivalent of four fighters, and this was a powerful argument, given the Government's political assumptions, for adopting the Treasury view that the Air Ministry should aim at defensive security in 1939 rather than bomber parity in 1942. This was the effect of the Cabinet decision of 7 November, which approved the whole of Scheme M's fighter proposals, specifying maximum production possible before April 1940, but which stated that only sufficient orders for bombers were to be placed to ensure that labour and plant were not unemployed.[127]

As it happened the desire to utilise industrial capacity to the full, combined with technical difficulties in producing new fighters, meant that bomber production continued to exceed that of fighters until 1940. Nevertheless, the Cabinet's decision of 7 November 1938 gave the Treasury the power to attempt to enforce the principle laid down by Inskip almost a year earlier, but ignored by the Air Staff, that fighters should have priority. The decision was a success for the Treasury view, as expressed by Fisher since December 1937, and for the effectiveness of financial restraint in forcing the Air Staff and Cabinet to allocate priorities between different parts of the rearmament programme. The Treasury's opposition to a bomber deterrent was not a priori, but represented recognition that military policy must be formed according to financial and economic means, the latter themselves being determined, in part, by the Government's ideas on domestic and foreign policies.

A New Army Policy, 1937

Developments with regard to the Army in 1937 can be understood only in the context of increasing urgency felt about the danger of air attack, and of the cost of maintaining and expanding the largest navy in the world. The Cabinet's decision on 22 December 1937 to accept Inskip's recommendation that: 'our first and main effort should be directed . . . to protecting this country against [air] attack, and to preserving the trade routes'[128] followed the Treasury's insistence that aggregate defence expenditure be limited, and was in line with Treasury views as to what priorities should be. The same cannot be said of

Inskip's recommendation, also accepted by the Cabinet on 22 December, that:

> Our third objective should be the maintenance of forces for the defence of British territories overseas . . . [and] our fourth objective, which can only be provided for after the other objectives have been carried out, should be co-operation in the defence of the territories of any allies we may have in war.[129]

Certainly Treasury insistence on there being a limit to defence expenditure created a need to define priorities, and the Treasury believed that air strength should have priority over the Field Force, but priority for Imperial defence ran counter to Chamberlain's and Fisher's earlier belief that measures to deter Germany were the best answer to threats from Japan and Italy. Priority for Imperial defence was the product of influences other than that of the Treasury.

Even priority for air defence required little influence on the part of the Treasury. As noted above, ministers, advised by the C.I.D. secretariat, had been showing concern about War Office allocation of gun-making capacity between anti-aircraft and field guns since late 1936, and on 8 November 1937 a meeting of ministers authorised Hore-Belisha to instruct his department to give anti-aircraft defence 'absolute priority over all other forms of war material'. A fortnight later, Inskip, while preparing his report, said it was difficult to imagine any rationing of finance for A.D.G.B.[130]

In the circumstances the Treasury's function was to restrain ministerial enthusiasm. A Cabinet decision on the 'Ideal Scheme' for A.D.G.B. of February 1937 had been held over, pending Inskip's review of defence, and in February 1938 Bridges advised that not all the scheme should be adopted forthwith, as it was beyond the War Office's ability to carry out in the immediate future, for want of industrial capacity. The War Office itself did not wish to devote all its efforts to A.D.G.B., and when the Home Defence Sub-Committee submitted a revised A.D.G.B. scheme to the C.I.D. in April 1938, calling for 640 heavy anti-aircraft guns, instead of 1264 in the 'Ideal' scheme, it was Hore-Belisha who opposed it as 'unfair', in that if the Army was held to its ration of finance, the increase in A.D.G.B. expenditure proposed for the next two years must impinge upon the Field Force. Nevertheless the C.I.D. and Cabinet approved what Fisher called the 'good and practicable' revised scheme.[131]

It is against this background that the Field Force's story must be understood. What Chamberlain had called for in October 1936 was a decision on whether the Territorial Army's twelve infantry divisions should be prepared for service in Europe, and if so, what priority should be given to their equipment. The War Office itself, by November 1936, wanted a decision, because of the stand taken by Treasury officials in the T.I.S.C. The War Office's plans for explosives factories, for example, were based on the needs of both Regular and Territorial contingents of the Field Force, but as preparations for the Territorial divisions had not been sanctioned by the Cabinet along with the rest of the rearmament programme in February 1936, Treasury officials would approve only proposals based on the needs of Regular divisions. The War Office found it difficult to recast its plans accordingly, nor indeed was it willing to do so, and delays resulted.[132]

In memoranda in December 1936 on the role of the Army the Secretary of State for War, Duff Cooper, argued that in war the maximum effort must be made with the minimum delay, and that therefore the twelve Territorial divisions should be equipped so as to be available to support the five Regular divisions as rapidly as possible. Although no more than a small part of the Territorial Army's equipment could be produced by industry by 1939, the knowledge that the Territorial Army was to be equipped would encourage firms to expand output and new armaments factories could be designed and built to the required scale. The War Office had no doubt that in war an expeditionary force would be required to support France and Belgium, as in 1914, and the experience of the autumn of 1914 had been that such an expeditionary force must be backed by reinforcements if it were not to be overwhelmed.[133] Duff Cooper was supported by the C.O.S., and in February 1937 Inskip felt unable to reject professional advice on the need to support the Regular expeditionary force with Territorial contingents.[134]

Chamberlain himself agreed in December 1936 that there was much to be said for Duff Cooper's case, if it were taken in isolation. Chamberlain's difficulty was that he could not see that the War Office's proposals for a 17-division Field Force were within the capacity of industry, or that, even if they were, that such a force would represent the best use of Britain's resources *at the outbreak of war*, whatever might be needed as the war progressed.[135] The Treasury wanted defence policy to take into account what was possible as well as what was desirable. Throughout 1936 and early 1937 the defence departments constantly petitioned the T.I.S.C., usually successfully, for *ad hoc* additions to their authorised programmes, with the result that the estimated total cost for all three departments had risen from £245 million in February 1936, when the rearmament programme was authorised by the Cabinet, to £426 million in January 1937.[136]. But, as Bridges pointed out, this process of allowing the defence programmes to grow willy-nilly was likely to lead to a slowing down of the rearmament programme as a whole, as industry fell behindhand with orders. If the combined programmes outgrew Britain's resources there was a real danger, Bridges thought, that 'money and effort would be wasted in building isolated parts of a structure planned on so gigantic a scale that it could not be completed'.[137]

What was essentially an interim decision was taken by the Cabinet on 5 May 1937, while Chamberlain was still Chancellor, so as to let War Office planning get ahead after it had been held up for six months by prolonged ministerial debate on the role of the Army. The Cabinet agreed that the Regular Army and the anti-aircraft units of the Territorial Army should be provided with their complete equipment and war reserves, but that the Territorial Army's twelve infantry divisions should receive only sufficient equipment to allow them to be trained in peace. No decision was made as to the speed with which this programme should be carried out, however, and, as usual, it was subject to Treasury approval in detail.[138]

It is hard to say at what point the idea arose that an expeditionary force prepared for Continental service might be deleted altogether from the rearmament programme. By October 1937 Chamberlain had read Liddell Hart's *Europe in Arms*, and had been sufficiently impressed by its conclusions on the Army to recommend them to Hore-Belisha.[139] Liddell Hart argued that Britain should 'eschew the idea of landing an army on the Continent', and should develop an air force which could intervene from its own shores at the outset of a war. 'The promise of such help', he wrote, 'would be more comfort to a threatened neighbour, and more deterrent to a would-be aggressor, than any force of the 1914 pattern – a mere drop in the bucket of a Continental struggle between mass armies'. Pownall may well have been right in thinking that Liddell Hart's writings were 'pounced upon' by Chamberlain and Simon to justify what the Treasury wanted on economic grounds.[140]

Certainly, prior to Inskip's review in October and November 1937, Treasury officials did not themselves challenge the need for an expeditionary force. Hopkins, in February 1937, while advocating rationing of defence departments' finance, noted:

> No one denies that we must have as soon as may be a very strong navy, a very strong air force, and a fully-equipped regular army. . . .[141]

Treasury officials concentrated on arguments why the Territorial divisions need not be prepared to take the field at the outbreak of war. Bridges questioned whether Territorial divisions could:

> be kept trained in peacetime up to the required pitch of efficiency . . . when soldiers have to handle not merely a rifle and machine guns [as in 1914] but so many modern contraptions.

He also thought that wastage in Regular units early in the war would mean that Territorials would be better used as drafts, rather than in their own formations.[142] Whatever may be said for or against Bridges' arguments, such arguments assumed that the Field Force would serve on the Continent. The strategic rationale for not preparing the Field Force for Continental service came from outside the Treasury.

By 10 November 1937 Chatfield, who was chairman of the C.O.S. Committee as well as First Sea Lord, had accepted that ever-growing

rearmament programmes would lead to national bankruptcy, and he
endorsed the view of his Director of Plans that:

> Can we, faced with the maintenance of a Navy and Air Force essential
> for our security as a Nation and as an Empire, afford to maintain a
> Field Force for service overseas? It is submitted that we cannot honestly
> maintain that such a force is vital to our security. . . . The Field Force
> should be reduced and our Army limited in general to those forces
> essential for garrison purposes.[143]

It will be noticed that, in this Admiralty view, preparation of an
expeditionary force to support potential European allies was placed
lower in priority not only than national finance, which reflected the
Treasury's influence, but also than Imperial defence.

Hankey, who seems to have been the adviser closest to Inskip during
that minister's review of defence, formed the same opinion as Chatfield
in November 1937. Hankey had previously been a defender of the Field
Force and, as recently as January 1937, had criticised Fisher's proposal
to limit its war strength to seventeen divisions.[144] But, faced with the
Treasury's financial calculations, Hankey observed on 23 November
that 'the dangers of the financial crisis of 1931 are so fresh in our
memories that I cannot advise a course which would bring them once
more within range of probability'. Accordingly, he recommended that:

> In future the role of the Field Force should be to provide for the military
> requirements of the Empire, and the additional provision made in
> previous programmes to equip it for service on the Continent of Europe
> should be cancelled.

As a concomitant the Territorial Army should no longer be regarded
as a reserve for a European campaign.[145]

Hankey's advice on 23 November seems to have been decisive, so far
as Inskip was concerned, for a memorandum written by Inskip on the
same day, and independently of Hankey's, showed that the minister
had not yet formed a clear order of priorities, and that he was still
open-minded on the question of an expeditionary force. Inskip merely
noted that 'a decision is required as to the scale of the Field Force which
we must provide fully equipped . . . for dispatch to the Continent'.[146]
Despite Hankey's arguments that Imperial commitments – the defence
of the Far East and Egypt, and the growing problem of maintaining
order in Palestine – threatened to absorb the whole of the Army's
resources in a major war, and that the Maginot Line meant that
France would not need assistance by land forces,[147] Inskip seems to
have been unhappy about placing the 'Continental hypothesis' last in
priorities, and wrote into his Interim Report of 15 December 1937 that:

> If France were again to be in danger of being overrun by land armies,
> a situation might arise when, as in the last war, we would have to
> improvise an army to assist her. Should this happen, the Government of
> the day would most certainly be criticised for having neglected to provide
> against so obvious a contingency.[148]

Nevertheless the report was received by the Cabinet on 22 December with what Hankey modestly described as 'general congratulations'.[149] The Government laid down that the Army's Estimates were to be drawn up on the assumption that the Field Force would not be committed to a European campaign at the outset of war. This was a more drastic reduction in the Army's role than anything contemplated by Chamberlain, while Chancellor, in 1936–7, although Chamberlain's arguments about the Field Force in 1934 suggest that it was a step which he was not unwilling to take. The outcome of Inskip's review of defence was partly a result of the Treasury's financial strictures, partly the product of fears of air attack, but also, so far as priority for Imperial defence was concerned, partly the result of Chatfield's and Hankey's advice.

Imperial Defence

Any doubts that it was the advice of Chatfield and Hankey, and not that of any member of the Treasury, which placed Imperial defence before support on land for European allies can be removed by a study of the Treasury's attitude to Imperial defence in the 'Thirties. From the D.R.C.'s first meetings in 1933–4 Fisher had argued for concentration of resources on the defence of the United Kingdom itself, excepting only Singapore, which he believed should be built up as a deterrent to Japanese aggression.[150]

The C.O.S. were inclined in 1934 and 1935 to argue the merits of particular projects, such as the renovation of Hong Kong's defences, but by 1936–7 the War Office and the Air Ministry were as anxious as the Treasury to concentrate on measures against Germany, and the Admiralty alone continued to take a wider view. As Chatfield wrote in November 1937 to Admiral Dudley Pound, then commanding the Mediterranean Fleet:

> I find it very difficult to move my two colleagues [the C.I.G.S. and the Chief of Air Staff] on the subject of the defence of Egypt, and we have been hampered by the absolute priority given by the Government to the anti-German problem. . . . The Air Force and anti-aircraft guns for A.D.G.B. . . . are behindhand, and as anything sent out to Egypt means a weakening of our position at home, there has been general obstruction in the C.I.D. to measures which the three Commanders-in-Chief [in Egypt] have so frequently represented as essential.[151]

Imperial defence, so far as British land and air forces were concerned, was, on the whole, a matter of what could be spared over and above home requirements. To return to the example of Hong Kong, only Chatfield in C.O.S.'s discussions in 1938 was keen on the colony's defence.[152]

The financial principles upon which Imperial defence rested were that the Dominions were responsible for their own defence, as was India, but financial adjustments were made in the case of India to allow for the facts that India utilised a large portion of the British Army, and that Indian forces might be used by the British Government outside India. Crown colonies contributed to the cost of their defence according to their means.[153] Since each part of the Empire was responsible for its own local defence the inference drawn by most of the Dominions was that the United Kingdom was responsible for the defence of the Empire as a whole. One result of this was that, in the first instance at least, plans had to be made for the reinforcement of Singapore from Great Britain, rather than from Australia, which was at least as interested in the defence of the naval base. If there was one thing which the C.O.S. and Treasury could agree on with regard to Imperial defence it was the need for a greater contribution from the Dominions. In 1938, when British defence spending reached £400 million, Australia's defence budget was about £21 million, Canada's £6·8 million, and New Zealand's and South Africa's both about £1·5 million. India, with a defence budget in 1938 of £34·5 million, made a more substantial contribution than the Dominions.[154]

Even in the case of Crown colonies there might be long bureaucratic wrangles over how much a given colony could be expected to pay towards local defence. For example, in 1930 the Governor of Kenya offered to raise a local coastal defence unit if two guns could be handed over from War Office stores as a gift to the colony. For five years there was spasmodic interdepartmental correspondence and discussion in the Overseas Defence Sub-Committee of the C.I.D. over who should pay for the setting up of the gun emplacements, the War Office seeking to place the cost (£9000) on the colony, the Treasury defending the Governor's opinion that this was beyond Kenya's means. By 1935 the War Office was willing to settle on the Governor's terms, but Treasury officials withheld approval for months more while they investigated whether these favourable terms would set a precedent for other colonies and territories. Final Treasury approval was granted only as an emergency measure during the Italo-Abyssinian crisis of 1935–6 – a period when not a few long-delayed Overseas Defence Sub-Committee schemes were implemented in the neighbourhood of Italy and her colonies.[155]

The greatest 'who pays what' battles, however, involved the War Office, the India Office and the Government of India, and the Treasury. The Treasury's attitude was that by the 'Thirties India, with its frontier and its internal political troubles, had become a defence liability, whatever her contribution to Imperial defence in the past, and that, financially, that liability should be kept to a minimum. When in 1933 a tribunal under Sir Robert Garran, the eminent Australian lawyer, recommended that Britain should make some contribution towards Indian military expenditure, mainly on the grounds that the Indian Army could serve outside India in an emergency, the Treasury successfully had the Secretary of State for India's claim for an annual £3 million cut by half.[156]

The whole question of subsidies was reopened in 1937 by two separate but related issues: the cost of mechanising British units in India, and the cost of improving the conditions of service for British troops. The first cost was incurred because of the Cardwell system whereby British units in India were interchangeable with those earmarked for the Field Force for European service. The second cost was incurred as a result of the War Office's attempts to improve recruitment in Britain. The Government of India claimed that it would be financially and politically impossible at the time to raise the necessary money, especially for improving the conditions of locally unpopular British troops. Bridges' advice in July 1937 was that while modernisation must go ahead, and while some contribution might be necessary from the British Exchequer, the real answer to India's problem was to reduce the number of British troops there. It seems hardly a coincidence, given Hore-Belisha's friendship with Fisher, that later the same month Hore-Belisha embarked on a major battle with the C.I.G.S., Deverell, when he asked the latter to investigate whether British troops serving in India might be released for service elsewhere.[157]

India and Burma in 1937 absorbed 45 of the 138 battalions of the British Regular Army. Whether any reduction would have been achieved if the Treasury had allowed subsidies to flow freely to Delhi is problematical. Deverell himself simply adopted the position that a heavy commitment of troops to India had always been accepted as necessary, while the War Office was acutely aware that the Indian Army, as organised before 1939, could not be relied upon completely to meet its Imperial commitments in the Middle and Far East in the event of war.* The Treasury, however, was careful to withhold subsidies for modernisation until after Indian defence had been reviewed in 1938, first by a C.I.D. sub-committee under Pownall, and then by a mission to India under Chatfield. Hopkins noted in July 1938 that 'in these times India is our eastern outpost and we have got to make up our minds to larger subventions than we had till recently contemplated', but unlimited subsidies would not encourage India to use her resources efficiently. Fisher had no doubt that Chatfield would find the higher direction of defence matters in India to be 'quite incompetent', and in fact Chatfield found that, in addition to four British battalions already transferred from India to Palestine and Malta, following Pownall's report, a further three British, and seventeen Indian battalions would be surplus to Indian requirements, if, as Pownall had recommended, greater use were made of aircraft instead of Army units for policing the North-West Frontier.[158]

---

* I am indebted to Dr. John Rawson of St. John's College, Oxford, for this information from his unpublished thesis on Indian defence policy between the wars.

Although the Cabinet did not approve Chatfield's report until June 1939 it is doubtful if the modernisation of India's defence forces was much impeded by the delay. British industry was unable to meet all British military requirements, far less those of India, and India's ability to produce her own arms or to import them from foreign countries was negligible. Moreover, on the promise that some subsidy would be forthcoming, the Government of India embarked upon the most urgent defence deficiencies four months before the Chatfield Report was adopted by the Cabinet.[159] On the credit side, Treasury 'meanness' forced a choice to be made, and the Pownall and Chatfield reports in 1938-9 precipitated a decisive shift in India's defence policy, from guarding the North-West Frontier to facing up to the Japanese menace. The Indian battalions rated as surplus in 1939 were not disbanded, but were made available for overseas garrison duties, and such duties were not hard to find in the Far East and in Egypt even before war broke out.[160]

Singapore, which was the key to British defence policy in the Far East, was certainly more in need of troops than the North-West Frontier. When early in 1934 Fisher had urged the completion of the Naval base at Singapore in 1938, instead of in 1939, it had been assumed by the defence departments concerned that Singapore could be attacked only by sea, and its defences had been planned accordingly. It was not until October 1937 that the War Office learned from the Army commander on the spot that landings on the east coast of Malaya would be feasible between October and March, and, therefore, that the defence of Singapore involved the defence of the whole of Malaya; and it was not until February 1939 that the War Office learned that the Admiralty expected that, because of the situation in Europe, it would take ninety, instead of the previous estimate of seventy, days for the Fleet to reach Singapore.[161] These new conditions entirely altered the scale of garrison required, so that although Fisher had envisaged Singapore as the main deterrent to Japan, the defences were in fact *planned* on an inadequate scale, which seems hardly to have been the Treasury's fault.

The Treasury's own records suggest that from April 1933, when the Cabinet decided that Singapore should be made secure against any Japanese *coup de main* by the end of 1936, the Treasury approved readily all proposals which could come under this heading. Indeed the only provision for the defence of Singapore at which the Treasury seems to have baulked concerned some anti-motor torpedo boat defences, proposed at the C.I.D. in January 1937, and about which Chamberlain expressed 'strong views' as an instance of the defence departments constantly adding to their defence programmes. Even so, once the War Office had worked out its proposals for these defences in detail, and submitted them to the T.I.S.C. in September 1937, Treasury officials ensured that there was no further delay, by allowing the War Office to place orders for guns and lights, and to acquire land, even though a strict interpretation of C.I.D. and Cabinet decisions might have enabled Treasury officials to delay approval until after Inskip had completed his review of defence in December.[162]

It will be recalled that – the Italo-Abyssinian crisis apart – the War Office and Air Ministry had not shown an inclination to give priority to the defence of Egypt, down to November 1937. But Inskip's Interim Report of December 1937 placed defence of Britain's overseas territories and interests before support on land for European allies, and this gave Egypt and the Suez Canal a higher priority than France or the Low Countries. At this point the story of Imperial defence leads one back to the question of the size and role of the Field Force. Inskip's Report of February 1938, and a paper by Hore-Belisha on the role of the Army the same month, suggested that the Regular Field Force should be equipped for what was called 'an Eastern theatre', which meant Egypt.[163] This, it was claimed, enabled 'substantial reductions' to be effected in the provision of tanks and ammunition, compared with the same size of force equipped for European operations. Nevertheless Treasury officials were hostile to the suggested new basis for Army preparations: Hopkins commented that the Army had been relieved of the requirement to fight in Europe only for the Foreign Office 'to conjure up a terrifying picture of an equally arduous African campaign', and Fisher dismissed the idea of a 'desert army' as 'merely silly'.[164] Bridges noted that the assumption of a desert campaign,

> if not quashed, is likely to result in our spending considerable sums of money on equipment etc. which is really only needed for a desert campaign. Surely what we want is a 'general purposes' Field Force.[165]

Accordingly Simon suggested to the Cabinet that the phrase 'for an Eastern theatre' be replaced by the phrase 'for general purposes', and he received support from the Foreign Secretary, Eden, who argued that the words 'for an eastern theatre' were 'politically undesirable'. Despite objections by Hore-Belisha and Inskip that some basis was required for planning, the Cabinet decided that in future the phrase 'for general purposes' should be used.[166]

Behind the form of words lay the question of the scale of equipment and reserves with which the Field Force should be provided. The question of the Army's role and organisation was considered by a sub-committee of the C.I.D. under Inskip, and its report was ready by 8 March.[167] While briefing Simon for the C.I.D.'s consideration of this report, Bridges noted:

> [In February] the War Office stated that the Field Force was 'assumed to comprise [three divisions] . . . maintained with a full scale of war reserves on the basis of an Eastern Campaign'. It now appears from . . .

the present paper that the reserves of ammunition in these divisions would, as it so happens, be to all intents on a Continental scale!

This is what we always suspected and feared, namely that the War Office in putting up their Eastern hypothesis haven't given us the savings which we expected. . . . They are still, in effect, clinging to an Army capable of fighting in the Continental role. . . .[168]

What the War Office wanted, and what the C.I.D. approved on 17 March, was a Field Force of two infantry and one mobile divisions, with equipment and war reserves on a Continental scale, but for defensive purposes only. A further two infantry divisions would have half the war reserves on that scale, and would be ready to embark in forty days, and there would also be a pool of equipment with which to despatch two further divisions, which might be Regular or Territorial, after four months. The equipment of such a force would make heavy demands on gun-making capacity, already strained by A.D.G.B. requirements, for, as Gort, the new C.I.G.S., explained to ministers, the Army's existing field artillery was outranged by that of foreign powers, and 'in these circumstances it would be murder to send our Field Force overseas to fight a first-class power', and as Hore-Belisha remarked: 'It must be recognised that if the Field Force had to fight in Libya [sic] it would meet a first-class enemy'.[169] In other words, the War Office wished to reserve some gun-making capacity to equip the Field Force for action, presumably offensive, in Libya, even though the Cabinet had directed that priority be given to A.D.G.B.

In approving the size of Field Force which the War Office wanted, however, ministers did not approve the purpose for which it was intended. Simon's phrase, 'for general purposes', was retained, and furthermore the Cabinet, in agreeing to the C.I.D.'s recommendations, made plain that the priorities as laid down in Inskip's Report of December 1937 held good, and that expenditure involved had to be found from within the Army's 'ration' of finance.[170] Accordingly, when Bovenschen, the War Office's Deputy Under-Secretary, wrote to Bridges in May 1938, asking whether the War Office was authorised to plan the equipment of the Field Force on the assumption of an 'Eastern theatre', Bridges replied that:

> After looking through the more recent records of decisions of the C.I.D. and other committees of Ministers . . . , I fear that I cannot put my finger on any definite pronouncement in favour of an Army organised to fight an Eastern Campaign. . . .[171]

Any proposals for heavy expenditure on equipment necessitated, whether as to type or scale, by the hypothetical requirements of an Eastern campaign, Bridges warned, would be resisted by the Treasury. The significance for the Army of Inskip's report of December 1937, so far as the Treasury was concerned, lay in the priority given to A.D.G.B., and not in that given to Imperial defence.

Continental Commitment, 1938–9

The General Staff's reluctance to give absolute priority to A.D.G.B. seems to have been founded on a belief that, if war came, the Cabinet would not long adhere to its decision not to send the Field Force to France. While giving evidence to the C.I.D. sub-committee on the organisation of the Army in February 1938, Gort explained that:

> If everything was to be sacrificed to A.D.G.B., we might find ourselves without any force at all to send to the Continent to help France if she were in danger of being defeated on land.[172]

By April 1938 Gort thought the Cabinet was slowly coming round to the view that an expeditionary force must be sent to France in the event of war with Germany.[173] No such decision had been taken by September, however, when war over Czechoslovakia seemed an immediate prospect, and when defence departments were asked to make proposals for immediate steps to be taken.

Treasury officials' response to different departments' emergency proposals brought out clearly their view of relative priorities, at that time, as between air defence and assistance to Continental allies. Substantially the whole of the Air Ministry's emergency proposals placed before the T.I.S.C. on 9 September were sanctioned at once, as proposals involving only the acceleration of the Air Ministry's approved programme. But sanction was withheld by Hopkins from some 40 per cent of the War Office's emergency proposals, on the grounds that the items in question were designed to prepare the Field Force to fight a European campaign, and that:

> so far as he was aware, no decision had been reached by ministers that there was a necessity to make special additional provision against the contingency that the Field Force might be engaged in a war on the Continent forthwith.[174]

Fisher spent 11 September, a Sunday, with Hore-Belisha, and discussed with him 'the question of the expeditionary force', and, according to Fisher, Hore-Belisha:

> agreed with the view that the whole idea was purely academic at the present time in view of the fact that the Germans would be good enough to come here. He appreciated the fact that the soldiers would remain here.[175]

Fisher believed the German air force would attack Britain at the outset of war, and that, until that attack could be contained, the Field Force would be unable to leave, and would be employed 'as general handymen' for A.D.G.B. and maintaining public order.[176]

Fisher had either misunderstood Hore-Belisha, or Hore-Belisha had had second thoughts by the next day, for then he raised in Cabinet the matter of the T.I.S.C. holding up War Office emergency measures. Simon seems to have felt that his officials had misjudged the occasion, for while he agreed with them that 'emergency provision for a winter campaign abroad cannot be regarded as the most urgent requirement in the existing situation', he refused to take up the Cabinet's time in squabbling over the disputed items, which would cost only £200,000.[177] Treasury sanction was duly granted.

While some might feel instinctively that 'never again' should British troops be committed to a renewed Western Front, Fisher's opposition to an expeditionary force at the time of Munich was based on his fears arising from German air superiority. In discussions, in October 1938, on the role of the Army in the light of the crisis, Fisher noted that there was 'too much talk' from the War Office about the Field Force, and not enough realisation that A.D.G.B. should have 'supreme priority'. At the same time, provided industrial capacity was not diverted from A.D.G.B. work, Fisher had no objections to sending *men* to France. He noted:

> I can see no reason why we should not call on the French for field artillery, tanks etc., for the force they would like us to land in France.[178]

Nor, apparently, did Fisher think that field formations need be restricted to Regular units. At any rate, he made clear in the C.I.D. that he 'deprecated any reduction in the strength of Territorial infantry battalions'.[179]

On 31 October 1938, in the light of what Hore-Belisha called the 'very marked desire of the French for the assistance of British Army formations on the Continent', the War Office asked for additional equipment at a cost of £200 million, to equip the Regular and Territorial Armies on a higher scale than under the authorised programme. This would enable two mobile divisions to be created out of the existing one, and a force of six divisions (including the mobile divisions) to be ready fourteen days after the outbreak of war. A further two infantry divisions, equipped on a lower scale, would be ready one month after the outbreak of war 'to support overseas garrisons', and the Territorial Army, organised into thirteen divisions, including one mobile and three motorised, would be available in from four to eight months after the outbreak of war.[180] Hopkins commented to Fisher that:

> We have been thinking that it would be right (subject to financial exigencies) to agree to some extension of army preparations, but certainly not an any such scale as this, nor for such a purpose as this.

Fisher agreed, noting that air defence and an adequate Navy were essential but that 'nothing else matters at this stage'.[181]

The War Office's proposals made no headway at Cabinet level before 1939, but this did not reflect Fisher's influence, for his close relationship with Chamberlain had been broken by Munich. The Cabinet was no less concerned than Fisher about the danger of air attack, and the failure of appeasement was not yet apparent. Discussions were held with the French at the end of November on co-operation in defence, but in these Chamberlain adhered 'to existing plans as to what would be available at the outbreak' of war – which meant two divisions.[182] In December 1938 and January 1939, however, the C.O.S. made out an overwhelming case for supporting France with a larger expeditionary force from the outbreak of war. France could no longer look to the Czech's thirty-five divisions for assistance, and the French Army was now outnumbered by the German. It would be difficult, the C.O.S. reported in January, to say how the security of the United Kingdom could be maintained if France fell, and, therefore, a contribution on land to the defence of France might be necessary for the defence of Britain.[183]

Fisher's comments on this C.O.S. report – which he described as 'sheer common sense' – suggest that progress with A.D.G.B., and the immediate prospect of war, had made him believe that the time for preparing the Army for European service had come. He noted:

> To have no Army at all is doubtless a possible policy. To have a small thoroughly efficient and equipped Army of the size favoured by the Chiefs of Staff is another possible policy. But to have a collection of human beings, numerically equal to the Chiefs of Staff proposal, un-equipped and unready for any military purpose of value is no policy at all, but just fatuous extravagance. Be it noted that the Chiefs of Staff are *not* proposing an Army on a continental scale; they accept the size and numbers of the existing Army (Regular and Territorial) practically as they are, but recommend that this shall be put into a position to function as an Army. I hope their report will be adopted.[184]

It will be recalled that Fisher had always advised that the preparation of the Regular and Territorial Armies for European service should be an 'ultimate objective'. What the War Office and C.O.S. were asking for in January 1939 was a Regular force only six divisions strong, including two mobile divisions, equipped on a Continental scale, with an immediate reserve of four Territorial divisions, and full training equipment for the rest of the Territorial Army. A further two divisions should be formed out of Regular units serving overseas, and equipped on a 'Colonial' scale.[185]

From a departmental point of view the Treasury was bound to be interested not merely in the size of the proposed Army, but also in its cost. More elaborate equipment, and rising costs due to inflationary pressures on industry, meant that the cost of an expeditionary force for Continental service had risen steadily over the years, and indeed the cost of the Field Force had been barely checked by the change in its role in 1938. As Compton pointed out on the same day as Fisher applauded the C.O.S.'s paper, the cost of a Regular expeditionary force for Continental service had been estimated at £72 million in October 1935, and £97 million in October 1937. In January and March 1938 the cost of the same size of force had been estimated at

£98 million on the hypothesis of an 'Eastern theatre', and £96 million for 'general purposes'. The revised estimate for the Continental role in January 1939 was £126 million.[186]

Hopkins and Phillips, in their advice to Simon, took a much more critical view of the C.O.S.'s paper on the Army than Fisher had done. The C.O.S. had taken the view that as 'only' about 30 per cent of British engineering industry was at present employed on armaments work, there should be ample capacity for increased Army demands, even after the full needs of the other services in war had been met. Hopkins and Phillips argued, however, that in war there would be enormous demand on engineering capacity for general repair work 'if destruction by air raids assumes any such magnitude as has been envisaged'. Moreover, if it were not possible to borrow from America, engineering capacity would be needed for increased exports to pay for the war, while warfare itself was more complex than in 1914-18 and required more industrial resources. 'It is true that we have left behind the time when we were attempting to cut our coat according to the cloth', Hopkins remarked, but a change in policy with regard to the Army 'may well prove the last straw', and the Cabinet should be warned of the seriousness of the country's financial position.[187]

After ministers had discussed the War Office's proposals on 2 February, however, Simon had to report back to his officials that no one in the Cabinet, except the Prime Minister, now placed much importance on finance as the fourth arm of defence, and when the War Office proposals came before the Cabinet again twenty days later the Chancellor had to agree that 'other aspects in this matter outweigh finance'. Even so, the Treasury, by pressing the financial issue, had been able to secure the deferment of some £16 million worth of the War Office's original proposals (costing £81 million altogether) mainly by delaying a decision on the formation of the two 'Colonial' divisions.[188]

The Army programme was greatly increased after the German occupation of Czechoslovakia. On 28 March Chamberlain was discussing with Hore-Belisha the necessity of taking some action which would show European countries that Britain intended to resist aggression, and Hore-Belisha, without first consulting the Army Council, suggested doubling the Territorial Army.[189] Wilson volunteered to discuss the proposal with the Treasury, and found Hopkins and Barlow very hostile to it. Simon, however, took the view that the matter must be looked at from a wider point of view than that of the Exchequer, and offered no opposition, so that a public announcement of the measure could be made the next day.[190]

In the circumstances Hopkins' and Barlow's objections had no impact, but had Simon been prepared to argue their case in the Cabinet it is possible that a less ambitious, but more easily attainable expansion of the Army might have been adopted instead. Barlow pointed out that the immediate military value of the new Territorial divisions would be nil, and far from deterring Hitler, they would be more likely to encourage him to strike before they were ready. Barlow would have preferred the money required for doubling the Territorial Army to be spent on the Regular Army. Hopkins observed that Hore-Belisha's plan had been invented in a few hours; was unrelated to any strategic plan, and was an 'important new step towards a commitment to fight the next war, like the last, in the trenches of France'.[191]

The final step towards that commitment came three weeks later when the Cabinet approved in principle a plan by Chatfield to increase industrial capacity and reserves of equipment to enable Britain to have a thirty-two-division Army in the field twelve months after the outbreak of war. In the same month of April compulsory military service was introduced, partly to provide for a speedier manning of the country's anti-aircraft defences than was possible with the exisiting Territorial anti-aircraft divisions, and partly to impress foreign opinion. In the months of crisis in 1939 the previous limits set to rearmament no longer applied, and the Treasury had lost its power to force ministers to choose between strategic priorities. As noted in Chapter III all that Simon and Hopkins could do in these circumstances was go to the Cabinet at the beginning of July and advise that in order to maintain the new scale of rearmament quasi-wartime controls over finance capital would be necessary before the end of the year. 'Conscription of wealth', as Chamberlain had remarked, was the 'corollary of conscription of manpower.'[192]

Summary

The Treasury influenced defence policy, in the first instance, by drawing attention to financial implications of unlimited rearmament, and persuading ministers to make choices which might otherwise have been avoided. 'Rationing' of finance led to Inskip's review of defence in 1937, and memories of 1931 were sufficiently recent to persuade not only the Cabinet, but also Chatfield and Hankey, that the coat of policy must be cut according to the cloth of finance. Not until 1939, when fear of war outweighed fear of a financial crash, did the Cabinet ignore Treasury warnings about finance.

Treasury advice on finance was in turn influenced by the object of government policy – which was to prevent war by appeasement and rearmament. So, too, was Treasury advice on what policy should be. Chamberlain and Fisher persuaded the Cabinet in 1934 to adopt a policy of long-term deterrence, based on air power. Down to 1937 the Treasury supported the Air Staff's policy of bomber 'parity'; but once it was clear that the aircraft industry was failing to match German output, the Treasury advocated a policy of making Britain secure against a 'knock-out blow' from the air, so that Germany would be deterred by the prospect of a long war in which Britain's financial and Imperial resources could be mobilised. Such a policy required sea power to defend trade routes, and while building up her air defences Britain maintained and developed the world's largest navy.

The heavy inroads on industrial capacity made by air and sea requirements dictated the extent and timing of Britain's military preparations. No doubt ministers wished to avoid a repetition of the Western Front of 1914–18, and in 1937 Chatfield and Hankey preferred Imperial defence to assistance to European powers, but the preparation of the Field Force for Continental service remained, at least for Fisher, an ultimate objective to be carried out once Britain was secure against air attack. Chamberlain concentrated on what could be done in peacetime to prepare forces for use at the outbreak of war, and both he and Fisher, down to 1939, believed that available industrial capacity would not be sufficient in peace even for the seventeen divisions which could be raised by voluntary recruiting, far less the thirty-two divisions projected by Chamberlain and Hore-Belisha after the occupation of Czechoslovakia.

It was the function of the Treasury to ensure that service planning did not go beyond the bounds of finance or industrial capacity, and by 1937 there was, as Bridges remarked, a real danger that 'money and effort would be wasted in building isolated parts of a structure planned on so gigantic a scale that it could not be completed'. Since defence departments were constantly seeking to expand their individual programmes, the Treasury sought to influence both policy-making, through financial rationing, and execution of policy, through detailed control of expenditure, to ensure that what it, and the Cabinet, considered to be the most important items received priority and were completed first. After Inskip had reviewed defence in 1937 this meant items against air and sea attack.

V

The Treasury's Influence on the Execution of Defence Policy

The Treasury's success in obtaining Cabinet decisions on defence priorities had to be followed up by Treasury control of expenditure to ensure that defence departments adhered to Cabinet decisions while carrying out different parts of the rearmament programme. Cabinet decisions were usually expressed in general terms, which left ample room for varying interpretations, especially when looked at from different departmental viewpoints. As noted in Chapter IV, the Admiralty aspired to build up to a two-power standard even when only a one-power standard was authorised by the Cabinet; the Air Staff continued to aim at building up a strategic bomber force even after the Cabinet had given priority to air defence, and the War Office was reluctant to allow priority for air defence to extinguish hopes of creating an expeditionary force. What follows is an attempt to show how far Treasury control of expenditure, as outlined in Chapter II, was effective in keeping departments to priorities agreed by the Cabinet (recorded in Chapter IV), interpreted by the Treasury in the light of the need to maintain financial stability (as explained in Chapter III).

Execution of growing rearmament programmes required creation of industrial capacity, and departments were obliged to submit for Treasury approval all contracts where public money would be used for this purpose, so that, by limiting industrial capacity, the Treasury could restrict a department's ability to spend even after financial control through the annual Estimates or through 'rationing' had weakened. The Treasury influenced the outcome of the rearmament programme by applying, or relaxing, Treasury control. Except where proposals threatened to be a particularly heavy strain on the balance of payments, the Treasury tended to relax its control over those parts of the programme to which the Cabinet had given priority, but not to relax control over other parts. At the same time, however, different departments were less or more subject to Treasury influence according to their need to expand industrial capacity. Broadly speaking, what happened was that Treasury control was most relaxed in the case of the Air Ministry, especially in 1935–8. The Admiralty, however, had least need to build up new industrial capacity, and was correspondingly less subject to Treasury control. The War Office came off worst, as it had

the greatest need for new productive capacity, while the Field Force
was given a low priority by the Cabinet and Treasury down to 1939.

This generalisation can best be tested by examining the Treasury's
influence on each department's programme in turn. In studying the
Treasury's influence one must bear in mind that Britain's resources were
limited compared with her defensive responsibilities. There were
bound to be gaps in the defences of Britain and her Empire, and it
cannot be assumed that each and every one of these gaps was due to the
malign influence of the Treasury. As the First Sea Lord, Backhouse,
observed in November 1938:

> The trouble is . . . that we are now trying to take on more than we are
> really able to . . . and we simply cannot produce more than we are
> doing.[1]

Defence departments themselves had to establish priorities, which
might in turn mean leaving gaps. The best examples of Treasury
influence are those where different courses of action were desired by
the Treasury and the defence department concerned, for thereby one
can see where Treasury influence made a difference to the execution of
defence policy.

The Air Force's Programme

The Air Ministry faced a wide range of difficulties while expanding
the Air Force: men had to be recruited and trained; sites had to be
selected for aerodromes, and men and aircraft had to be accommodated
on these sites, which were usually far from conveniently situated from
the point of view of securing building labour. The Treasury could have
added greatly to these difficulties by maintaining strict standards of
Treasury control. For example, down to 1934 the Air Ministry had been
required to submit to the Treasury details of proposed new barracks, or
renovations, right down to heating arrangements, and delays seem to
have resulted. But from 1934 Fisher made it clear to his officials that
they were not to hold up expansion, and Air Ministry finance officers
were given much wider discretion.[2] Again, the Treasury did not even
attempt to exercise effective control over establishments, for, as Bridges
observed, there was not 'any danger that the supply of personnel will
ultimately outrun the supply of machines'.[3]

The Treasury's influence on Air Force expansion is best told with
reference to 'the supply of machines', for it was upon aircraft production
that Treasury officials concentrated. One of the paradoxes of rearmament was that, while Chamberlain and Fisher advocated an 'air
deterrent', the ministers responsible for expansion of the Air Force
found they had not a free hand to spend as much money as they
would have wished.[4] The key to this paradox was that priority for the
Air Force was subject to the need to maintain Britain's economic and

financial strength. By a Cabinet decision of February 1936 rearmament was not to interfere with normal trade and industry, and until that rule was revoked in March 1938 the Air Ministry had to compete for industrial resources not only with other defence departments, but also with civil industry, which was enjoying growing consumer demand down to late 1937. In 1937 the Secretary of State for Air, Swinton, thought that this policy of non-interference – which was government, and not simply Treasury, policy – would delay completion of the Air Ministry's current programme from 1939 to 1941.[5]

A good example of how the Treasury sought to reconcile the needs of the 'fourth arm of defence' with those of the Air Ministry, and sound administration, is provided by the case of the Aluminium Company of Canada. On 15 March 1939 the Air Ministry requested Treasury sanction, at twenty-four hours' notice, of an agreement reached with that company for guaranteed purchase of aluminium. Given the guarantee, the company would set up a factory at its own expense. Waley took the view that the proposed cost in foreign exchange of aluminium purchase – £3½ million or more – would be such that the alternative of spending £600,000 on creating equivalent industrial capacity in Britain would not be unattractive. The Treasury refused to be rushed, and consulted the Board of Trade, and it was not until 4 April that agreement was reached, on the basis of another alternative scheme whereby a shadow factory for the British Government would be set up in Canada. This factory would be operated by the Canadian company, but equipment would be sent out from Britain so as to reduce the drain of foreign exchange.[6]

For the most part, however, Treasury control on Air Ministry spending had only a gentle braking effect, and Treasury records make it clear that from May 1935 finance flowed freely into the Air Force programme. The Air Ministry was allowed to place long-term contracts in advance of Parliamentary approval, provided the Treasury was informed, and the size of Supplementary Estimates, in Bridges words, 'depended on the extent to which aircraft manufacturers kept up to date with their contracts'.[7] No money was refused the Air Ministry in the Estimates or Supplementary Estimates of 1935 and 1936, and swift Treasury approval of proposals for expenditure led Swinton to write to Chamberlain at the beginning of 1937:

> I would like to express my very grateful thanks . . . to the departmental Treasury for their unfailing readiness to help us in the unprecedented difficulties of the time.[8]

A £3 million cut was made, at Bridges' suggestion, in the 1937 Sketch Estimates (for over £85 million), in respect of a proposed increase in bomber strength which had not yet been submitted to the C.I.D. or Cabinet. But Bridges said it would be made clear to the Air

Ministry that this cut need not debar them from obtaining a Supplementary Estimate for the proposal later. Barlow thought that 'a gentle
brake will not hurt', and indeed for three years the Air Ministry had
been unable to spend all the money voted for aircraft.[9]

It was a good deal easier for the Air Ministry to draw up a paper
programme than it was for industry to carry it out, and it was the fact
that the current programme – Scheme F – was in arrears that led the
Treasury to resist proposals for greater schemes in 1937-8, prior to
Scheme L of April 1938. The reasons for difficulty in spending money
on aircraft were a subject of controversy at the time, but the Air
Ministry's problems may be divided broadly into those relating to the
development of new types, and those relating to production. Swinton
recalled that 'there were not wanting manufacturers who would like
to have built a lot of old Hinds and Harts' [biplane light bombers],
'death-traps which could have been turned out in quantity and would
have produced a nice fraudulent balance sheet'. He, however, made a
deliberate decision in 1935 to go for quality rather than quantity,
waiting for new types, often ordered off the drawing board, and he
suffered much criticism as a result because 'few people realise (or did
then) how heartbreaking are the delays in getting out a new type'.[10]

How far was the Treasury responsible for the lack of suitable types
to order in 1935, or earlier? A memorandum by Swinton's successor,
Sir Kingsley Wood, in October 1938, following Fisher's attacks on the
Air Staff's competence, claimed that during the period of the Geneva
Disarmament Conference of 1932-3: 'all development work on the
larger types of aircraft had been discontinued in deference to the views
of the Treasury and the Foreign Office'. In the early 'Thirties the
Foreign Office entertained hopes of limiting the size of bombers by
treaty, and, in 1935, Ellington explained that the Air Staff had not
proceeded with new heavy types 'owing to the fact that the limited
money available had had to be spent on aircraft falling within the
[proposed three-ton] restriction'.[11] The absence of modern heavy types
meant that the expansion schemes of 1934 and 1935 provided for more
light bombers, and fewer heavy bombers, than the Air Staff would have
wished. Undoubtedly the Treasury must take its share of the blame for
this state of affairs, but the Germans also had problems while bringing
modern bomber types into production. At first they had to rely on
converted commercial aircraft, and almost half the German output of
bombers in 1938 was of obsolete or obsolescent types.[12] Air Force
expansion came at a time of revolution in aircraft design, and another
way of putting financial restrictions on research before 1934 into
perspective is to note that almost none of the modern types of 1937-9 in
Britain or Germany appeared on the drawing board until 1934.

Aircraft deliveries were delayed by more than Swinton's policy of
waiting for modern types. Deliveries even of established types were

behindhand in 1936, and it was not until September of that year that Swinton felt he could say that so important a firm as Vickers 'were at last fully alive to the necessity of straining every nerve to carry out their orders'.[13] The position was worst with new types from new factories, and here again the Air Ministry was inclined to blame industry. One report in 1937 to Air Council members regarding production at Fairey's new Stockport Factory of that firm's new Battle bomber spoke of:

> Bad organisation. . . . There was so much finished and partly finished work in the shops that unless aircraft began to come out very shortly there would be no space left in which to work.[14]

Delays in that case were so bad that the Air Council cancelled part of the order.

Aircraft manufacturers, however, blamed the Air Ministry for delays, and by March 1938 their representatives had persuaded Wilson that:

> the chief difficulty arises owing to what the firms feel to be a persistent habit on the part of quite a large number of individuals in the Air Ministry to come down to the works and give directions to quite minor changes to be made in planes that are under construction.

A month later criticism in Parliament and the press moved Wilson to point out to Chamberlain that 'a wave of dissatisfaction with the Air Ministry is developing fast'.[15] In May Swinton resigned.

In the midst of all these recriminations no one attempted to blame Treasury officials for delays. Swinton later described Bridges as a 'good ally', who, while making sure of value for money, also made sure money was made available.[16] Indeed, as already noted, the Treasury allowed Air Ministry contractors to receive rather more favourable terms than other departments' contractors. It was well understood in the Treasury that Air Force expansion involved expanding the aircraft industry. It was known from the beginning that Scheme C of 1935 would absorb the whole of existing capacity, and that there would be no margin for increased production should the scheme prove inadequate, as it did, to match German expansion. For that reason Trenchard had advised Fisher before Scheme C was adopted that drastic reorganisation and immediate expansion of productive capacity was necessary, and that Weir was the man to carry this out, and that advice was passed on to Chamberlain. At the time the Air Ministry seems to have given ministers no hint that it was thinking in such terms.[17]

Even when Weir was advising the Air Council it was found there was a limit to what could be done, for private firms were reluctant to expand plant at the risk of having surplus capacity once the expansion scheme was over. By May 1936 Swinton had decided the time had come for the formation of a government-owned shadow industry for aircraft and engines. The Air Ministry originally estimated that it would spend only £530,000 on shadow factories in 1936, but Bridges made sure that additional money was forthcoming through a special Supplementary Estimate when the Air Ministry found it could spend £2 million.[18]

While creating a government-owned shadow industry the Air Ministry and the Treasury were not unsympathetic to the needs of private industry. For example, in May 1937 the firm of Nash and Thompson, which was responsible for most turrets for new aircraft, was in financial difficulties. The Treasury agreed to the cost of certain additional plant recently installed by the firm being borne by the Air Ministry, and this, together with other advances, eased the firm's position.[19] That was a step designed to maintain the pace of the expansion programme. Then early in March 1938 the Air Ministry asked to be allowed to negotiate a formal subsidy for a private aero-engine firm, Alvis, even though there was no need for Alvis capacity for the expansion programme. The firm was in danger of bankruptcy and of being broken up, and it was argued that it would be cheaper to maintain Alvis capacity than to build a government-owned war reserve factory. Barlow recognised this as a departure from the Robinson Committee's recommendation that the Government should own plant it paid for, and deferred decision in the T.I.S.C., but after a fortnight's delay the Air Ministry received approval to go ahead.[20]

On 27 April 1938 the Cabinet authorised the Air Ministry to accept as many aircraft as it could obtain from the British aircraft industry, up to a maximum of 12,000 machines in the next two years. Following upon the Cabinet's decision the previous month to relax the assumption that rearmament should not interfere with normal trade and industry, this marked a new departure in the history of the expansion of the Air Force – and it was one much desired by the Treasury. On 2 April Fisher had written to the Prime Minister, drawing attention to the 'appalling facts' that estimated British output of aircraft in 1938 was 2,100 to 2,250 whereas the estimate for German output was 6,100. For 1939 the estimated figures were 5,000 and 7,250 respectively. (It is now known that the correct German figures were 5,235 for 1938 and 8,295 for 1939.)[21] The situation was discussed by Chamberlain and Swinton, and before 27 April they and Simon had agreed that an Air Council Committee on Supply should be set up, with a Treasury official as a member. This official, Bridges, would have full financial authority to sanction expenditure on the 12,000-aircraft programme, including expenditure on necessary building and plant, and the Committee's decisions would be reported only subsequently to the T.I.S.C.[22]

Bridges was authorised to reserve a decision when he felt that a case had not been made by the Air Ministry, or that a matter required further investigation in detail by the T.I.S.C. But he understood well that speed was of the essence, and he risked P.A.C. disapproval in his use of his power to authorise expenditure. He suggested, for example, that the Air Ministry pay a price for a service depot so much higher than that estimated by a valuer that the normal course would have been to go to arbitration. This gave the Air Ministry immediate entry instead of waiting for long-drawn-out arbitration procedure. He agreed to an order for 500 small elementary training machines not being counted among the authorised 12,000 aircraft, thus in effect increasing the number authorised by the Cabinet. He agreed to an approach being made to a firm to act as sub-contractors to Rolls Royce, even though the firm, the British United Shoe Co. Ltd., had been allocated by the C.I.D.'s supply organisation to the War Office and Admiralty lists of industrial capacity for use in war. The Supply Board was to be asked to change its plans later.[23]

Bridges had to do this work while still carrying the full load of his other departmental duties, involving every other aspect of defence. Although not given to expressing personal feelings he did write to one civil servant at the time:

Many thanks for your manuscript note about the Cabinet Committee on the Defence of India. This happens to be one of these horrible days when I sit all day on the Air Council Supply Committee, and I have only just seen your note when looking in at the office at lunch-time; consequently I am afraid I shall not give you a very satisfactory answer. . . .[24]

As a result of the Air Council Supply Committee's work orders worth £43 million were placed for aircraft, including over £6 million for contracts in the United States, in the two months from 29 April, but less than £7 million had been devoted to new industrial capacity in the same period.[25] Prior to the adoption of Scheme L Bridges had tried to encourage the Air Ministry to spend money on expanding industrial capacity for use in war, rather than on building up reserves of aircraft. But the Air Ministry had preferred in Scheme L to pile up orders so as to encourage manufacturers to carry out their promise of producing 12,000 aircraft in two years with existing capacity. By July, however, deliveries had fallen behind promises, and the Air Ministry wanted to create new industrial capacity. The trouble, as Bridges told Fisher, was that by then it was so late that:

I am bound to say that I think the number of machines to be produced out of the new capacity now proposed by March 1940 will not be very large.[26]

Quite apart from the question of going beyond what the Cabinet had authorised, Bridges knew the Supply Board was seriously perturbed at the extent to which Air Ministry demands would impinge on other departments in wartime. Bridges asked:

If it is impossible to find the money and resources to put behind the first line Air Force (to which we are now building up) adequate reserves and war potential, does it not look rather as though we are allowing ourselves – under stress of the parity argument – to be persuaded into an attempt to build up too big a force; and that we should really be stronger if we had a rather smaller force with adequate resources behind it? And, incidentally, a force with a larger proportion of fighters?[27]

As already noted, the Treasury and Air Ministry had been in dispute as to the proportion of fighters to bombers since Inskip's Report eight months earlier. Now, by refusing authority to proposals which could not be justified under the existing programme the Treasury could force the Air Ministry to put new proposals for a balanced expansion scheme before the Cabinet. This action did not affect the Air Ministry's ability to spend in the immediate future. As the Air Ministry's records for October 1938 noted, the lack of Treasury sanction for some £2 million-worth of war potential proposals was causing no delay as 'none of the proposals covered by this sum were quite ready for action'.[28] The Treasury continued to be liberal in 1938–9 towards proposals for increasing industrial capacity, and it has been estimated that floor space for aircraft production rose by about 60 per cent between August 1938 and September 1939. As a result, in September 1939 British monthly production of aircraft overtook Germany's.[29]

Nevertheless the stand taken by Treasury officials towards part of the unauthorised war potential helped to force the Cabinet battle in the autumn of 1938 on priorities between fighters and bombers. The Cabinet's decision of 7 November, which approved the whole of Scheme M's fighter proposals, specifying maximum production possible before April 1940, but which laid down that bomber orders were only to be sufficient to ensure that labour and plant were not unemployed, was a success in principle for the Treasury view. Hitherto the Air Ministry had not really given fighters priority, as the Inskip Report had recommended. This is reflected in the orders approved by the Air Council Committee on Supply. In its most productive first two months the Committee placed orders under Scheme L for 884 bombers compared with only 561 fighters. Bridges could not challenge this policy on the Committee because Swinton had arranged that the Committee would be concerned only with the means of giving effect to decisions in principle taken beforehand by Air Council members alone. Of the 561 fighters ordered initially by the Committee 300 were Gladiator biplanes, and the Air Staff's reluctance to order more of an obsolescent type was undertandable. The remaining 261 were Spitfires and Defiants, and as both types were still under test some reluctance to risk ordering large numbers of possibly unsuccessful aircraft was also understandable. Less understandable was why it took the Munich crisis in September to move the Air Staff to place an order for 1000 Hurricanes, the best type in service at the time, in addition to the 900 ordered down to March 1938.[30]

The Cabinet's decision in November 1938 gave the order of priorities that the Treasury wanted, but Treasury officials rightly anticipated difficulty in enforcing the Cabinet's decision. As Gilbert, Bridges' successor at D.M., observed:

> The Cabinet's approval of the programme gives the Treasury the right to watch commitments in bombers, which were away with the lion's share of the money in the Air. I am not sure that we shall be able to do much, unless the political outlook [abroad] changes. . . .[31]

Gilbert's doubts were justified. A month after the Cabinet's decision the Air Ministry presented proposals for its new heavy bomber programme. The Air Ministry anticipated that the new aircraft would be ready for production from August 1939, and planned immediate creation of all the productive capacity required for the full programme in Scheme M, within the original time-scale (completion in 1942). At an inter-departmental meeting on 9 December 1938 Gilbert observed that this plan 'made no concession to the views of the Cabinet that the increased fighter programme should be approved, and the current one accelerated, at the expense of some retardation of the bomber programme'. The Air Ministry representative admitted that 'the original objective remained unchanged', but explained that the Air Ministry's Finance Branch was retaining control of financial commitments so that a further approach would be made to the Treasury when orders for aircraft came to be placed. Gilbert was persuaded, and told Barlow: 'we have got to accept . . . that control at [that] stage can be real control'.[32] On this basis the Treasury agreed on 20 December that the Air Ministry should order jigs to provide for peak production of the new bombers.

The question of aircraft orders too was soon settled, although not without a rearguard action by Fisher. Wilson thought it 'somewhat difficult to argue . . . against experts' on the technical merits of the new bombers, and Barlow believed the Treasury could not carry its opposition to the new bombers further. Fisher, however, attempted to argue against the experts, pointing out that the Air Staff reached its conclusions in favour of big bombers by comparing the performance of a heavy bomber, the Stirling, which was not yet in production, with an older type of medium bomber, the Wellington, which was already in service. 'Is it necessarily the case that a Medium Bomber must be slower than a bigger size?' he asked. Fisher's challenge seems to have carried no weight in the Prime Minister's Office, however, and in January the Treasury sanctioned the Air Ministry's proposed orders.[33] Since jigs and materials approved in December were still being assembled no delay resulted from Fisher's challenge. On the other hand the Air Ministry had been too optimistic as to when the new heavy bombers would be ready for production – in July 1939, when production should have been about to begin, these types were already nine months behind schedule. Technical factors imposed delay where Fisher could not, and for the time being the Air Ministry had to be content with continuation orders for existing types.[34]

Similarly technical factors made it difficult for the Air Ministry to carry out the Cabinet's policy of priority for fighters. The Treasury approved promptly all orders for fighters, but industry found it easier to continue producing existing types of bombers than to introduce new types of fighters on to assembly lines. Air Ministry figures showed that at the end of 1938 deliveries of obsolescent medium bombers were ahead of schedule, whereas those of fighters were behindhand. As a result it was not until February 1940 that fighter production exceeded that of bombers.[35]

On balance, it must be said that technical problems of bringing new types of fighters and bombers into service did more than Treasury control to dictate how Scheme M was carried out. At the same time, the Air Ministry was not impervious to the Cabinet's instruction that fighters should have priority, and whereas in October 1938 Britain had had 406 first-line fighters, most of them obsolescent biplanes, in September 1939 the figure was 608, and most were monoplanes. First-line bomber strength increased in the same period from 492 to 536. In September 1939 Germany had 1,750 first-line bombers capable of attacking Britain, and the R.A.F. was further than ever from the goal of 'parity' with Germany,[36] but at last Britain had adequate protection against air attack, so that British industry could realise its war potential – and enough industrial capacity had been created so as to enable the British aircraft industry to outbuild the German in war. This state of affairs was due to the considerable efforts of the Air Ministry and the aircraft industry, but credit is also due to the Treasury, which had both urged the reorganisation of the industry since 1935, and which, by relaxing Treasury control more in the case of the Air Ministry than of other departments, had given the Air Ministry a distinct advantage in securing industrial resources. Air Ministry expenditure rose both absolutely and relatively more than either other defence department between 1935 and the outbreak of war, so that between 1936 and 1938 the Air Ministry moved from being the least to the greatest spender among the defence departments.[37]

The Navy's Programme

The importance of a department's access to industrial capacity is further illustrated by the case of the Navy. The Admiralty had enjoyed pre-eminence among the defence departments before 1934, and the effects of retrenchment, although drastic enough, had nevertheless left the Navy with fewer production problems than its sister services. The Admiralty was correspondingly less subject to Treasury control, which concentrated on the creation of new industrial capacity, and, therefore, the Admiralty was better able to pursue its own policy without Treasury interference. It will be recalled that the Admiralty wished to build to a standard of naval strength which would enable the Navy to oppose the Japanese and German navies simultaneously, but the Cabinet avoided authorising the Admiralty's proposed two-power 'New-Standard'. What follows shows how successful the Admiralty was in building towards the two-power standard, despite Treasury control.

The Treasury supervised proposals for industrial capacity by the Admiralty, as in the case of other departments, and there was the occasional check to the Admiralty's plans. For example, in 1936 the Admiralty tried to break away from a well-established policy whereby filling factories (for explosive shells) were a common service to all three services, administered by the War Office. The Admiralty wished to establish its own factory, but the Treasury – and the Secretary of State for War – were opposed to the idea, and Inskip adjudicated against the Admiralty. By way of contrast when, in the same year, the Air Ministry proposed to negotiate a contract with I.C.I. for filling bombs, and the War Office objected, Barlow persuaded the T.I.S.C. to agree to the Air Ministry's proposal on the grounds that 'immediate provision . . . of bombs was of paramount urgency'.[38]

Nevertheless the Admiralty had, or planned to acquire, sufficient industrial capacity to enable it to embark in 1936 on a programme greater than that required for the authorised one-power standard. Detailed Treasury control, although irksome to the Admiralty, was not a wholly effective brake in this connection. For example, in April 1936 the Treasury approved an Admiralty proposal, made to the T.I.S.C., whereby the rearmament of the main fleet with anti-aircraft equipment was to be accelerated, so as to be complete by the end of 1938 instead of 1945. In June 1937 the Admiralty submitted a further programme, to the D.P.R.C., to equip trade protection vessels with similar equipment, and this was approved by ministers subject to Treasury sanction of the expenditure involved. When Treasury officials looked at the proposals they discovered that the Admiralty had already provided for the necessary industrial capacity when placing orders under the earlier main fleet programme. It was pointed out to the Admiralty that it had not referred specifically to the inclusion of the trade protection requirement when it had put forward its earlier proposals for productive capacity, and the Admiralty agreed it had been at fault in this.[39] The result was that even although the trade protection requirement was considered a major addition to the authorised rearmament programme, and therefore, by the Cabinet decision of 30 June 1937, subject to delay until after Inskip had completed his review of defence, Treasury officials found they had to approve orders for anti-aircraft equipment under this requirement to prevent industrial capacity standing idle in the meantime.

The Treasury did restrict the Admiralty's finance through the Estimates more strictly than the Air Ministry's. Although the Admiralty benefited from the general relaxation in strict Budgeting from late 1935, the Admiralty's sketch Estimates continued to be cut by the Treasury – by about £1½ million from £107 million in 1937, and £4½ million from £131 million in 1938 – forcing the Admiralty to eliminate some items in the usual manner.[40] Rationing of finance was also imposed on the Admiralty in 1938-9, as it was not in the case of the Air Ministry.

In considering the Treasury's influence on the execution of naval policy one has to bear in mind that Cabinet decisions on naval standards were not always crystal-clear. While avoiding authorisation of a two-power standard the Cabinet did not deny its desirability or prevent steps being taken towards implementing it. Fisher himself did not believe that naval rearmament should be limited to the authorised one-power standard, although he thought a two-power standard too much, and it cannot be assumed that any shipbuilding in excess of the one-power standard represented either defiance of the Cabinet's wishes or weakness on the part of the Treasury.

The Admiralty's D.R.C. programme for the financial years 1936-9 inclusive, approved by the Cabinet in February 1936, was supposed to represent what was possible in these years with available industrial capacity. The Admiralty was asked to do no more than work out the programme required for the new standard of naval strength proposed by the D.R.C., and to make suggestions as to any items in that programme that could be put in hand before 31 March 1940.[41] Four months later, however, Admiral R. G. H. Henderson, the Third Sea Lord, called at the Treasury, asking for approval of an acceleration of the 1936 new construction programme, and he left papers which showed Hopkins that the increased rate of construction would be continued in the following three financial years. Hopkins discussed the matter later on the phone with Henderson, who claimed that acceleration in the 'Thirties could be balanced by reduced programmes in the 'Forties. This 'seemed a little thin' to Hopkins, and Henderson himself seems to have had doubts about the wisdom of his arguments, for he called at the Treasury the next day to withdraw all previous statements and papers. What Henderson then proposed to do was to lay before ministers in the D.P.R.C. 'for their information' the total acceleration which could be achieved over the next four years and 'to reserve the right to discuss with the Treasury the substitution of new programmes for the existing D.R.C. programmes' for 1937, 1938 and 1939.[42]

The Treasury wished to know if the acceleration would impede the progress of the other services' programmes, for example by taking up gun-making capacity. The First Lord, Hoare, at the D.P.R.C. meeting on 2 July, said he thought not. The Treasury also wished to know whether the acceleration meant any increase in the naval programme. Hoare said 'he wished to make clear that it was only a speeding up of the existing approved programme'. On this assurance the D.P.R.C. approved the acceleration of the 1936 new construction programme, but, on Chamberlain's suggestion, deferred consideration of the rest of the proposed acceleration for when individual year's programmes came to be examined.[43]

The 1937 new construction programme which came before the Treasury the following January amounted to a 50 per cent increase on the original D.R.C. programme. Bridges observed:

> We know that the Admiralty do not want to force the issue of the new standard . . . and that they want to go on as long as they can with building programmes which can be regarded as simply acceleration of the already approved programme. My own impression is that it is becoming more and more difficult to regard the Admiralty's proposals as simply acceleration of the approved programme.[44]

While Hopkins and Barlow shared Bridges' suspicions, Fisher felt 'sure that there can be no conscious intention to conceal on the Admiralty's part'. Bridges made enquiries at the Admiralty, and elicited the information that the Naval Staff wished Hoare to press for a two-power standard, but, it was said, the First Lord preferred to burke the issue, during 1937 at least, on the grounds that if it were known that Britain was to aim at a larger fleet the Germans might plan a corresponding increase in their fleet. Bridges commented that: 'I am bound to say that I cannot avoid a suspicion that the Admiralty have not been altogether frank with us in this matter'.[45]

Bridges' belief that the Admiralty had already decided to exceed the authorised programme was well-founded. A secret internal note by the Admiralty's Head of Estimates Branch in November 1936, for example, stated clearly: 'The Defence Programme to which the Admiralty is now working is generally larger than that which was laid down in D.R.C. 37' [the programme approved by the Cabinet in February 1936].[46] As late as December 1937 the Naval Staff was in no hurry to tell the Treasury, or the Cabinet, that an increase in the authorised programme was planned. As Phillips, the Director of Plans, observed:

> All our proposed 1938 Building Programme can be justified on the basis of the D.R.C. Fleet except one Flotilla of destroyers and three submarines.
> Admittedly such justification assumes that after the 1938 Building Programme we should almost have to have a 'Building holiday' for several years in . . . all main categories except aircraft carriers.
> It does not seem necessary, however, to stress this point now. Sir T. Inskip [then reviewing defence expenditure] is well aware of it.[47]

So, of course, were Treasury officials. Hopkins had never been impressed by Admiralty arguments that an increase in construction in 1936–40 would be balanced by reductions later, and following Bridges' enquiries in January 1937 Hopkins felt that 'the true nature of the Admiralty construction programme has crystallised'.[48] The Treasury did not wish existing industrial capacity to be idle, but on the other hand it was felt that naval orders should not be allowed to grow to the point where they drew scarce supply factors such as skilled labour and machine tools away from the programme of the other services, or interfered with merchant shipbuilding. The Admiralty's finance was limited accordingly. After prolonged negotiations the Admiralty's 1937 programme was accepted subject to a reduction in the cost to fall on 1937 itself. In other words the Admiralty were to start some ships later in the financial year than proposed, and, as the Admiralty found that in any case it wished to postpone orders for five cruisers so as to incorporate recent technical improvements, financial stringency did not bear very hardly on the programme.[49]

A bigger battle was looming by the time the 1938 programme came to be considered. The Cabinet had accepted Inskip's recommendation in December 1937 that for the present the Admiralty should not incur expenditure which committed them to a fleet beyond the D.R.C. programme, leaving the decision as to an increased standard to be taken in a year's time. But the Admiralty's new construction proposals for 1938 took them to within £20 million of the whole £225 million planned by the D.R.C. for the seven years to 1942.[50] Hopkins, realising the implications for the trade cycle, told Fisher:

> A perverse fate has led the Admiralty to propose a programme which of all possible programmes is one which suits anticipated circumstances least well. A heavy programme of ships to be laid down in 1938 will involve heavy expenditure in 1939 and 1940, and a good deal still in 1941, and only a small remnant after that. . . . So great a decrease in an important section of industry, added to the anticipated falling off in house-building and in expenditure on aircraft factories and the like, can only be described as calamitous.[51]

The Admiralty was well aware of these reasons why there could be no 'building holiday' after the 1938 programme – the point had been put to their representatives by Wilson during Inskip's review[52] – but of course the Admiralty had no intention that there should be a building holiday. As a memorandum by its Director of Plans in November 1937 made clear: 'A Navy capable of fighting Japan and Germany simultaneously is our present definition of adequate strength'[53] Reviewing the 1938 new construction programme Hopkins observed to Fisher:

> I think it is clear that the Admiralty have not sincerely and honestly accepted the Cabinet's decision that substantially they are to work on the D.R.C. Programme unless and until it is decided in a year's time from now that a greater programme can be sanctioned. . . .[54]

The size of the new construction programme to be sanctioned for 1938 should not, Hopkins thought, be such as to prejudice ministers' decisions. Feelings were aroused in the interdepartmental battle which followed, with Hopkins describing one proposed Cabinet Paper by the First Lord, Duff Cooper, as 'outrageous in its misstatements of facts'.[55] No agreement could be reached between Duff Cooper and Simon on the size of the 1938 new construction programme before the Estimates were due to be presented to Parliament, and the Estimates had to go forward without the programme, which was presented in the summer with a Supplementary Estimate. The Admiralty had proposed in December 1937 the sum of £3,100,000 as the cost of new construction to fall on the financial year 1938. Simon in February 1938 had said that the amount he had in mind was about £1 million less. By May 1938 the Admiralty had found that for industrial reasons it would be able to spend only £1,773,000 – or less than the Chancellor was willing to give![56]

As already noted, a compromise was hammered out in the summer of 1938 whereby the Admiralty's ration of finance for the next three years was fixed at an intermediate level between that required for the D.R.C. Fleet and that required for the New Standard. The 1939 new construction programme was in accordance with financial rationing, but, at least so far as major fleet units were concerned, industrial capacity, not finance, continued to be the real limiting factor. As the First Lord, now Lord Stanhope, wrote to Simon in December 1938:

> Two capital ships represent the largest programme it is possible for us to undertake in 1939, having regard to . . . the limitations of our productive capacity for heavy guns, gun mountings and armour. . . .[57]

What, then, was the influence of the Treasury on the execution of naval policy? It is, of course, true that the industrial limits imposed on the Admiralty owed much to the effects of retrenchment on the Navy's suppliers before 1934, and finance continued to be an important limiting factor until 1936. But once rearmament proper had begun the Admiralty was able to lay down almost all the major fleet units it planned to lay down in 1936–9 for the New Standard. Industrial factors determined how quickly money was spent.

Turning to the various categories of ships one finds this to be particularly true of capital ships, even though Chamberlain had argued in 1934 for postponing capital ship replacement, and Hopkins in 1938 had questioned the value of further orders for ships which took four years to build, when Cabinet policy called for concentration on defence preparedness before April 1940.[58] When building up to the New Standard the Admiralty planned to lay down no more than ten capital ships in the financial years 1936–9, and although, under rationing of finance, one capital ship was dropped from the 1939 programme, industrial factors would have imposed that decision anyway.[59] The other nine were sanctioned by the Treasury, but only the five laid down under the 1936 and 1937 programmes were completed in time to take part in the war. The other four were postponed or abandoned when the War Cabinet decided to give priority to vessels which could be brought into service against Germany sooner. Hopkins' doubts as to the value of these vessels proved justified.

Under the London Naval Treaty of 1930 the first new capital ships of the 1936 programme could not be laid down before January 1937, and far from being obstructive the Treasury agreed to steps to speed their construction. In 1942 Churchill and Chatfield quarrelled over the causes of delay in bringing these vessels – the *King George V* class – into service, the argument turning on decisions and design delays regarding the ships' guns. Chatfield claimed the guns had not caused delay because he had 'obtained special permission of the Treasury actually to commence their construction six months in advance of the London Treaty date. Far from there being delay, therefore, we gained six months by this step.'[60] The Treasury also agreed to tenders for capital ships of the 1937 programme being invited in advance of parliamentary approval of that programme, so that orders could be placed in April 1937 instead of later in the financial year.[61] Whatever delays occurred, they were not the result of Treasury control.

Again, in the case of cruisers, although only fifteen were to be laid down in the three financial years 1936–9 under the D.R.C. programme, all twenty-one cruisers which the Admiralty wished to order while aiming at the New Standard were approved. This was a priority which must have given Chatfield some satisfaction, for on taking over as First Sea Lord in 1933 he had made one of his three main tasks an increase in the Navy's authorised cruiser strength from fifty to seventy. His other main objectives, by his own account, were to rebuild the battlefleet and to have Fleet Air Arm transferred from Air Ministry to Admiralty control.[62]

Not included among these main priorities was the formation of a nucleus on which to build the huge anti-submarine force needed in war. This received a rather low priority – in 1932 it was planned that future annual building programmes should include three cruisers but only two anti-submarine escorts.[63] In 1936 ministers considering the D.R.C. programme were told by the First Lord, Sir Bolton Eyres-Monsell, that 'the Admiralty thought submarines had not today the same importance as in the past', and, when the 1936 Estimates were presented, Parliament was told that modern equipment meant that 'fewer destroyers could do the work formerly done by many'.[64] From all this one may infer that the small numbers of anti-submarine vessels ordered before 1939 reflected not so much financial restraint, but Admiralty priorities, for such vessels cost a mere fraction of the sums being spent on main fleet units, such as aircraft carriers, designed primarily with a war with Japan in view. Large-scale orders of anti-submarine vessels only began to be placed after Munich, and were then approved by the Treasury readily enough.[65]

In fairness to the Admiralty, Germany was slow to rebuild her U-boat fleet, and as late as September 1939 had as few as twenty-six submarines suitable for operations in the Atlantic.[66] The Admiralty did not know that from 1940 German submarines would be able to operate from the coast of France. Nor was the Admiralty alone in underestimating the danger from submarines. The Air Staff thought it desirable that the largest proportion of aircraft possible should be employed in strategic bombing, and Bridges was told by his friends at the Admiralty that they thought plans put before the C.I.D. for what was later called Coastal Command were 'of exceptional modesty'.[67] What the neglect of anti-submarine warfare does seem to show is that despite the efforts of Fisher and Chamberlain to concentrate the Admiralty's collective mind on war with Germany, the Admiralty persisted in giving at least equal priority to preparation for a war against Japan before 1939. In this respect the Treasury's influence was quite unavailing. Roskill blames 'financial stringency' for the deficiencies in anti-submarine defences at Scapa Flow which made possible the sinking of the *Royal Oak* in 1939.[68] Yet the Admiralty spent large sums on defences at Singapore and else-where, and neglected Scapa Flow, which it decided was to be the main fleet base only in January 1939.[69] It is all too easy to make 'Treasury meanness' an excuse for failure to give priority to what mattered most. Part of the reason why the Navy was not altogether ready for war with Germany in 1939 was that the Admiralty had pursued a policy of building a fleet capable of fighting Japan and Germany simultaneously.

The Treasury's financial restraint was designed primarily to ensure that naval rearmament was kept down to a scale which did not threaten the economy or draw scarce industrial resources away from the other services' programmes, and the Admiralty, like the other depart-ments, was not able to do all it wished. Nevertheless industrial capacity, rather than finance, was the limiting factor. An Admiralty paper in October 1938 estimated that most firms engaged on the rearmament programme were 'working their machines about 85 per cent', and only 'some small increase' in production would be possible even if com-mercial work were cancelled.[70] The Admiralty had not been kept on too tight a financial leash, and Churchill, on taking over as First Lord in September 1939, thought that what was still the world's largest Navy had the situation well under control.[71]

The Army's Programme

The War Office's problems in the Nineteen-Thirties owed much to the fact that, after the initial reduction of all three services after 1918, the Army had borne the brunt of the years of financial stringency. The result, as Lord Hailsham, the Secretary of State for War, wrote in December 1932, was that at that date the Army was 'not in a satisfactory position either on a peace footing or as an instrument of policy in an emergency' – a view which the Treasury official examining the 1933 Estimates found 'not possible to contest'.[72] By 1933 much of the War Office's munitions from the First World War had been sold off as surplus to requirements, and it was a sign of a new attitude when in November of that year Creedy, the Permanent Under-Secretary, argued against further such sales. Although, as he told the Army Council, 'unable from a strictly financial point of view to advocate the retention of stores reported to be surplus', he felt justified on 'arguments of military expedience'. At the time the War Office was planning on the basis of a twelve-division expeditionary force, and the decision meant that the Army entered the period of rearmament with enough old field guns and howitzers, which later proved capable of modernisation, for a larger force than that.[73]

Equipping the Army with modern weapons, however, proved to be the most frustrating of all major tasks connected with rearmament. In assessing the Treasury's responsibility for this it is relevant that the performance of the War Office itself has been criticised much more than that of either of the other defence departments. The War Office struck Ismay in 1933 as 'hidebound, unimaginative, impersonal and overpopulated', and Hore-Belisha saw one of his main tasks on taking over in 1937 as the 'vitalisation of a stagnant atmosphere'. Such 'vitalisation' could take forms which antagonised soldiers and officials, and, on being appointed to succeed Creedy in 1939, Grigg found the War Office 'by no means a happy family'.[74] The War Office had the greatest supply problems of the defence departments, and, until after 1936, the staff and organisation least able to cope with inexperienced suppliers. When considering changes in the organisation of the War Office in October 1937 Weir noted that even 'with organisation equal to, or even better than, that of the Admiralty, the War Office could not place itself in the same favourable supply situation'.[75]

The Army also suffered far greater recruiting problems than either of the other departments. When the rearmament programme was announced in 1936 both the Regular and Territorial Armies were well below their peace establishment, and recruitment was below wastage. Nevertheless for political reasons the Prime Minister felt obliged to pledge that there would be no conscription, and the Army continued to rely on voluntary recruitment until April 1939. Duff Cooper's displeasure at the Treasury's refusal to give instant and entire approval to his proposals in 1936 for improving recruitment has already been noted.[76] Nevertheless recruitment did improve in 1937, and, after a vigorous campaign by Hore-Belisha, even more so in 1938, so that perhaps the Treasury's influence was not too detrimental in this respect.[77]

It is easy to understand Duff Cooper's frustration regarding the War Office's programme to improve barracks – a fundamental part of any move to improve recruitment. In September 1936 Duff Cooper wanted to replace Raglan Barracks at Devonport with new barracks at Tavistock, at the cost of £400,000, instead of reconstructing the existing barracks for £240,000. The Treasury official, Compton, reviewing the proposal noted that:

> The decision to move to Tavistock is the Secretary of State's, arrived at against the preponderance of opinion at the War Office, which was in favour of reconstructing Devonport. I have reason to believe that Treasury objection would be welcomed. . . .[78]

The Treasury did object to the proposal, and for general as well as particular reasons. As Bridges observed:

> We have [already] warned the War Office unofficially that we feel the urgent pressure on building labour for works essential to the completion of the Defence programme (i.e. factories, and new accommodation for the increased numbers of the R.A.F., who would otherwise have nowhere – not even Victorian barracks – to lay their heads) may lead to the postponement of barrack reconstruction which, however desirable, can at a pinch be postponed.[79]

Down to 1939 the Treasury was not prepared to agree to overtime work on Army barracks, and insisted on being informed before each contract was placed. The Treasury's insistence on priority for factories rather than barracks does seem to have been justified, since the size of expeditionary force which Britain could send abroad was dictated by the equipment, rather than the manpower, available. During the Czech crisis in 1938, for example, the Adjutant General suggested that personnel arrangements should be worked out on the basis of the Regular Army plus five Territorial Army divisions, but the C.I.G.S., Gort, took the view that this plan went 'too far beyond our means . . . from the point of view of the provision of the necessary equipment', and reduced the figure for Territorial divisions to three.[80] It is in terms of industrial capacity and the supply of munitions that the Treasury's influence can be discussed most significantly.

Since the Army's sources of supply had been pared to the bone by retrenchment much depended upon the creation of new industrial capacity. Here the basic problem from the point of view of Treasury control was that the Field Force did not enjoy the same priority as the Air Force. When the T.I.S.C. came to consider the Air Ministry's proposals on 20 March 1936 for placing orders for aircraft for delivery in 1937 and 1938 the War Office representative had to admit that:

The War Office were a few weeks behind the Air Ministry in completing their detailed plans, but they would soon be bringing before the Committee proposals comparable to the Air Ministry's.[81]

Hopkins and Barlow drew attention to 'a possible pre-emption by the Air Ministry of the available sources of supply to the detriment of the War Office and Admiralty', and the War Office representative said that 'the War Office could not agree to the Air Ministry programme being launched till they knew how the War Office would be affected as regards machine tools'. Treasury officials consulted Inskip, but the Air Ministry were naturally anxious to get ahead and on 1 April Hopkins sanctioned enough contracts to let them do so, even though the War Office representative thought that this decision 'seemed to prejudice the whole question of priority of supply'.[82]

The question of priority of supply had, indeed, been prejudiced in part already, for the Air Ministry had been given freedom by the Treasury to place additional contracts in advance of Parliamentary approval since May 1935, whereas it was only after March 1936 that the War Office enjoyed the same freedom.[83] The Air Ministry's rearmament programme was already in motion before 1936, whereas the same cannot be said for that of the War Office. As Pownall remarked in May 1936:

> Over two months since [the War Office] got authority and contracts not placed yet. It's partly due to delay in getting Treasury approval for the terms of contract, the Treasury want to put in a 'break clause' which no manufacturer could possibly accept. But even then I fear the War Office machine is working very slowly.[84]

Treasury insistence on a 'break clause' – that is provision for termination of production – was not restricted to War Office contracts, and in any case the Treasury relaxed this requirement in June 1936. But since the Air Ministry's rearmament programme was already in motion, any delays in contract procedure tended to bear more hardly on the War Office. This was not a Treasury plot against the Army, but rather it was the case that priority for expanding the Air Force, which was certainly desired by the Cabinet, was bound to be at the expense of the other force most dependent on the creation of new industrial capacity, that is the Army.

Control of expenditure on new industrial capacity, as in the case of the other departments, was the most effective form of Treasury control after 1936. Treasury examination of proposals for the Royal Ordnance Factories run by the War Office seems to have been very detailed. As late as the autumn of 1938 the War Office was still coming to the Treasury for approval of a comparatively minor item like flameproof magazine fittings in one factory. Sanction was usually forthcoming promptly, but where War Office proposals were greater than what was necessary for the authorised D.R.C. programme Treasury officials were bound down to July 1937 to withhold sanction – and, as already noted, the War Office found this a serious blow to its plans to equip the Territorial Army.[85] From July 1937 Treasury officials were authorised by ministers 'to consider and sanction particular orders submitted by the War Office which go beyond the hypothesis at present approved, if they are satisfied that they offer sufficient economic advantages',[86] but so general an instruction left ample room for disagreement at the official level.

As part of the policy of non-interference with normal trade the Treasury tried to stop the War Office from broadening the basis of its supply by bringing in new firms into gun production, urging that the work should be postponed and done later when the new Royal Ordnance Factories had been completed. This, and other restrictions on the same theme, meant that the Director-General of Munitions Production was unable to place all the orders that had been authorised.[87]

It cannot be said that Treasury officials showed themselves over-anxious that new Royal Ordnance Factories should be completed in the shortest possible time. In February 1938 the War Office pressed that contractors should be made to work overtime at nights to speed the construction of these factories, but the Treasury would not agree. Bridges commented:

> I think we should oppose the night work idea strenuously. After all, the dates for completion of the defence programme as a whole – still more of particular items in it – are not 'laid up in Heaven'.[88]

The Treasury took its stand on the expense of night work, and the likely deterioration in workmanship, and at the T.I.S.C. extracted from the War Office representatives a promise that the Treasury would be consulted before any special measures were taken at any Ordnance Factory. The Treasury did agree in April 1938 to night work on one portion of one factory, where delays would otherwise have put back the date of the whole factory's completion by two months. But this was the only exception for some months thereafter.[89]

The priority given from 1936 by the Treasury to the creation of a shadow industry, or 'war potential', for aircraft also implied a lower priority for similar war potential for the Army. The War Office would plan factory sites on a scale sufficient to allow for immediate expansion in war, but, in general, provision for the actual construction of war potential had to be excluded from all projects for factories submitted to the Treasury for approval. The Treasury's reasoning was that the P.S.O.C. had reported in November 1936 that sufficient skilled labour was not available for the full war potential programmes of all three services, and that there was uncertainty whether the War Office hypothesis – based on Western Front fighting on the scale of 1918 from the outbreak of war – should stand without amendment.[90] Uncertainty was removed when the Cabinet decided in December 1937 that the Army was *not* to be prepared to fight on the Western Front at the outbreak of war.

The Territorial Army's field units were supposed to receive lowest priority of all. Nevertheless the Cabinet agreed in February 1937 that Territorial training equipment should be the same as the Regular Army's. Under authority of this decision the War Office was able to order training equipment sufficient to provide by April 1940 two more Regular divisions, thus virtually raising the authorised five-division programme to a seven-division one. According to the official historian of British War Production, successive Secretaries of State and the Director-General of Munitions Production used Territorial Army requirements as a means of creating equipment and war potential, sometimes surreptitiously.[91] Nevertheless, Treasury control over the creation of new industrial capacity, together with P.S.O.C. planning, did ensure that the Air Ministry had priority. Moreover, it was this detailed control of industrial capacity which largely determined the growth in the War Office's Estimates from 1936.

The importance of industrial capacity as the limiting factor in Army expansion is underlined by the fact that the War Office was unable to spend all the money made available to it through the Estimates. Despite talk in the C.I.D. of multi-million pound programmes the stern reality was that in 1934 and 1935 the War Office found itself unable to spend all its modest allocations for warlike stores, because of manufacturing delays.[92] The War Office received virtually all it could spend in 1936 – only five barracks improvement schemes and three churches being deleted from the Supplementary Estimate in July. A substantial cut was demanded by the Treasury of the War Office's Sketch Estimates in 1937 – from £97 million to £90 million – but the cut was made by the War Office on the assumption of a lag in the erection of Ordnance Factories and in production, which the Secretary of State hoped would not occur.[93] Supplementary Estimates could be counted upon to cover any extra cost should the programme be on schedule, but, as it happened, the War Office underspent its Vote for warlike stores in 1937 by £5,981,000 whereas the Air Ministry overspent its allocation for aeroplanes and spares in the same year by £121,000.[94]

As noted in Chapter IV, financial restraint led to major changes in defence priorities in December 1937, and a net reduction in War Office *plans*, in 1938. But once ministers had been forced to settle priorities Treasury officials showed no desire to obstruct the *execution* of the Army's new programme, so far as available industrial capacity allowed. Indeed rationing of finance was in practice a good deal more flexible, even in the case of the War Office programme, in 1938-9 than might appear from Cabinet papers. After the *Anschluss* the War Office asked if Inskip's recent request for an £82 million cut in its planned expenditure for the four years 1938–41 still held good. At a meeting on 1 April Bridges told Hore-Belisha that as far as the Treasury was concerned that was the position, but added that he thought it was possible that Inskip might agree to the cut being regarded as being made on the Army's programme as a whole – which extended beyond 1941 – and not on the allocation for the first four years.[95] In other words if the War Office could accelerate authorised expenditure with its share of industrial capacity the Treasury would not stick rigidly by annual rations of finance.

The reductions in War Office plans after Inskip's reports in the winter of 1937–8 were a curious interpretation of the Cabinet's decision that air defence should have priority over Imperial defence or assistance to possible Continental allies. The War Office did indeed propose in April 1938 to cut the capital cost of the Field Force by £15¼ million during the period of financial rationing – but that was less than the cut of £28¾ million made by the War Office in provision for A.D.G.B.[96] The explanation for this anomaly, as already noted, lay in the War Office's reluctance to sacrifice all gun-making capacity to anti-aircraft guns, at the expense of field artillery requirements, and it was not until the autumn of 1938 that the Treasury felt any need to question War Office proposals for anti-aircraft gun orders.

The alarms of the Munich crisis revealed that the War Office was behindhand even with the limited 640-gun A.D.G.B. programme of April 1938. Nevertheless Hore-Belisha, in Pownall's words, 'ran amok' at a Cabinet Sub-Committee on 27 October 1938 and demanded authority for all the guns necessary to complete the full 1264-gun Ideal Scheme, or twice the number he had been advised to ask for by his professional advisers in the War Office. Ministers in the Committee were in general extremely ready to give authority, but Hopkins, through Simon, made the point that it was necessary first to create new industrial capacity and, while Hore-Belisha's proposal might be approved in principle, there was no need to authorise the actual placing of anything like the total orders asked for until their manufacture could begin many months hence. This was accepted, and, after consultation between the Director-General of Munitions Production and Treasury officials, the conclusion of the Cabinet on 7 November was that the War Office was authorised to create capacity for carrying out the Ideal Scheme and to place orders accordingly, but 'Treasury approval for the proposals should be obtained in the ordinary way'. Meanwhile the T.I.S.C. had already, on 4 November, approved an interim proposal for 320 3·7-inch guns – the number which, according to War Office representatives, would be sufficient to secure the creation of the required industrial capacity.[97]

According to Pownall, Hore-Belisha was 'taken to task' by the Government for so far exceeding professional advice. If so, Hore-Belisha's understandable impatience at any further delay was perhaps tinged with personal feeling. At any rate he made a fuss at the C.I.D. on 19 January 1939, after Barlow, at a T.I.S.C. meeting two days previously, had withheld immediate approval of a War Office proposal to order a further 366 3·7-inch anti-aircraft guns. Hore-Belisha claimed that Cabinet approval had been given for these guns, and that his actions in carrying out the Cabinet's wishes were being delayed.[98] What had happened at the T.I.S.C. on 17 January was that Barlow had noted that whereas the Ideal Scheme of A.D.G.B., approved in principle by the Cabinet on 7 November 1938, specified 1264 guns of 3·7-inch or larger calibre, the 366 guns now proposed would bring total orders under this head to 1361. Moreover, whereas the Ideal Scheme provided for the *replacement* of existing 3-inch anti-aircraft guns by guns of larger calibre, the 366 3·7-inch guns now proposed were to be in *addition* to the 3-inch guns, which were to be retained, thus raising the total of guns of 3-inch and over to 1661, or 397 more than specified in the Ideal Scheme. The War Office representatives explained that the Ideal Scheme was now regarded by the War Office as under-insurance, but Barlow felt that so large an addition to the authorised programme must be referred to the Chancellor. The available industrial capacity was fully employed on the orders placed two months earlier, and there was time for consideration by Simon, Chatfield and Hore-Belisha, and, despite the attempt by the last named to rush matters at the C.I.D. on 19 January, T.I.S.C. approval for the 366 3·7-inch guns in question was not forthcoming until 2 February.[99]

The incidents in October 1938 and January 1939 concerning anti-aircraft guns illustrate the power of Treasury officials to delay action by referring matters to the Chancellor. The power of Treasury officials lay in their ability to advise ministers as to what was possible, and to hold up departments while ministers came to a decision. In addition, the Treasury's knowledge of the over-all financial picture seems to have led to what Pownall, while serving at the War Office, described in December 1938 as:

> . . . a very marked tendency [on the part of ministers] to say in effect, 'yes, that's a very good idea, off you go and see if you can get the money out of the Treasury'. . . . Admittedly the Treasury often play up very well, but surely it's the negation of Ministerial authority.[100]

The test of the power of the Treasury to delay action was the equipment of the Field Force. The Cabinet, advised by the Treasury and others, gave this aspect of rearmament a lower priority in December 1937 than air or trade defence, but the General Staff seems to have been reluctant to give the Field Force a low priority. It is difficult to measure the impact of financial rationing on the equipment of the Field Force in the financial year 1938, but the example of tanks is interesting as it illustrates most clearly the interactions of the Treasury's influence with other factors. Armoured fighting vehicles bore the brunt of the War Office's proposed reductions in the cost of the Field Force at the beginning of 1938, savings under that head exceeding the total of all others such as field guns and infantry transport. In line with the requirement of a North African campaign the reduction in tanks was at the expense of heavier – and more costly – types designed for Western European operations. Compared with the authorised D.R.C. programme there were to be 340 infantry tanks, instead of 833, and no medium tanks, instead of 247. The cut in infantry tanks did represent a genuine cut in *planning*, but since even in December 1938 only sixty were expected to be delivered by March 1939 the cut was hardly at the expense of current production. The cut in medium tanks is even more interesting. The medium design was not expected to be ready for production before mid-1939, whereas a lighter, but similarly armed, cruiser tank was expected to be available in the autumn of 1938. What the War Office now planned was to offset the cut in medium tanks by increasing orders for cruiser tanks from 350 to 585. In other words the War Office would be able to order more of the type which could be produced in the immediate future. Nor was ultimate production of medium tanks sacrificed. Hore-Belisha wrote to Chamberlain that the type's development would continue, and preparations would be made for its production in war.[101]

The Treasury was by no means solely responsible for the shortage of tanks in 1938–9. There were a number of reasons why design, development and deliveries of new tanks were slow, including a shortage both of materials and of draughtsmen, and the death in an air accident of Britain's leading tank designer, Sir John Carden, in 1935.[102] Again, the War Office's decision in 1938 to plan for fewer and cheaper tanks bore as much the mark of War Office priorities as of financial restraint. The General Staff sought economy at the expense of tanks while continuing to re-equip, and expensively motorise, infantry divisions, and it had also rejected a suggestion by Hore-Belisha, prompted no doubt by Liddell Hart, in the summer of 1937, that the implications of an expeditionary force of two mobile divisions for use in a western theatre be worked out.[103]

As noted in Chapter II, Treasury officials were prepared in 1938, however unenthusiastically, to modify contract procedure to keep tank producers in business.[104] In one important respect, however, Treasury influence was inimical to tank production. On 27 April 1939 the Director-General of Munitions Production told the C.I.D. that:

> ... until recently tank production had not been given a very high degree of priority. The work conflicted with locomotive and railway wagon work. The powers to be given to the Ministry of Supply should improve the position. . . .[105]

Here in a nutshell is one of the major themes in considering the Treasury's influence on rearmament. The Government had been attempting to arm for war with the minimum of disturbance in the peacetime economy, and when normal civil industrial resources began to be diverted to rearmament the expansion of the Air Force had been given first priority. The high priority given by the Cabinet to the maintenance of normal economic activity and to the Air Force both reflected the Treasury's views, and Treasury control over industrial resources, partly through control of finance but increasingly through control of new industrial capacity, ensured that departments conformed, on the whole, to Cabinet priorities. The low priority given to the Field Force compared with other aspects of rearmament is surely best summed up by the fact that until 1939 locomotive and railway wagon work could impede tank production.

A changed attitude was made necessary, however, by the Cabinet's decisions in February, March and April 1939, which raised the requirement for field units' equipment from that of an Army of up to seven divisions for general Imperial defence purposes, to one of thirty-two divisions for European operations. From the point of view of Treasury control the most important change came on 23 March, when a Cabinet Committee laid down that munitions production for the enlarged Army was to have priority over normal trade – as the Air Force programme had had for a year. Then on 29 March the Cabinet authorised a doubling of the strength of the Territorial Army, and when the same day a request came from the War Office to the Treasury for approval of machine tool orders Gilbert observed

> some argument could have been put up . . . a few days ago, but in view of today's sanction on the Territorial Army it seems quite clear that our future requirements are such as to remove all argument as to the necessity for getting on with these machine tools forthwith.[106]

The Treasury showed no desire to obstruct the War Office once Cabinet policy had changed. The Treasury agreed that plans should be put forward piecemeal and that instalments should not be delayed until the whole plan for the Expeditionary Force had been worked out. An instalment of nearly half the £65 million proposals authorised by the Cabinet Committee on 23 March was approved by the Treasury on 4 April.[107] On the other hand, the rapid expansion of the Army caused great administrative and industrial problems. The administrative process could be speeded up in the case of accommodation for conscripts, as happened from May onwards when the Treasury agreed that the War Office could use quasi-wartime arrangements for putting up the necessary camps, delegating authority to local Commands, and dispensing with competitive tenders.[108] Industrial problems relating to the supply of equipment were less easily solved, and the Treasury continued to keep a tight reign on War Office expenditure where creation of new industrial capacity was involved.

On 4 May the War Office came to the T.I.S.C. with proposals to implement a Cabinet decision of 19 April to provide war equipment and reserves for ten Territorial Army divisions, at a total cost of £19 million in addition to expenditure already authorised. Barlow said that he did not think that the committee could deal with the complete programme before the War Office produced an estimate of their demands for new industrial capacity, and, as an interim measure, the War Office was authorised by the Treasury only to order such equipment within the total of £19 million as could be placed as continuation orders with existing capacity. Bovenschen, the Deputy Under-Secretary of State at the War Office, wrote to Barlow subsequently, describing himself as 'somewhat perturbed' at this limited sanction as the War Office could not get firms to expand capacity without orders.[109]

The Treasury reply, drafted by Gilbert though signed by Barlow, noted that:

> We fully appreciate the point which you make that the creation of extra capacity and orders for reserves go hand in hand. . . . [But] in my view . . . the proposal . . . is (or appears to be) starting at the wrong end, and that the right way to begin is to think more in terms of the potential to be created than of orders to be given. . . .
>
> I may mention that Sir Arthur Robinson [chairman of the Supply Board] wrote to me recently and told me that the War Office would want about £20 million worth of machine tools for their expanded programme. This is in itself about twice the present annual output of the industry even if all manufacture for export were stopped. You are not, however, the only competitors in the field, as the Air Ministry have large orders in view.
>
> I think you should be aware of this position when giving your orders for the expanded programme. If any question should arise of purchase abroad, we should like to be consulted in advance, as there are special difficulties at the present time in the way of purchases involving foreign exchange.[110]

The full War Office proposals of 4 May were not sanctioned by the Treasury until 26 June. It is hardly surprising that, from the War Office's point of view, the continued tight Treasury control of the execution of policy was very frustrating. On the other hand, without the Treasury's control of expenditure, it is hard to see how, even with the P.S.O. organisation doing its best to keep up with changing programmes, interdepartmental competition, and confusion in industry, could be avoided.

As matters were, with the new Royal Ordnance Factories coming into production in 1939, delays in preparing the Expeditionary Force for service in France were much less than might have been expected, given changes in Cabinet policy in 1937–9. The authorised D.R.C. programme of February 1936 had aimed at equipping five divisions by March 1941. By May 1940, however, there were ten infantry divisions and a tank brigade in France, and other divisions were being prepared in Britain or were serving in Norway. The sudden increase in the total authorised strength of the Army in 1939 to thirty-two divisions had diverted much equipment from the Expeditionary Force so that the new divisions might be trained, and inevitably there were deficiencies.[111] Nevertheless the War Office had achieved more by 1940 than it had hoped to do by that year in 1936. This achievement did not really reflect failure of Treasury control, however, for this force equipped for European operations had been created only after Britain's air and sea defences had been made secure.

Summary

The Treasury's influence on the execution of defence policy, as on the formation of that policy, was strongest at the level of broad priorities between departments. Selective application, and relaxation, of the brake of Treasury control enabled the Air Ministry to become the biggest spender of the three defence departments. The Treasury could not prevent a department aiming at goals beyond what the Cabinet had authorised, but the Treasury could limit that department's new industrial capacity, and therefore its ability to achieve unauthorised goals. At the same time the Treasury found it difficult to hold up orders when industrial capacity would be made idle thereby, and almost impossible to make a department order more of a particular weapon, for example fighters, than that department wished to order.

Treasury control did not operate in a vacuum, but conformed to Cabinet decisions, and was subject to ministerial supervision. Certainly ministers were much influenced by the Treasury while deciding policy, but a remarkable aspect of rearmament was the degree to which defence departments pursued individual policies which suggested priorities somewhat different from those agreed by the Cabinet. Weaker Treasury control could only have increased this tendency, and the most likely result would have been less well co-ordinated deliveries of equipment, and less balanced and less complete defence forces. The defence departments' ever-growing demands were more than industry, or the P.S.O.C.'s plans, could cope with, and the Treasury's rationing of finance was in effect a means of rationing real industrial resources. Frustrating though Treasury control must have been seen from within any one defence department, the Treasury seems to deserve credit for ensuring that Britain's minimum requirements for air and trade defence were met first.

VI

Conclusion

The Treasury had a duty to ensure that public expenditure conformed
to Cabinet policy and parliamentary votes, but the attitudes and actions
of Chamberlain, Fisher, Hopkins and Bridges make it absurd to write
of 'the dead hand of the Treasury' in 1933–9, however apt that phrase
may have been in earlier years. Defence policy had to be guided by two
considerations: on the one hand, there seemed to be a danger of
attempting to spend too much, thereby 'undermining ourselves' by
bringing about 'another 1931'; on the other, there was a danger that
Britain might not be ready for war if and when it came. No doubt more
might have been spent before 1936 had the Treasury been less orthodox
in its economic beliefs, but the D.R.C., while drawing up what became
the rearmament programme of 1936, was not inhibited by financial
considerations. Within a year that programme, calculated to cost
£1038 million over five years, had grown so much that it was estimated
to cost £1500 million, and the level of borrowing necessary to carry out
such a programme, £400 million over five years, was thought by
Keynes in 1937 to entail 'a risk of what might fairly be called inflation',
if the full rate of expenditure began immediately, and if it were not
carefully planned. In 1938 and 1939 an adverse current balance of
payments, an outflow of gold and depreciation of the pound against the
dollar, all indicated strain on the economy and a decline in foreign
confidence in Britain's financial stability, and while Treasury fears of
'another 1931' may have been exaggerated, there seems to have been
good reason to anticipate growing difficulty in importing essential raw
materials and food.

For industrial reasons defence departments found it difficult to
spend even their voted funds. Retrenchment since 1919, which the
Treasury had advocated, and the Ten Year Rule, which the Treasury
had strengthened in 1928, had reduced the specialised armaments
industry to a skeleton by 1933, while Treasury obstruction had held up
P.S.O.C. planning for wartime mobilisation of industry. Although
there had been powerful political demands for retrenchment down to
the early 'Thirties, the Treasury cannot be absolved from much of the
blame for Britain's inability to rearm without extensive industrial
investment and concomitant inflationary pressures. On the other hand,
by 1935 the Treasury had grasped the importance of industrial capacity,
and subsequently relaxed the brake of Treasury control on expenditure

designed to create capacity which the Treasury believed to be essential. At the same time continued Treasury control forced defence departments to think in terms of an orderly flow of orders and production.

Contemporary criticism of the National Government often tended to assume that Britain was the 'most powerful nation and Empire in the world',[1] and most subsequent critics of rearmament seem to have shared an implicit assumption that Britain ought to have been as powerful as Hitler's Reich, and that she had the means of making herself so. But industrial capacity set narrow limits to British rearmament in the short term – while new munitions factories were being brought into production – and comparative figures of output in key industries suggest that even in the longer term Britain's capacity for rearmament was inferior to Germany's. For example, Britain's annual average output of steel in 1935-9 was 11·8 million metric tons; that of Germany was 20·4 million metric tons. Since at the beginning of 1936 the British steel industry was reported to be approaching its full capacity to produce, and since even in 1940-4 Britain's annual average output of steel was still only 12·9 million metric tons, it does not seem that Britain's inferiority in this respect simply reflected Treasury 'meanness' in 1936-9.[2] Another key industry was the production of machine tools, and here the disparity between British and German output was even more striking. It has been estimated that in 1939 British output of machine tools was less than a fifth of Germany's, and since Britain was a net importer of machine tools in 1939 the disparity seems to have had more deep-seated causes than Treasury restrictions on defence expenditure.[3]

In the short term, that is the period 1936-9, paper pounds alone could not remove industrial bottlenecks and enable British rearmament to match Germany's. Ironically, at a time of mass unemployment, the main limiting factor was seen as the supply of skilled labour. At the beginning of 1936 the Government was advised by Weir and the Ministry of Labour that industry, as then organised, could not cope with the D.R.C. programme, although that programme envisaged a maximum level of expenditure of less than half of what Germany's current rearmament expenditure was believed to be, and less than a quarter of what Germany was believed to be capable of spending. From the point of view of rearmament, the tragedy of the inter-war years seems to have been not simply that successive governments did not provide more Budget deficits and undifferentiated public works, but rather that the unemployed were not trained in the skills which would have made them an effective reserve either for armaments industries or for new export industries to help pay for rearmament. There was, of course, the question of trade union standards, which were relaxed only gradually even after 1936.

Lack of government powers over private investment also made it difficult to concentrate Britain's limited resources on rearmament. Use was made of public funds to expand the armaments industry, and from 1937 the Government levied taxes on income which were unprecedented in peacetime, but which, even so, were at much lower rates than in Germany. The political problems in substituting guns for butter were very great. It is in the light of industrial, and related political and economic, problems that the financial limits set by the Treasury to defence departments' expenditure have to be judged. It was the P.S.O.C., not the Treasury, which first warned that there was not sufficient skilled labour available to maintain in war all the forces projected by the defence departments in 1936. Financial rationing was imposed by the Treasury so that decisions would have to be made as to priorities within the rearmament programme. The figure of £1500 million for five years for all three defence departments given by the Treasury in 1937 was a bargaining counter, modified early in 1938 to £1570 million, with both the Treasury and, apparently, the Cabinet believing that further upward revision might be necessary. Actual expenditure by defence departments in the financial years 1938 and 1939 was far above the level implied by a £1500 million 'ration', for five years, a total of £382 million being spent by the three departments in 1938, and £642 million in 1939.[4]

If, as Bridges remarked, there were 'physical limits to what [could] be provided in a limited period', then priorities had to be established as to which parts of the rearmament programme should, on strategic grounds, be completed first. The C.O.S., however, in the absence of guidance from the Cabinet, seem to have preferred simply to add up the different departments' requirements. Although retrenchment down to 1933 had created something in the nature of *tabula rasa* upon which a new defence policy might be written, it was not until 1937 that Chatfield advised that, in order to give the Navy and Air Force sufficient priority, the Army should no longer be prepared to fight in Europe. Even then he gave the advice privately as First Sea Lord, and not in his capacity of chairman of the C.O.S. Committee, and was persuaded not only by the Treasury's financial arguments, but also by his desire to prepare the Navy against both Japan and Germany.

There was, therefore, a case for the Treasury forming 'independent and constructive views' on policy, and there was certainly a need to see that 'strategical problems [were] thoroughly worked out by the strategists'. Defence policy had to take into account what British industry, and possible enemies, could accomplish in a given period. By 1936 British intelligence reports suggested, accurately enough, that German industry could not equip an army larger than the combined French and Belgian armies much before 1940. But as early as 1935 German aircraft production, compared with British and French production, was causing concern, and by the end of 1937 the C.O.S.

were agreed that Germany might be tempted to gamble on her advantage in the air. Again, defence policy had to be tailored to political requirements, which meant that a deterrent to German aggression had to be found without putting British industry on a war basis. The Treasury view in 1934-7 was that the best deterrent would be a superior air force, capable of counter-offensive operations, and concentrated against Germany (and not, as the First D.R.C. Report had suggested, in penny packets around the Empire). It was only once it had become apparent by 1937 that the British aircraft industry could not match German output, at least in the short term, that the Treasury advocated an air defence policy designed to make Britain 'a sufficiently unattractive hedgehog' to deter a direct German attack.

An effective deterrent to German aggression, however, must convince the Germans that they would lose any war in which Britain intervened. The C.O.S. themselves said in 1937 that Britain and France could not hope to overpower Germany in a short war, and the inference drawn by Fisher, among others, was that Britain must plan on the basis of a war in which she would have time to mobilise the resources of her Empire and to bring economic pressure to bear on Germany through blockade. This required not only adequate air and trade defence to avoid defeat at the outset, but also, in the Treasury's view, sufficient international purchasing power with which to buy those materials which Britain could not produce herself but which would be essential for victory. Beyond a certain limit, the bigger the defence forces created, the less able Britain would be to maintain them in war. While there might be some dispute as to where that limit lay, Britain's dependence on American aid by 1941 suggests that the Treasury was correct in principle, and, of course, American aid could not be counted upon before the war.

It was in the light of the needs of air defence and the Navy, and finance as the 'fourth arm of defence', that the Treasury wished the role of the Army to be decided. Fisher argued that the Air Force must have first call on new industrial capacity, but he believed that a Field Force of seventeen divisions, ready for operations in the Low Countries on or near the outbreak of war, should be an 'ultimate policy'. In 1936 Fisher thought that seventeen divisions should be the limit of Britain's effort on land in war, but Chamberlain, who seems to have believed that five divisions were all that Britain could prepare in peace, did not set a limit to expansion in war, and, indeed, agreed to thirty-two divisions being prepared once, in March 1939, he believed international relations had become a 'mockery' of peace. So long as Germany's superiority over France lay in air, and not in land, power, there was much to be said for the logic of the Treasury's priorities, and if the logic seemed too cold, given France's reasonable wish that Britain too should be prepared to make *un effort du sang*, then Fisher, at least, had no objection to sending troops to France, if the French would equip them.

If priorities were to be set, the Treasury had to persuade the Cabinet to make decisions – hence the £1500 million 'ration' proposed for defence expenditure in 1937–42 – and then persuade the Cabinet what these decisions should be. Given popular fear of air attack and revulsion against the mass conscription, and slaughter, of 1916–18, it was not difficult to persuade ministers to give priority to the Air Force over the Army. On the other hand, the Treasury did not have a monopoly of advice, and the priority accorded in Inskip's Report in 1937 to Imperial defence over assistance to possible allies reflected Chatfield's and Hankey's influence. Without Treasury influence, however, the Cabinet might have avoided choices, and certainly without Treasury control of expenditure it would have been harder than it was to prevent different services pursuing their own policies regardless of over-all policy laid down by the Cabinet. By greater or lesser restrictions on different departments' expenditure the Treasury was able to influence broad priorities as between departments.

It is hard to measure influence, but the difference between proposed and actual expenditure by departments gives some indication of the impact of the Treasury's influence. Had the priorities recommended by the D.R.C. in 1934 and 1935 prevailed, the Air Ministry would have continued to have had a smaller share of total defence expenditure than the Admiralty or War Office. As it happened, Air Ministry expenditure overtook that of the War Office in 1937, and that of the Admiralty in 1938, and this reflected the Treasury's influence combined with the Cabinet's own preferences. From the point of view of the influence of Treasury control of expenditure, the interesting years are 1936 and 1937, for while in these years all defence departments accelerated and made *ad hoc* additions to their D.R.C. programmes, over-all policy as recommended by the D.R.C. did not change until the end of 1937, and no major new scheme for aircraft production was approved until 1938. Yet whereas the Air Ministry exceeded its D.R.C. forecasts by 11 per cent in 1936 and 36 per cent in 1937, the War Office exceeded its forecasts by less than 1 per cent in 1936, and by only 26 per cent in 1937.[5]

Turning to the significance of the Treasury's influence on rearmament, one is bound to note that German aggression was not deterred in 1936, 1938 or 1939. But Germany's military leaders seem to have been reluctant to risk war in any of these years,[6] and Hitler's successes in 1936 and 1938 seem to have been due to his restriction of his demands to what the British and French governments would be reluctant to fight for. If military weakness persuaded Britain not to fight in 1938, that weakness was the one which the Treasury was most anxious to see remedied, namely air defence. When the test of war came Britain was able to contribute to the Allied cause the world's largest navy, an aircraft industry which out-produced Germany's in 1940, and an army which was just large enough to deny the German Army any decisive advantage in men or quantity of equipment.[7] Does it seem more likely, then, that the débâcle of 1940 was due mainly to Treasury 'meanness', or to the different strategy, tactics and design specifications of the rival armed forces? The British Army understandably complained of a lack of munitions, but the same complaint was made by the German Army, which faced a major munitions crisis after the Polish campaign in 1939.[8] Germany's one major numerical advantage was in the air, yet one wonders whether France would have been saved even if the R.A.F. had had more aircraft. To Ismay 'it almost seemed as though the Air Staff would prefer to have their forces under Beelzebub rather than anyone connected with the Army', while Slessor, with manly frankness, has admitted that while the R.A.F. was not trained to intervene directly on the battlefield, Bomber Command's techniques and training were not yet sufficiently advanced for it to be effective in its chosen strategic role either.[9]

It is also worth asking what might have happened if industry had been asked to produce more bombers or to arm more warships or Army field units. Given the tendency down to 1939 for deliveries to lag behind orders even when the Treasury made finance available, might not the result have been fewer fighters and anti-aircraft guns, and by how much narrower a margin could the Battle of Britain have been won? Of course more could have been produced for all services if the Government had had greater powers over finance and industry before the war, but the Government felt unable to take such powers. Unanswerable arguments can be advanced by military men for increased armaments, if each service is taken in isolation, and if over-all financial, industrial and political aspects are ignored. The Treasury did not ignore these aspects, and rightly brought them to the attention of those responsible for policy. Far from being paralysing, the Treasury's use of the power of the purse forced ministers and military men to come to decisions about priorities, and thereby ensured that essential elements in Britain's defences were completed first.

Notes

CHAPTER I
Unless otherwise stated, all publishers in notes have London offices.

1. R. J. Minney, *Private Papers of Hore-Belisha* (Collins, 1960), p. 171. Rae was an Under-Secretary.
2. Derek Wood and Derek Demptster, *Narrow Margin* (Arrow Books, 1969), p. 37; Correlli Barnett, *Britain and Her Army* (Allen Lane, 1970), p. 421.
3. D. C. Watt, 'Air Force View of History', *Quarterly Review*, October 1962, pp. 428ff.
4. Duff Cooper, 'Spend to Rearm', London *Evening Standard*, 26 Oct. 1938.
5. 'Cato' [Michael Foot, Peter Howard and Frank Owen], *Guilty Men* (Gollancz, 1940), pp. 6, 9–16, 44–46, 86–89, 100 and 113.
6. Sir John Wheeler-Bennett, *Munich, Prologue to Tragedy* (Macmillan, 1948), p. 265.
7. Sir Keith Feiling, *Life of Neville Chamberlain* (Macmillan, 1946), pp. 258 and 292.
8. Keith Middlemass, *Diplomacy of Illusion* (Weidenfeld and Nicolson, 1972), p. 81f.
9. Viscount Simon, *Retrospect* (Hutchinson, 1952). Sir Warren Fisher, 'Beginnings of Civil Defence', *Public Administration* (1948) xxvi. 212; *The Times*, 3 Mar. 1942, p. 5. *Lessons of British War Economy*, ed. Sir Norman Chester (Cambridge U.P., 1951), pp. 1–4. Lord Bridges, *Treasury Control* (University of London Press, 1950) and *The Treasury* (Allen and Unwin, 1966).
10. War Cabinet minutes, 15 Aug. 1919, quoted in *History of the Second World War, U.K. Military Series*: N. H. Gibbs, *Grand Strategy* (1976), i. 3.
11. *Parl. Papers* 1924–25, xxiv, Cmd. 2207.
12. The long-standing dilemma of British defence policy, whether to give priority to the overseas Empire or to Western Europe, is considered in Michael Howard, *The Continental Commitment* (Temple Smith, 1972).
13. Gibbs, *Grand Strategy*, i. 51.
14. Letter to *The Times*, 9 Aug. 1946.
15. *Parl. Papers* 1932–33, xvii, Cmd. 4259; *H.C. Deb.*, 5th series, 1933–34, vol. 281: 47.
16. P.R.O., Treasury Papers, Series 175, file 35 [hereafter T.175/35]: Hopkins to P. J. Grigg (Churchill's Principal Private Secretary), 1 May 1928.
17. Gibbs, *Grand Strategy*, i. 58.
18. For a critique of British financial policy in these years see Susan Howson, *Domestic Monetary Management in Britain 1919–38* (Cambridge U.P., 1975).
19. T.175/28: Waterfield to Fisher and Churchill, 15 Sept. 1928. By the Kellogg–Briand Pact, signed at Paris on 27 Aug., 15 states, followed by 45 others by 1930, renounced war as an instrument of national policy.
20. Lord Chatfield, *It Might Happen Again* (Heinemann, 1947), p. 13.
21. For example, see *History of the Second World War, U.K. Military Series*: Basil Collier, *Defence of the United Kingdom* (1957), pp. 6–8, 21f.; Correlli Barnett, *Collapse of British Power* (Eyre Methuen, 1972), p. 278; Peter Dennis, *Decision by Default* (Routledge and Kegan Paul, 1972), pp. 18f., 28f., 31.
22. R. A. C. Parker, *Europe 1919–45* (Weidenfeld and Nicolson, 1967), p. 260.
23. Derived from Berenice A. Carroll, *Design for Total War* (Mouton, the Hague, 1968), p. 184.
24. P.R.O., Cabinet Office Papers, Series 23, vol. 70 (hereafter CAB.23/70): Cabinet minutes, 10 Feb., and 23 Mar., 1932, esp. pp. 242 and 391.
25. CAB.16/109: D.R.C.14, 28 Feb. 1934, table A1. The figure includes expenditure proposed for the Fleet Air Arm, but excludes proposed shipbuilding, which was estimated at a total of £20 million for the quinquenium over and above the 1933 level of expenditure for that purpose.

26. CAB.24/250: C.P.205 (34), 31 July 1934, para. 51.
27. CAB.16/112: D.R.C.37, p. 41, table 4; CAB.16/123: D.P.R.(D.R.) 9, 6 Feb.' 1936.
28. CAB.16/112: D.R.C. 37, para. 122.
29. CAB.16/112: D.R.C.37, table 4, and CAB.16/123: D.P.R.(D.R.) 9, p. 11.
30. *Parl. Papers* 1936–37, xvii, Cmd. 5374; *H.C. Deb.*, 5th series, 1936–37, vol. 320: 1209.
31. CAB.23/88: Cabinet minutes, 30 June 1937, pp. 330ff.; CAB.23/90A: Cabinet minutes, 22 Dec. 1937, p. 346; CAB.24/274: C.P.24 (38), 8 Feb. 1938, p. 10.
32. *History of the Second World War, U.K. Civil Series*: M. M. Postan, *British War Production* (1952), pp. 471, 484.
33. Alan S. Milward, *German Economy at War* (Athlone Press, 1965), pp. 6, 28.

CHAPTER II

1. *Parl. Papers* 1935–36, vi. 63ff.
2. *Parl. Papers* 1935–36, v. 431.
3. Bridges, *The Treasury*, p. 38.
4. Conversation with Sir Thomas and Lady Padmore, 15 Mar. 1975, and letter from Sir Thomas to the author, 25 Aug. 1975 (See Note on Sources). The expression 'confidential adviser' was Chamberlain's (CAB.23/95: Cabinet minutes, 26 Sept. 1938, p. 247).
5. Feiling, *Neville Chamberlain*, p. 258; Lord Ismay, *Memoirs* (Heinemann, 1960), p. 90; Iain MacLeod, *Neville Chamberlain* (Muller, 1961), p. 164.
6. University of Birmingham Library, Neville Chamberlain Papers (hereafter N.C.) 2/23A: Chamberlain's diary, Jan. 1934 (no day).
7. *Essayez, Memoirs of Marquis of Zetland* (John Murray, 1956), p. 228; Viscount Templewood, *Nine Troubled Years* (Collins, 1954), p. 329f.
8. Simon, *Retrospect*, p. 227; CAB.23/100: Cabinet minutes, 5 July 1939, pp. 117ff.; Hankey's diary, 23 Aug. 1939, quoted in Stephen Roskill, *Hankey, Man of Secrets* (Collins, 1974), iii. 413.
9. In order of appointment, Messrs. Leslie Hore-Belisha, A. Duff Cooper, W. S. Morrison, John Colville, D. Euan Wallace and H. Crookshank.
10. Letter from Sir Edward Playfair to the author, 18 July 1975 (see Note on Sources).
11. Churchill College, Cambridge, Sir (Percy) James Grigg's Papers 2/23/2: Wilson to Grigg, 31 Jan. 1938.
12. Minney, *Private Papers of Hore-Belisha*, p. 70f.
13. Grigg Papers 2/20/33: Grigg to Sir Findlater Stewart, 2 Jan. 1938, and 2/23/1: Grigg to Wilson, 16 Jan. 1938.
14. Letter of Nov. 1937, quoted in Minney, *op. cit.*, p. 71.
15. *Parl. Papers* 1945–46, xx. 159.
16. Feiling, *Neville Chamberlain*, p. 314f.
17. N.C.18/1/951: Chamberlain to his sister Ida, 14 Mar. 1936; PREM.1/250: Simon to Chamberlain, 25 Oct. 1937.
18. Franklyn A. Johnson, *Defence by Committee* (Oxford U.P., 1960), p. 249, and Lord Chatfield, *It Might Happen Again*, p. 170.
19. N.C.18/1/980: Chamberlain to Ida, 10 Oct. 1936; T.175/97: Hopkins to Fisher, 4 Feb. 1938; T.161/855/S.48431/01/3: Bridges' note, 14 Feb. 1938.
20. *Parl. Papers* 1935–36, v. 431.
21. *Ibid.*, 433, 438, 440f.
22. Sir Roy Harrod, *Life of John Maynard Keynes* (Macmillan, 1963), p. 421f.; Sir Wilfred Eady, 'Sir Richard Hopkins', *D.N.B.* 1951–60.
23. Letter from Sir Edward Playfair to the author, 18 July 1975.
24. *Parl. Papers* 1935–36, v. 442.
25. Sir Frederick Leith-Ross, *Money Talks* (Hutchinson, 1968), p. 152; *Collected Writings of John Maynard Keynes* (Macmillan, 1972), x. 330f.
26. Conversations with Sir Edward Playfair, 21 Apr. 1975, and with Lord Trend (see Note on Sources), 26 June 1975.

27. *Parl. Papers* 1935–36, v. 439; T.199/50c: minutes of Treasury Organisation Committee, 9 Mar. 1937, p. 4, and conversation with Sir Thomas Padmore, who was secretary of that committee, 15 Mar. 1975.
28. Leith-Ross, *Money Talks*, pp. 145–7.
29. King's College, London, Liddell Hart Papers, 11/1937/54: Liddell Hart's note on talk with Bullock, 25 June 1937. Conversation with Sir John Winnifrith, 31 Jan. 1975 (see Note on Sources).
30. T.199/50c: Treasury List of Staff (booklet for office use only), p. 10.
31. T.199/50c: draft report of Treasury Organisation Committee, 2 Nov. 1937, p.4.
32. CAB.23/93: Cabinet minutes, 1 June 1938, p. 375f.; Lord Swinton, *Sixty Years of Power* (Hutchinson, 1966), p. 118; Ismay, *Memoirs*, p. 89.
33. For example, a letter from Bridges to Hopkins, relating to the 1937 Defence White Paper, but written while Hopkins was away celebrating an anniversary, begins: 'First of all, we have discovered your secret and wish you all very many happy returns of the day . . .' (T.161/778/S.41729/1, 13 Feb. 1937).
34. Simon, *Retrospect*, p. 231.
35. Sir John Winnifrith, 'Baron Bridges', *Biographical Memoirs of Fellows of the Royal Society*, xvi (Nov. 1970), 55f.
36. T.161/855/S.48431/01/2: Bridges' memorandum, 17 Dec. 1937.
37. Conversation with Sir John Winnifrith, 31 Jan. 1975.
38. Treasury Establishment Officer's files (T.199) and conversation with Mr. George Oram, 21 Mar. 1975 (see Note on Sources).
39. *Parl. Papers* 1935–36, v. 434, and conversation with Sir John Winnifrith, 31 Jan. 1975.
40. N.C.18/1/1002: Chamberlain to Ida, 17 Apr. 1937. Conversation with Sir John Winnifrith, 31 Jan. 1975.
41. T.161/932/S.42750: Hopkins' comment on memorandum by Compton, 15 Dec. 1937.
42. Cambridge University Library, Baldwin Papers, volume I, folio 40: Hankey to Baldwin, 23 Aug. 1934.
43. CAB.21/424: Fisher to Baldwin, 13 Jan. 1936; N.C. 18/1/949: Chamberlain to Ida, 16 Feb. 1936.
44. Johnson, *Defence by Committee*, p. 264.
45. CAB.21/424: Fisher to Chamberlain, 15 Feb. 1936.
46. Roskill, *Hankey*, iii. 366.
47. Churchill College, Cambridge, Hankey Papers 1/8: diary, May 6–16, 1938; *Chief of Staff: Diaries of Lieutenant-General Sir Henry Pownall*, ed. Brian Bond (Cooper, 1972), i. 149 (hereafter cited as *Pownall Diaries*).
48. Lord Hankey, *Government Control in War* (Cambridge U.P., 1945), p. 77.
49. British Library of Political and Economic Science, Fisher Papers 2/13: Fisher to Wilson, 15 May 1939. Lord Trenchard retired as Chief of Air Staff in 1929. Lord Milne retired as C.I.G.S. in 1933.
50. A. Boyle, *Trenchard, Man of Vision* (Collins, 1962), p. 68of.; Grigg Papers 2/21/1: Trenchard to Grigg, 2 Mar. 1935.
51. National Maritime Museum, Greenwich, Chatfield Papers 3/1: Hankey to Chatfield, 3 June 1938. Hankey Papers 24/1: notes for Hankey's evidence on the Central Organisation of Defence, 12 Oct. 1954.
52. PREM.1/250: Simon to Chamberlain, 25 Oct. 1937.
53. T.161/855/S.48431/01/3: note by Hopkins, 11 Feb. 1938.
54. Fisher Papers 2/13: Fisher to Wilson, 15 May 1939.
55. T.161/891/S.26350/01: Bridges to Barlow and Hopkins, 11 Mar. 1935.
56. CAB.16/133: A.D.R. 55, p. 3.
57. CAB.12/3: Home Defence Committee minutes, 23 Nov. 1937, p. 1f.; Ismay, *Memoirs*, p. 80.
58. T.175/35: Fisher's memorandum, 25 Feb. 1925; CAB.2/6(1): C.I.D. minutes, 16 Apr. 1935, p. 189.
59. T.161/876/S.19907/3: Barlow's note, 22 Feb. 1935.
60. CAB.60/32: minutes of 55th meeting, p. 7f.
61. Johnson, *Defence by Committee*, p. 257.
62. T.161/624/S.36130/34: Fisher's note, 3 Feb. 1934.

63. T.161/736/S.22793/2: Fisher to Simon, 28 July 1937, and Bridges' and Barlow's comments on C.P.199 and 199A.
64. Conversation with Sir John Winnifrith, 31 Jan. 1975.
65. Sir Charles Walker, *Thirty-Six Years at the Admiralty* (Lincoln Williams, 1934), p. 216.
66. Viscount Norwich, *Old Men Forget* (Rupert Hart-Davis, 1953), p. 199f.; CAB.23/86: Cabinet minutes, 2 Dec. 1936, pp. 201ff.; CAB.23/87: Cabinet minutes, 20 Jan. 1937, pp. 61ff., and T.162/436/E.34161/2 to 4: 8D files.
67. T.161/989/S.42212: Duff Cooper to Simon, 27 June 1938, and Rowan to Bridges, 28 June 1938.
68. Duff Cooper, 'Spend to Rearm', London *Evening Standard*, 26 Oct. 1938, p. 7.
69. T.161/856/S.49094/01: Gilbert's memorandum, 2 Nov. 1938; T.161/923/S.40760/03/3: Wilson to Hopkins, 20 July 1939; CAB.23/100: Cabinet minutes, 26 July 1939, pp. 237–41.
70. Harold Macmillan, *Winds of Change* (Macmillan, 1966), p. 353.
71. T.161/877/S.19907/5: Barlow's memorandum, and Hopkins to Fisher and J. H. E. Woods (Simon's Principal Private Secretary), 25 Oct. 1938.
72. Bridges, *The Treasury*, p. 206.
73. T.199/50c: minutes, 2 Nov. 1936.
74. PREM.1/346: note by Hopkins, 28 Apr. 1938; CAB.23/77: Cabinet minutes, 8 Nov. 1933, p. 204.
75. T.161/717/S.40250/01: Bridges' memorandum, 16 Nov. 1935.
76. *Ibid.*, Fisher to Sir P. Cunliffe-Lister, 12 Sept. 1935, and minutes of first T.E.E.C. meeting, 16 Sept. 1935, pp. 1 and 6.
77. CAB.16/123: minutes, 6 Feb. 1936, p. 321.
78. *Parl. Papers* 1935–36, xvi. 860.
79. T.161/1315/S.40700/1: T.I.S.C. minutes, 1 Apr. 1936, p. 4.
80. See *History of the Second World War, U.K. Civil Series*: William Ashworth, *Contracts and Finance* (1953), pp. 11–13.
81. Conversation with Sir John Winnifrith, 31 Jan. 1975.
82. T.161/718/S.40780: T.I.S.C. minutes, 16 Mar. 1936, p. 2f.; T.161/783/S.48431/02/1: Bridges' memorandum, 13 Jan. 1937.
83. T.161/783/S.48431/02/1: Hopkins' marginal comment on memorandum by Bridges, 29 June 1937.
84. T.161/624/S.36130/34: Bridges to Barlow, 11 Oct. 1934.
85. T.161/783/S.48431/02/1: Bridges to Hopkins, 14 Jan. 1937.
86. *Parl. Papers* 1935–36, v. 432. Also T.161/580/S.35164/33: Grieve to Strohmenger, 21 Dec. 1932, where the head of 5D wrote: 'I think the Treasury has every reason to be grateful to the Army Council for its consistent co-operation during the last few years'.
87. CAB.23/79: Cabinet minutes, 31 July 1934, p. 372.
88. T.161/718/S.40780: minutes of 1st T.I.S.C. meeting, 16 Mar. 1936.
89. CAB.24/270: C.P.165(37), p. 272.
90. T.161/783/S.48431/02/1: memorandum by Bridges, 13 Jan. 1937, and memorandum prepared for Chancellor, May 1937 (no day).
91. T.161/783/S.48431/02/1: Bridges to Hopkins, 14 Jan. 1937; T.161/855/S.48431/01/3: Bridges' memorandum, 14 Feb. 1938.
92. T.161/783/S.48431/02/1: Hopkins' memorandum, 19 Jan. 1937, and memorandum prepared for Chancellor, May 1937 (no day); T.161/855/S.48431/01/2: Hopkins' memorandum, 17 Dec. 1937.
93. T.161/783/S.48431/02/1: Bridges' notes, with Fisher's comments, 29 June 1937.
94. CAB.24/273: C.P.316(37), para. 31.
95. T. 161/855/S.48431/01/3: Hopkins' memorandum, 11 Feb., and Bridges' memorandum, 14 Feb. 1938; T.175/97: Hopkins' memorandum, 12 Jan. 1938. The sum adopted by the Cabinet in February 1938 as the ceiling for defence expenditure in the quinquennium beginning 1 Apr. 1937 was £1650 million, but of this only £1570 million was for the defence departments, the balance being for Air Raid Precautions, for the accumulation of stocks of food and raw materials, and for the payment of interest on the Defence Loans (CAB.24/274: C.P.24(38), p. 9).

96. T.161/923/S.40760/03/2: T.I.S.C. – Air Ministry memorandum No. 242, 25 July 1938.
97. CAB.16/182: C.P.24(38), p. 133f.
98. T.177/42: draft memorandum for Fisher and Simon, June 1938 (no day).
99. CAB.23/90A: Cabinet minutes, 27 Oct. 1937, p. 59.
100. Viscount Norwich, *Old Men Forget*, p. 222.
101. T.161/949/S.49094/2: Hopkins' note, 4 Nov. 1938; T.161/905/S.35170/39: Simon to Sir Kingsley Wood, 25 Jan. 1939.
102. T.161/904/S.34610/39: Barlow to Hopkins, 20 Jan. 1939.
103. P.R.O., Admiralty Papers (ADM.), series 116, file 3631: memorandum signed by H. V. Markham (Principal Private Secretary to the First Lord), 29 July 1938. T.161/949/S.49094/2: Hopkins' note, 4 Nov. 1938.
104. CAB.23/100: Cabinet minutes, 5 July 1939, p. 114.
105. Fisher Papers 2/13: Fisher to Wilson, 15 May 1939.
106. ADM.205/3: Backhouse to the Earl of Cork and Orrery, 12 Dec. 1938.
107. Ashworth, *Contracts and Finance*, p. 6.
108. CAB.16/123: minutes of interdepartmental meeting held at Treasury, 6 Feb. 1936, p. 321. For Fisher's administrative reforms see Sir H. P. Hamilton, 'Sir Warren Fisher and the Public Service', *Public Administration*, (1951), xxix. 5ff.
109. Lord Eustace Percy, *Some Memories* (Eyre and Spottiswoode, 1958), p. 183. *Pownall Diaries*, i. 181.
110. T.161/863/S.4248/1: Bridges to Sir A. Carter, 7 May 1938. On 'cost plus percentage' contracts a contractor was guaranteed an agreed percentage of his total costs as profit.
111. CAB.16/123: D.P.R.(D.R.)C. minutes, 31 Jan. 1936, p. 216f.
112. T.161/948/S.49086/01: Report of Treasury Sub-Committee on Contract Procedure.
113. T.161/1169/S.2920/09: Gilbert to Barlow, 5 Sept. 1939.
114. CAB.16/123: D.P.R.(D.R.)C. minutes, 30 Jan. 1936, pp. 195–201; T.161/948/49086/01: Report of Treasury Sub-Committee on Contract Procedure, Note by Treasury Representatives.
115. *H.C. Deb.*, 5th series, 1935–36, vol. 315: 70f.; T.161/718/S.40730: note by Hopkins, 18 Feb. 1936.
116. *Parl. Papers* 1938–39, viii. 465.
117. T.161/876/S.19907/3: Hopkins to Fisher and Ferguson, 23 Mar. 1936. *History of the Second World War, U.K. Civil Series*: J. D. Scott and Richard Hughes, *Administration of War Production* (1955), pp. 25–27.
118. T.161/937/S.43899: esp. T.I.S.C. minutes, 9 Dec. 1937, item 3.
119. T.161/935/S.43475 *passim*.
120. ADM.116/3988: Report of Shakespeare Committee on Financial Control in the Admiralty, 4 Aug. 1939, *Parl. Papers* 1936–37, vii. 52.
121. *Parl. Papers* 1936–37, vii. 40–49. T.175/104 (Part 1).
122. P.R.O., Air Ministry Papers (AIR.), series 6, vol. 31: minutes of Secretary of State's progress meeting, 25 Oct. 1937, item 5; Viscount Swinton, *I Remember* (Hutchinson, 1948), p. 118f.
123. T.161/922/S.40730/04: Sir Arthur Street (Air Ministry) to Barlow, 20 Feb. 1939. *H.C. Deb.*, 5th series, 1938–39, vol. 344: 744ff., 943ff. and 2394ff.
124. T.161/922/S.40730/04: Bridges to Barlow, 16 Dec. 1936.
125. *Ibid.*, Barlow to Sir E. Forbes, 13 Apr. 1937; Barlow's memorandum, 18 Oct. 1937; Compton to Gilbert, 1 Dec. 1938; Barlow's memorandum, 17 Feb. 1939.
126. T.161/950/S.51936: Bridges to Barlow, 4 July 1938.
127. T.161/1316/S.40700/8: T.I.S.C. minutes, 29 Sept. 1936, p. 10.
128. *H.L. Deb.*, 1942–43, vol. 125: 269. For similar allegations see same debate, cols. 252, 289 and 311, and Sir Alexander Legge-Bourke, *Master of the Offices* (Falcon Press, 1950), esp. pp. 13–15 and 28–39.
129. Fisher Papers 1: note prepared by Fisher for P.M., March 1926 (no day).
130. Hamilton, 'Sir Warren Fisher', *Public Administration* (1951), xxix. 27.

131. Baldwin Papers, vol. 169, folios 194–6: Fisher to Baldwin, 8 Dec. 1934; London-derry to Baldwin, 10 Dec. 1934.
132. Liddell Hart Papers 1/129: notes on the case of Sir Christopher Bullock, compiled by Bullock, 10 Mar. 1938.
133. *The Times*, 6 Aug. 1936, p. 15.
134. Liddell Hart Papers 1/129: Bullock to Liddell Hart, 12 Aug. 1936 and 11 Mar. 1938. For other accounts of this sad episode see Roskill, *Hankey*, iii. 209n and 360f., and H. Montgomery Hyde, *British Air Policy Between the Wars* (Heine-mann, 1976), p. 386f.
135. Bridges, *The Treasury*, pp. 171 and 175.
136. Scott and Hughes, *Administration of War Production*, p. 11.
137. AIR.6/34: Secretary of State's progress meeting, minutes, 11 July 1938, p. 11, and AIR. 6/35: minutes, 7 Sept. 1938, item 3.
138. D. C. Watt, *Personalities and Policies* (Longmans, 1965), p. 102.
139. *Ibid.*, p. 103, note 4.
140. *Pownall Diaries*, 15 Feb. 1934. Baldwin Papers 1/40: Hankey to Baldwin, 23 Aug. 1934.
141. Conversation with Sir Edward Playfair, 21 Apr. 1975.
142. N.C.7/11/29/20: Fisher to Chamberlain, 1 June 1936. For record of Chequers weekend see N.C.18/1/1059: Chamberlain to his sister Hilda, 9 July 1938.
143. PREM.1/252: Fisher to Chamberlain, 1 Oct. 1938.
144. Watt, *Personalities and Policies*, pp. 5 and 100ff. Watt defends Fisher against the charge.
145. Conversation with Sir Thomas and Lady Padmore, 15 Mar. 1975.
146. Fisher Papers 2/7: Fisher to Wilson (for Chamberlain), 17 Sept. 1938.
147. Fisher Papers 2/9: Fisher to Simon and Chamberlain, 1 Oct. 1938; N.C.18/1/1070: Chamberlain to Hilda, 2 Oct. 1938, and (regarding Fisher and Wilson) conversation with Sir Thomas and Lady Padmore, 15 Mar. 1975.
148. T.175/104 (Part 2): Hopkins to Fisher and Simon, 15 Apr. 1939; Minney, *Private Papers of Hore-Belisha*, p. 195.
149. Fisher Papers 2/13: Fisher to 'My dear H.J. (for N.C.)', 15 May 1939.
150. *Ibid.*
151. King's College, London, Library, Ismay Papers V/F3/1.
152. Sir John Wheeler-Bennett, *John Anderson, Viscount Waverley* (Macmillan, 1962), p. 233.
153. For an account of this episode see *The Times*, 2 Apr. 1942, p. 2, and 14 Apr., pp. 2 and 5.
154. Lord Vansittart, *Mist Procession* (Hutchinson, 1958), p. 443.
155. PREM.1/252 *passim*.
156. Sir James Grigg, *Prejudice and Judgement* (Jonathan Cape, 1948), p. 53.

CHAPTER III

1. Conversation with Sir Edward Playfair, 21 Apr. 1975; Sir Henry Clay, *Lord Norman* (Macmillan, 1957), p. 469.
2. Leith-Ross, *Money Talks*, pp. 147f. For E.A.C. papers see P.R.O., Cabinet Papers, Series 58.
3. J. M. Keynes, *The General Theory of Employment, Interest and Money* (Macmillan, 1936), pp. v–vi.
4. H. D. Henderson, *The Inter-War Years and Other Papers* (Oxford U.P., 1955), p. 161.
5. *Collected Writings of John Maynard Keynes*, xiii. 565–633; T.208/195: Hawtrey's criticism of *General Theory*.
6. Susan Howson, *Domestic Monetary Management in Britain*, pp. 143, 145. Susan Howson and Donald Winch, *The Economic Advisory Council 1930–1939* (Cam-bridge U.P., 1977), p. 109.
7. T.160/885/F.17545: Hopkins to Fisher, 17 May 1939, *et seq.*
8. T.175/104 (Part 1): Note on 26th E.A.C. Report, 22 Dec. 1938.
9. *The Times*, 4 Oct. 1933, p. 14.

10. See Appendix IV, Table D.
11. CAB.16/109: Note by Fisher, 29 Jan. 1934, p. 379.
12. CAB.23/100: C.P.149(39), para. 3, p. 138; CAB.58/23: E.A.C.(E.I.)209, p. 4.
13. CAB.23/92: Cabinet minutes, 16 Feb. 1938, p. 134. What follows is based on paras. 7–14 of Inskip's Interim Report, C.P.316(37), in CAB.24/273.
14. C.P.316(37), para. 8.
15. CAB.16/182: D.P.(P.)2, 'Planning for War with Germany', report by C.O.S., Feb. 1937.
16. PREM.1/236: Hopkins to Simon, 29 Oct. 1938, para. 8.
17. CAB.23/100: Cabinet minutes, 12 and 26 July 1939, pp. 159, 216 and 270f.
18. Churchill College, Cambridge, Vansittart Papers 1/10: C.P.104(34), p. 13; CAB.27/508: D.C.M. minutes, 30 Apr. 1935, p. 128.
19. CAB.23/92: Cabinet minutes, 14 Mar. 1938, p. 371.
20. N.C.18/1: Chamberlain to his sister, 14 Nov. 1936.
21. Sir Winston Churchill, *Great Contemporaries* (Thornton Butterworth, 1937), p. 225.
22. CAB.4/21: C.I.D. Paper 1087B, 'Treasury Comments on C.O.S. 1932 Review', 11 Mar. 1932; CAB.23/70: Cabinet minutes for 10 Feb. and 23 Mar. 1932, esp. pp. 242 and 391; T.171/296: Hopkins to Chamberlain, 21 Mar. 1932. T.161/560/S.18917/016/1: Strohmenger to Fisher, 12 July 1932, *et seq.*
23. CAB.16/109: D.R.C. minutes, 14 Nov. 1933, p. 46.
24. CAB.23/78: Cabinet minutes, 7 Feb. 1934, p. 108.
25. Hankey Papers 1/7, p. 57 (diary, 22 Feb. 1934).
26. Baldwin Papers 131/194.
27. CAB.27/511: D.C.M.(32)120. para. 3; CAB.27/507 (vol. iii): D.C.M. minutes, 24 July, 1934, pp. 394 and 399.
28. CAB.27/148: N.C.M.(35)10, para. 3; *H.C. Deb.*, 5th series, 1933–34, vol. 289: 675f.
29. CAB.27/507 (vol. iii): D.C.M. minutes, 25 and 26 June, 1934, pp. 270, 278 and 295.
30. CAB.23/78: Cabinet minutes, 19 Mar. 1934, p. 282f.; Templewood, *Nine Troubled Years*, pp. 138, 196; G. M. Young, *Stanley Baldwin* (Rupert Hart-Davis, 1952), p. 199.
31. Vansittart, *Mist Procession*, pp. 443 and 507.
32. CAB.16/109: D.R.C. minutes, 23 Jan. 1934, and D.R.C. 12, pp. 143 and 379; Baldwin Papers 1/80: Fisher to Baldwin, 26 Feb. 1935.
33. CAB.64/22: Printed record of meeting between Secret Deputation and Prime Minister, 29 July 1936, p. 30f.
34. C. L. Mowat, *Britain Between the Wars* (Methuen, 1955), p. 553.
35. T.172/1526 and T.172/1527: Chancellor's speeches, 1934 and 1935; *The Times*, 4 Oct. 1935, p. 8; N.C.2/23A: Chamberlain's diary, 2 Aug. 1935.
36. E. M. Robertson, *Hitler's Pre-War Policy and Military Plans* (Longmans, 1963), pp. 35 and 45.
37. Roskill, *Hankey*, iii. 251.
38. *Sunday Telegraph*, 22 Sept. 1974, p. 23.
39. Roskill, *op. cit.*, p. 289, n. 4, quoting T.172/1853.
40. T.172/1853: note by Phillips, 25 Feb. 1937.
41. *Ibid.*, note by Hopkins, 25 Feb. 1937.
42. *H.C. Deb.*, 5th series, 1933–34, vol. 292: 2421.
43. T.161/642/S.19907/04: Hopkins to Fisher, 21 Jan. 1935.
44. T.172/1837: Fisher to Phipps, 21 Feb. 1935.
45. *Ibid.*, Phipps to Fisher, 27 Feb. 1935.
46. *Ibid.*, Hopkins to Fisher, 7 Mar. 1935.
47. T.172/1830: Fergusson to Chamberlain, 27 Apr. 1935.
48. CAB.16/112: D.R.C. minutes, 11 July 1935, p. 79f., and 19 July, p. 92.
49. T.161/783/S.48431: note by Bridges, 27 July 1935; Feiling, *Neville Chamberlain*, p. 266.
50. CAB.16/112: D.R.C. 37, Table 4.
51. CAB.16/123: D.P.R.C. minutes, 13 Jan. 1936, p. 96 and D.P.R.(D.R.) 9, p. 11.
52. T.172/1832: Hopkins to Fisher and Chamberlain, 7 Oct. 1935.

53. T.171/324: Fisher to Chamberlain, 2 Dec. 1935.
54. Sir J. A. R. Marriott, *Modern England* (Methuen, 1963 – first published 1934), p. 378f.
55. T.208/201: note by Phillips, 29 Apr. 1939, based on notes by Hawtrey on 'Borrowing and Inflation', same date.
56. Sir Ralph Hawtrey, *A Century of Bank Rate* (Frank Cass and Co., 1962), p. xi.
57. T.175/94 (Part 2): Phillips to Hopkins, 31 Dec. 1936.
58. T.175/96: Hopkins' notes on the Borrowing Bill, 23 Feb. 1937. A table in T.175/115 gives Treasury figures for national debts per head of population at July 1939 as:

	£s
United Kingdom	172
United States	64
France	57
Italy	52
Germany	33
Japan	11

59. T.172/1832: Hopkins to Fisher and Chamberlain, 7 Oct. 1935.
60. *Ibid.* and T.177/25: Phillips to Fraser, 27 Nov. 1936.
61. T.175/94 (Part 2): Phillips to Hopkins, 31 Dec. 1936. Phillips believed that in the long run the factor which told in establishing world prices was the supply of gold. Measured in pounds or dollars, the supply of gold available for monetary purposes at the end of 1936 was twice as great as before the Depression, and Germany and China were unable to absorb gold for political reasons. As it happened, 1938 saw Britain experiencing a sharp recession, and Bank Rate continued at 2 per cent until August 1939, when it was raised, briefly to 4 per cent. Bank Rate returned to 2 per cent after the outbreak of War, and continued at that level until 1951. In 1936 Phillips regarded 3½ per cent as 'normal' for Bank Rate.
62. T.175/96: memorandum by Hopkins, 29 Dec. 1936.
63. Appendix III, Table A2, and Appendix IV, Table A1.
64. CAB.24/270: C.P.165(37), p. 271.
65. T.175/96: Hopkins to Fisher and Chamberlain, 4 Feb. 1937.
66. T.172/1853: Woods to Hopkins, 5 Feb. 1937.
67. T.175/96: Hopkins to Woods, 16 Feb. 1937.
68. *Economist*, cxxii. 575; *H.C. Deb.*, 5th series, 1936–37, vol. 320: 1223–9.
69. T.175/96: Hopkins' notes on the Second Reading of the Borrowing Bill, 23 Feb. 1937.
70. T.172/1853: *passim*, including cutting from *The Times*, 25 Feb. 1937, of Keynes' address to the National Mutual Life Association Society.
71. CAB.24/270: C.P.165(37), p. 273.
72. T.175/94 (Part 2): Phillips to Hopkins, 31 Dec. 1936. For annual trends see below, Appendix IV, Table C.
73. CAB.24/265: C.P.339(36), p. 281.
74. N.C.18/1/1003: Chamberlain to Hilda, 25 Apr. 1937; T.161/783/S.48431/02/1: Fisher's marginal comment on Hopkins to Chancellor of the Exchequer, 1 June 1937; T.161/855/S.48431/01/2: note by Bridges, 17 Dec. 1937.
75. *The Times*, 11 Mar. 1937, p. 17f.
76. CAB.24/260: E.A.C.(S.C.), Report, 10 Feb. 1936, p. 285.
77. *The Times*, 13 Jan. 1937, p. 13.
78. CAB.16/123: minutes, 13 Jan. 1936, p. 86f. Weir, a Glasgow businessman, had been appointed Scottish Director of Munitions in 1915 and thereafter had risen steadily in the organisation of wartime production, before being appointed Secretary of State for Air in 1918.
79. CAB.24/261: C.P.96(36), p. 322, and CAB.23/83: Cabinet minutes, 8 Apr. 1936, p. 452.
80. CAB.23/92: Cabinet minutes, 14 Mar. 1938, p. 372.
81. See Alan Bullock, *Life and Times of Ernest Bevin* (Heinemann, 1960), i. 624ff. and 635.

82. CAB.24/260: C.P.57(36), p. 349; CAB.16/136: D.P.R.C. minutes, 26 Nov. 1936, p. 354f.; T.161/735/S.21842/085: Contracts Co-ordinating Committee minutes, 17 Dec. 1936, p. 5.
83. CAB.16/123: minutes, 13 Jan. 1936, pp. 87–98.
84. Swinton, *I Remember*, p. 118.
85. *H.C. Deb.*, 5th series, 1935–36, vol. 309: 1094.
86. CAB.16/140: D.P.R. 107, p. 314; CAB.23/85: Cabinet minutes, 29 July 1936, p. 170; CAB.24/262: C.P.117(36), p. 43; CAB.24/265: C.P.339(36), p. 277.
87. T.177/37 (Part 2): Inskip to Brown (Minister for Labour), 14 June 1937. See also CAB.23/100: Cabinet minutes, 5 July 1939, p. 131, for alarm expressed by Lord Maugham, the Lord Chancellor, even at that date, at a suggestion by Hopkins that housebuilding might have to be restricted through control of building society loans.
88. T.177/56: Phillips to Hopkins and Wilson, 20 June 1940.
89. T.161/720/S.49175: H. P. Hamilton (Board of Trade) to Hopkins, 17 Oct. 1936; memorandum by Bridges, Phillips and Hopkins, 10 Nov. 1936.
90. CAB.24/265: C.P.339(36), p. 280.
91. T.160/729/F.12829/2: Waley to Leith-Ross, 23 Oct. 1936, *et passim*.
92. T.160/878/F.16056: Waley to Hawtrey, 16 Nov. 1938.
93. T.161/720/S.49175: memorandum by Bridges, Phillips and Hopkins, 10 Nov. 1936; CAB.24/265: C.P.339(36), p. 281.
94. *History of the Second World War, U.K. Civil Series:* Sir Keith Hancock and M. M. Gowing, *British War Economy* (1949), p. 114.
95. T.175/94 (Part 3): Hopkins to Simon, 2 Sept. 1937, and Woods to Hopkins, 9 Sept. 1937. The Anglo-American debt settlement of 1922 had been for repayment of £978 million over 62 years, at 3 per cent interest for 10 years, and 3½ per cent thereafter.
96. T.161/841/S.41106: memorandum by Bridges, 20 Oct. 1936.
97. T.161/877/S.19907/4: note by Bridges on P.S.O.C.–1275B, 18 Nov. 1936.
98. Feiling, *Neville Chamberlain*, p. 292; T.172/1856 *passim*.
99. T.175/95: Hopkins to Fisher and Simon, 21 Feb. 1938; T.161/855/S.48431/01/3: note by Hopkins, 11 Feb. 1938, para. 27.
100. Robertson, *Hitler's Pre-War Policy*, p. 84.
101. T.161/783/S.48431/02/1: memorandum prepared for Chancellor, May 1937 (no day).
102. CAB.24/270: C.P.165(37), paras. 3, 14 and 15.
103. T.161/783/S.48431/02/1: note by Hopkins, 19 Jan. 1937.
104. CAB.24/270: C.P.165(37), para. 16.
105. CAB.23/83: Cabinet minutes, 2 Mar. 1936, p. 206; CAB.23/94: minutes, 20 July 1938, p. 184.
106. B. E. V. Sabine, *British Budgets in Peace and War* (Allen and Unwin, 1970), p. 123; Earl Winterton, *Orders of the Day* (Cassell, 1953), p. 249; T.161/783/ S.48431/02/1: Bridges' notes on C.P.165(37), 29 June 1937.
107. CAB.24/273: C.P.316(37), p. 4f.
108. *The Times*, 12 and 14 Jan. 1937, both p. 13f.
109. T.161/783/S.48431/02/1: Phillips to Hopkins, 19 Jan. 1937; T.177/38: Hopkins to Rowan, 13 Mar. 1937, and Phillips to Hopkins (undated).
110. CAB.27/640: P.C.E.(37) 10, addendum to the report, 20 Dec. 1937.
111. T.177/42: Barlow to Hopkins, 22 June 1938.
112. T.161/855/S.48431/04: minutes of Inskip review, 25 Nov. 1937.
113. T.161/855/S.48431/01/1: memorandum by Inskip, 23 Nov. 1937.
114. See Appendix IV, Table D.
115. *The Times*, 13 Jan. 1937, p. 13f.
116. CAB.24/273: C.P.316(37), paras. 23 and 24.
117. T.161/855/S.48431/01/2: note by Hopkins, 17 Dec. 1937; T.161/855/S.48431/ 01/3: note by Hopkins, 11 Feb. 1938.
118. T.161/855/S.48431/01/2: Fisher to Simon, 18 Dec. 1937.
119. T.175/97: Simon to Hopkins, 16 Mar. 1938, and Hopkins to Simon, 17 Mar. 1938.
120. CAB.16/182: C.P.24(38), para. 48.

121. CAB.23/93: Cabinet minutes, p. 73.
122. CAB.23/92: Cabinet minutes, 12 Mar. 1938, p. 353, and 14 Mar. 1938, p. 369.
123. CAB.23/93: Cabinet minutes, 6 Apr. 1938, p. 125.
124. T.175/97: Hopkins to Simon, 17 Mar. 1938.
125. CAB.23/94: Cabinet minutes, 15 June 1938, p. 12.
126. T.161/949/S.49094/2: notes by Gilbert, 4 Nov., and Hopkins, 5 Nov., 1938; CAB.23/96: Cabinet minutes, 7 Nov. 1938, p. 155f.
127. T.208/196: note by Hawtrey, 13 Feb. 1937, on article by Keynes in *The Times*, 13 Jan. 1937; T.208/201: note by Hawtrey, 28 Apr. 1939, on letter by Keynes to *The Times*, 26 Apr. 1939.
128. T.172/1910: article sent by Harrod to Simon, 5 July 1939.
129. CAB.23/96: Cabinet minutes, 7 Nov. 1938, p. 162.
130. T.175/104 (Part 1): Hopkins to Simon, 23 Dec. 1938; T.175/104 (Part 2): Phillips to Hopkins, 15 Dec. 1938; *Parl. Papers* 1938–39, xxi, Cmd. 5944.
131. T.161/949/S.49094/2: Phillips to Hopkins, 4 Nov. 1938.
132. *The Times*, 1 Dec. 1937, p. 22; Grigg Papers 2/23/2: Wilson to Grigg, 31 Jan. 1938.
133. T.161/949/S.49094/2: Phillips to Hopkins, 4 Nov. 1938; CAB.23/97: Statement by the Chancellor of the Exchequer, 18 Jan. 1939, pp. 32ff. (Hopkins' draft is in T.175/104 (Part 2)).
134. CAB.23/97: Chancellor's statement, 18 Jan. 1939, p. 32f.; T.175/104 (Part 1): Hopkins to Simon, 23 Dec. 1938.
135. T.161/949/S.49094/2: Gilbert to Fisher and Woods, with note by Hopkins, 5 Nov. 1938; PREM.1/236: Hopkins to Simon and Barlow, 29 Oct. 1938.
136. CAB.58/23: E.A.C.(E.I.) 201.
137. T.160/878/F. 16056: Waley to Hawtrey, 16 Nov. 1938.
138. CAB.58/23: E.A.C.(E.I.) 209, 16 Dec. 1938, para. 9.
139. T.175/104 (Part 1): note by Phillips, 21 Dec. 1938.
140. CAB.58/23: E.A.C.(E.I.) 209, para. 6.
141. T.175/104 (Part 1): 'Views of Treasury and Bank of England on suggestions made in para. 23 of E.A.C. Report of 16 Dec. 1938'.
142. T.160/871/F.15777: letters to Waley, 27 Oct. 1938, and 2 Nov. 1938.
143. CAB.23/97: Cabinet minutes, 18 Jan. 1939, pp. 32–34.
144. Clay, *Lord Norman*, p. 402f.
145. CAB.23/100: C.P.149(39), p. 138. T.175/104 (Part 2): note by Hopkins, 3 Jan. 1939; Clay, *op. cit.*, pp. 435 and 441. See also R. S. Sayers, *The Bank of England 1891–1944* (Cambridge U.P., 1976), ii. 561–7, 571f.
146. CAB.23/99: C.P.118(39), 23 May 1939, p. 235.
147. T.171/341: Fisher to Simon, 3 Jan. 1939.
148. *H.C. Deb.*, 5th series, 1938–39, vol. 346: 976, 978, 987–9; T.175/112: Gilbert to Hopkins, 4 Jan. 1939, and Hopkins to Fisher and Simon, 6 Jan. 1939.
149. T.175/112: press cuttings.
150. *H.C. Deb.*, 5th series, 1938–39, vol. 346: 999 and 1355. CAB.23/99: Cabinet minutes, 24 Apr. 1939, pp. 6 and 10.
151. CAB.23/100: Cabinet minutes, 5 July 1939, p. 117.
152. T.208/201: note by Hawtrey, 20 Apr. 1939, on J. M. Keynes, 'Crisis Finance', *The Times*, 17 and 18 Apr. 1939; Keynes, 'Will Rearmament Cure Unemployment?', *The Listener*, 1 June 1939; T.175/115: Hawtrey to Hopkins, 20 June 1939; Clay, *Lord Norman*, p. 441.
153. CAB.16/209: S.A.C. minutes, p. 75f.
154. CAB.23/100: Cabinet minutes, 5 July 1939, p. 87.
155. CAB.23/100: C.P.149(39), p. 138; CAB.23/99: Cabinet minutes, 24 Apr. 1939, p. 8.
156. CAB.23/100: Cabinet minutes, 5 July 1939, pp. 117ff. and C.P.149(39), para. 40, p. 138.
157. T.175/115: Hopkins to Padmore (Private Secretary to Wilson) and Wilson Smith (P.P.S. to Simon), 3 July 1939.
158. *Ibid.*, Most Secret Paper No. 2, 13 June 1939, and unsigned, undated memorandum (for Income Tax quote); CAB.23/100: Cabinet minutes, 5 July 1939, pp. 114 and 117.

159. CAB.23/100: Cabinet minutes, p. 119f.
160. Berenice A. Carroll, *Design for Total War*, p. 159.
161. Parker, *Europe, 1919–45*, p. 238.
162. CAB.23/97: Cabinet minutes, 25 Jan. and 2 Feb. 1939, pp. 66f. and 182.
163. CAB.23/100: Cabinet minutes, 5 July 1939, p. 124. CAB.23/97: Cabinet minutes, 22 Feb. 1939, p. 311.
164. T.175/115: Phillips to Hopkins, June 1939 (undated).
165. Fisher Papers 2/11: Fisher to Simon, 3 Jan. 1939.
166. CAB.23/95: Cabinet minutes, 3 Oct. 1938, p. 304.

CHAPTER IV

1. *Parl. Papers* 1934–35, xiii, Cmd. 4827.
2. *H.C. Deb.*, 5th series, 1937–38, vol. 332: 1600–8 and 2169. CAB.27/507 (vol. iii): minutes of Disarmament Committee (Ministerial) [henceforth cited as D.C.M.], pp. 276 and 318f.
3. Norman Gibbs, 'British Strategic Doctrine, 1918–39' in *Theory and Practice of War*, ed. Michael Howard (Cassell, 1965), p. 194.
4. T.161/580/S.35164/33: 'Defence Expenditure 1933'.
5. *H.C. Deb.*, 5th series, 1932–33, vol. 270: 632.
6. T.175/47: Grieve's memorandum, 30 Mar. 1933.
7. Letter to *The Times*, 9 Nov. 1948. T.175/28: A. P. Waterfield to G. C. Upcott, 5 Feb. 1931 (Waterfield was then in charge of 5D).
8. Baldwin Papers 168/190: MacDonald to Baldwin, 10 Aug. 1933.
9. CAB.2/6(1): C.I.D. minutes, p. 110; T.161/620/S.35164/34: Hailsham to Chamberlain, 2 Jan., and Grieve to Fergusson, 17 Jan. 1934.
10. CAB.16/109: C.O.S.310, p. 295, and D.R.C.9, p. 369.
11. *Ibid.*, D.R.C. papers, esp. pp. 71, 78, 433 and 444ff.
12. CAB.16/109: D.R.C. papers, pp. 107, 109 and 432f. CAB.29/148: N.C.M.(35)3. CAB.23/79: Cabinet minutes, 25 Sept. 1934, p. 335.
13. For obstacles to Anglo-Japanese understanding see Ann Trotter, *Britain and East Asia, 1933–37* (Cambridge U.P., 1975).
14. CAB.29/148: N.C.M.(35)3, 23 Apr. 1934, p. 3f.
15. *Diplomacy of Illusion*, p. 80.
16. CAB.16/109: D.R.C.2 and D.R.C.19. CAB.21/369: Montgomery-Massingberd to Hankey, 11 Sept. 1933. Chatfield Papers 3/1: Chatfield to Fisher, 4 June 1934.
17. T.161/621/S.35171/35: Fisher to Chamberlain, 14 Nov. 1934. Chatfield Papers 3/1: Chatfield to Fisher, 4 June, and Fisher to Chamberlain, 12 Nov. 1934; 3/2: Chatfield to Sir Charles Madden, 4 Oct. 1934.
18. T.161/779/S.41815: Bridges' note of 1 Dec. 1937; T.161/849/S.42779: Fisher's comment on note by Bridges, 12 Jan. 1938.
19. Fisher Papers 2/2: Fisher to Baldwin and Chamberlain, 5 July 1935; Hankey Papers 1/7: diary entry, 25 Nov. 1935.
20. T.161/779/S.41815: note by Bridges, 1 Dec. 1937. For wrangles within Whitehall, see Earl of Avon, *Facing the Dictators* (Cassell, 1962), *passim*.
21. CAB.2/6(2): C.I.D. minutes, 5 July 1937, p. 517.
22. T.161/842/S.41152.
23. N.C.18/1/865 and 965: Chamberlain to Hilda, 24 Mar. 1934 and 14 June 1936.
24. CAB.27/507(vol. iii): D.C.M. minutes, 3 May 1934, p. 30; T.161/844/S.41622: note by Bridges, 8 Feb. 1938; CAB.2/8: C.I.D. minutes, 1 Dec. 1938, p. 91.
25. CAB.23/78: Cabinet minutes, 19 Mar. 1934, p. 284.
26. T.161/855/S.48431/01/3: Bridges' note, 14 Feb. 1938.
27. T.161/780/S.42000: 'Admiralty Memorandum on New Standard' and Bridges' note, 27 Apr. 1937.
28. CAB.16/109: D.R.C.14, Table A2, and D.R.C.16, p. 433.
29. *Ibid.*, D.R.C. papers, pp. 143 and 365–9.
30. Chatfield Papers 3/1: Chatfield to Fisher, 4 June 1934; Baldwin Papers 131/198ff.

31. CAB.27/511: D.C.M.(32) 120, para. 15; CAB.27/507(vol. iii): D.C.M. minutes, 25 June 1934, p. 279f. Hankey Papers 1/7: diary entry, 9 Aug. 1934. Boyle, *Trenchard*, p. 681.
32. CAB.27/507 (vol. iii): D.C.M. minutes, 25 and 26 June, and 24 July, 1934, pp. 260–71, 298 and 391–7. CAB.23/79: Cabinet minutes, 31 July 1934, pp. 354–6.
33. Baldwin Papers 1/40: Hankey to Baldwin, 23 Aug. 1934.
34. CAB.27/507 (vol. iii): D.C.M. minutes, 25 June 1934, p. 280; CAB.27/514: D.C.M.(A.F.) minutes, 6 July 1934, p. 1.
35. Pownall diary entry, 30 July 1934, quoted in Middlemass, *Diplomacy of Illusion*, p. 88. CAB.27/507 (vol. iii): D.C.M. minutes, 24 July 1934, p. 388.
36. T.161/920/S.40150: note by Bridges, 6 June 1935; CAB.2/8: C.I.D. minutes, p. 154.
37. CAB.16/112: D.R.C. minutes, 10 and 14 Oct. 1935, pp. 132–55; CAB.16/123: D.P.R.C. minutes, 20 Jan. 1936, p. 141.
38. T.161/755/S.36130/37: Fisher's comments on Bridges' note of 8 Feb. 1937; T.161/780/S.42000: Bridges' notes of 27 Apr. and 8 May 1937.
39. Stephen Roskill, *Naval Policy Between the Wars* (Collins, 1976), ii. 347.
40. CAB.24/273: C.P.316(37), para. 57.
41. T.161/855/S.48431/01/2: Fisher to Simon, 18 Dec. 1937; T.175/97: Hopkins to Fisher, 19 Jan. 1938.
42. PREM.1/346 *passim*; T.161/909/S.36130/39: Rowan's note, 3 Jan. 1939.
43. ADM.116/3863: memorandum by Captain V. H. Danckwerts, D. of P., 5 May 1939. CAB.2/8: C.I.D. minutes, 2 May 1939, p. 207.
44. See Appendix III, Table A2.
45. T.161/855/S.48431/04: minutes of Inskip review, 2 Dec. 1937.
46. ADM.116/3631: 'Notes on Defence Expenditure Papers', by Phillips, with note from Chatfield to Duff Cooper, 10 Nov. 1937.
47. T.175/28: Waterfield to Lt.-Com. Maund, C.I.D., 3 Apr. 1929.
48. *H.C. Deb.*, 5th series, 1922–23, vol. 165: 2142; 1933–34, vol. 286: 2078; 1934–35, vol. 295: 883; 1932–33, vol. 270: 632.
49. CAB.27/508: D.C.M. minutes, 30 Apr. 1935, p. 135.
50. Watt, *Personalities and Policies*, pp. 102 and 114. T.172/1830: Fergusson to Chamberlain, 9 May 1935; T.161/770/S.40467: Fisher's note, 5 June 1935.
51. Boyle, *Trenchard*, p. 681f. CAB.16/109: D.R.C. minutes, 30 Jan., and 16 and 26 Feb., 1934, pp. 182–98, 257–58, and 284–89; D.R.C.14, pp. 10 and 35.
52. Vansittart, *Mist Procession*, p. 443.
53. Baldwin Papers 131/195f: Fisher to Chatfield, 11 July 1934. PREM. 1/252: Fisher to Chamberlain, 1 Oct. 1938; CAB.27/507 (vol. iii): D.C.M. minutes, 10 May 1934, p. 124.
54. CAB.27/511: D.C.M.(32)120. N.C.18/1/877: Chamberlain to Hilda, 1 July 1934. Chamberlain suggested a cut in the Army's programme from £40 million to £19 million, and in the Navy's from £88 million to £68 million.
55. CAB.21/434: Hankey to Baldwin, 29 June 1934. CAB.27/514: D.C.M.(32)123.
56. CAB.27/514: minutes, 6 July 1934, pp. 9–15, and D.C.M.(32)123, p. 8.
57. Hankey Papers 1/7: diary entry, 9 Aug. 1934. Marquess of Londonderry, *Wings of Destiny* (Macmillan, 1943), p. 139.
58. Feiling, *Neville Chamberlain*, p. 313; CAB.23/80: Cabinet minutes, 26 Nov. 1934, p. 238.
59. T.172/1830: Fergusson to Chamberlain, 9 May 1935; T.161/671/S.40019: Hopkins' comment on note by Bridges, 4 July 1935.
60. Sir John Slessor, *Central Blue* (Cassell, 1956), p. 184.
61. *The Times*, 3 Oct. 1936, p. 7.
62. Sir Warren Fisher, 'Beginnings of Civil Defence', *Public Administration*, xxvi. 214. A.R.P. was the responsibility of the Home Office and local authorities, and is beyond the scope of a study of the Treasury and the defence departments. There were wrangles over how much of the cost of A.R.P. should be borne on the Exchequer, and how much on local rates, but large sums were voted for A.R.P. following the Air Raids Precautions Act of 1937. The manifest deficiencies in A.R.P. in September 1938 were due, at least partly, in the Treasury

view, to the Home Office's preoccupation with gas attack, to the neglect of preparations to deal with high-explosive bombs (T.161/916/S.39299/053: Rowan to Gilbert, 28 Oct. 1938, and note by Gilbert, 29 Oct. 1938).

63. CAB.16/109: D.R.C. minutes, 25 Jan. and 16 Feb. 1934, pp. 169f. and 248–50.
64. T.161/838/S.40760/1: Fisher's and Chamberlain's comments on Bridges' note of 10 Sept. 1936. CAB.2/6(2): C.I.D. minutes, 29 Oct. 1936, p. 356.
65. Boyle, *Trenchard*, p. 681.
66. CAB.63/52: memorandum by Hankey, 18 Jan. 1937.
67. CAB.16/109: D.R.C. minutes, 23 Jan. 1934, pp. 149 and 158f., and D.R.C. 14, para. 99.
68. *Pownall Diaries*, i. 29.
69. *The Times*, 28, 29 and 30 Aug. 1933 (all p. 11f.), filed in T.161/571/S.30040.
70. CAB.16/109: D.R.C. papers, pp. 153–5 and 371; T.175/48: Fisher's comment on memorandum by Grieve, 14 Mar. 1932.
71. Baldwin Papers 131/195: Fisher to Chatfield, 11 July 1934.
72. CAB.27/511: D.C.M.(32)120, para. 13; N.C.2/23A: Chamberlain's diary, 6 June 1934; N.C.18/1/877: Chamberlain to Hilda, 1 July 1934.
73. Howard, *Continental Commitment*, p. 107.
74. See p. 19.
75. CAB.27/507 (vol. iii): D.C.M. minutes, 3, 10 and 15 May, 1934, pp. 20ff., 30ff., 107, 118f., 136 and 144.
76. N.C.18/1/877: Chamberlain to Hilda, 1 July 1934; CAB.27/511: D.C.M. (32)120, paras. 9 and 10.
77. CAB.23/79: Cabinet minutes, 31 July 1934, pp. 357ff.
78. Howard, *Continental Commitment*, p. 107; Dennis, *Decision by Default*, p. 113.
79. Liddell Hart Papers 1/159: Chamberlain to Liddell Hart, 8 Mar. 1937. *Europe in Arms* was published in 1937 by Faber and Faber.
80. *Daily Telegraph*, 25 June 1934, p. 11.
81. CAB.63/52: note by Hankey, 18 Jan. 1937; CAB.64/35: Chamberlain to Inskip, 24 Dec. 1936.
82. CAB.16/112: D.R.C. minutes, p. 95f., and D.R.C.37, p. 36.
83. T.161/876/S.19907/3: Bridges to Fisher, 19 Dec. 1935.
84. See p. 83.
85. CAB.16/123: D.P.R.C. papers, pp. 263ff. Weir's papers contain cuttings of Liddell Hart's articles in *The Times* of 25, 26 and 27 Nov. 1935 (Churchill College, Cambridge, Weir Papers, 17/10).
86. *Pownall Diaries*, vol. i, p. xx, and 27 Jan. 1936 entry. T.161/1071/S.42580/1: Weir to Chamberlain, 7 Dec. 1936.
87. CAB.16/123: D.P.R.C. minutes, pp. 97, 102f., 119f., 164–6 and 173. N.C.2/23A: Chamberlain's diary, 19 Jan. 1936.
88. Howard, *Continental Commitment*, p. 114.
89. *The Times*, 3 Oct. 1936, p. 7.
90. CAB.21/509: Chamberlain to Inskip, 13 May 1937. See also CAB.24/265: C.P.334(36), by Chamberlain, 11 Dec. 1936.
91. T.161/718/S.40780: Hopkins to Fisher and Fergusson, 2 Apr. 1936.
92. T.161/929/S.41671: note by Bridges, 27 Jan. 1936. T. 161/842/S.41152: Fisher's comment, 28 July 1936, on C.I.D.–1247B.
93. CAB.64/3: Ismay's memorandum, and Hankey to Inskip, 21 Sept. 1936. Ismay, *Memoirs*, p. 84f.
94. CAB.64/3: extract from D.P.R.C. minutes, 26 Nov. 1936.
95. T.161/856/S.49094/02.
96. N.C.2/23A: Chamberlain's diary, 25 Oct. 1936.
97. T.161/1071/S.42580/1: Fisher to Chamberlain, 23 Oct. 1936.
98. *Ibid.*, Chamberlain to Fisher, 30 Nov. 1936.
99. T.161/855/S.48431/04: minutes of meetings 28 Oct.–2 Dec. 1937.
100. CAB.24/273: C.P.316(37), para. 42.
101. What follows is based on T.161/777/S.41648 and Slessor, *Central Blue*, p. 184.
102. CAB.16/140 and CAB.16/141 *passim*.
103. CAB.64/9: Air Ministry note, 22 Oct. 1937.

104. T.161/778/S.41764: note by Bridges, 26 Oct. 1937. CAB. 64/3: Hankey to Inskip, 27 Sept. 1937.
105. T.161/855/S.48431/01/2: Swinton to Simon, 12 July 1937.
106. T.161/855/S.48431/04: minutes of Inskip review.
107. CAB.64/30: Inskip to Swinton, and Swinton to Inskip, 4 Nov. 1937.
108. T.161/779/S.41815: note by Bridges, 16 Nov. 1937; T.161/855/S.48431/01/1: memorandum by Hankey, 23 Nov. 1937.
109. T.161/855/S.48431/04: minutes, 2 Dec. 1937.
110. Roskill, *Hankey*, iii. 285.
111. CAB.63/52: 'Future Programmes of Our Defence Services'.
112. CAB.63/52: Hankey's draft, 3 Dec. 1937. T.161/855/S.48431/01/1: *Aide-Mémoire*.
113. *H.L. Deb.* 1937–38, vol. 107: 443.
114. T.161/855/S.48431/01/1: Fisher's marginal comments on 'Defence Review Draft Copy No. 8', 8 Dec., and note by Air Staff, 11 Dec. 1937.
115. CAB.24/273: C.P.316(37), para. 98.
116. Slessor, *Central Blue*, pp. 166 and 180.
117. T.161/855/S.48431/01/3: notes by Bridges and Fisher, 14 and 15 Feb. 1938.
118. T.161/923/S.40760/03/1: note by Bridges, 5 Apr. 1938; CAB.23/93: Cabinet minutes, 6 Apr. 1938, p. 121.
119. Slessor, *op. cit.*, p. 184.
120. T.161/923/S.40760/03/2: Fisher to Air Marshal Freeman, 30 Sept. 1938.
121. Slessor, *op. cit.*, p. 184; PREM.1/236: Hopkins to Simon, 29 Oct. 1938.
122. PREM.1/236: Hopkins to Simon, 29 Oct. 1938.
123. Fisher Papers 2/10: Fisher to Chamberlain and Simon, 5 Nov. 1938.
124. PREM.1/252: Fisher to Chamberlain, 1 Oct. 1938; T.161/950/S.53066: Fisher's comment on note by Bridges, 19 July 1938.
125. PREM.1/236: Wilson to Woods, 1 Nov. 1938.
126. CAB.23/96: Cabinet minutes, 7 Nov. 1938, p. 164.
127. CAB.23/96: Cabinet minutes, 26 Oct. and 7 Nov. 1938, pp. 58 and 147–72; T.161/923/S.40760/03/2: Hopkins to Simon, 31 Oct. 1938, and note of conclusions reached with the Prime Minister, 3 Nov. 1938.
128. CAB.24/273: C.P.316(37), para. 42.
129. *Ibid.*, paras. 43–4.
130. CAB.64/7: C.I.D. Paper No. 271–A; T.161/855/S.48431/01/1: Inskip's memorandum, 23 Nov. 1937.
131. T.161/855/S.48431/01/3: memorandum by Bridges, 14 Feb. 1938; CAB.2/7: C.I.D. minutes, 7 Apr. 1938, p. 5f. For A.D.G.B. schemes see p. 126f.
132. CAB.2/6(2): C.I.D. minutes, 19 Nov. 1936, p. 370.
133. CAB.24/265: C.P.326(36) and C.P.337(36).
134. CAB.24/267: C.P.46(37).
135. Italics added. CAB.24/265: C.P.334(36), p. 266.
136. CAB.24/270: C.P.165(37), p. 272.
137. T.161/780/S.41999: Bridges to Barlow, 19 Apr. 1937.
138. CAB.23/88: Cabinet minutes, pp. 178 and 183.
139. Minney, *Private Papers of Hore-Belisha*, p. 54.
140. *Europe in Arms*, p. 78f.; *Pownall Diaries*, i. 125.
141. T.161/1071/S.42580/2: note by Hopkins, 2 Feb. 1937.
142. *Ibid.*, Bridges to Woods, 15 Dec. 1936, passages in typescript underlined by Chamberlain.
143. ADM.116/3631: 'Notes on Defence Expenditure Papers', by Phillips, 10 Nov. 1937, paras. 33, 34 and 46.
144. CAB.63/52: 'Role of the British Army', note Hankey, 18 Jan. 1937.
145. T.161/855/S.48431/01/1: 'The Cost of Defence', memorandum by Hankey, 23 Nov. 1937.
146. *Ibid.*, memorandum by Inskip, 23 Nov. 1937.
147. T.161/855/S.48431/01/1: Hankey's memorandum, 23 Nov. 1937, and T.161/855/S.48431/04: minutes of Inskip Review, 16 Nov. 1937.
148. CAB.24/273: C.P.316(37), para. 75.
149. CAB.23/90A: Cabinet minutes, p. 356.

150. See p. 109f.
151. Chatfield Papers 4/10: Chatfield to Pound, 23 Nov. 1937.
152. CAB.53/9: minutes of C.O.S. meetings, 4 Apr. and 13 June 1938, pp. 9–12 and 116–23.
153. T.161/903/S.34388/4: note on Imperial expenditure on military defence, 27 May 1932.
154. Royal Institute of International Affairs, *Political and Strategic Interests of the United Kingdom* (1939), pp. 292–5, quoted in Susan Strange, *Sterling and British Policy* (Oxford U.P., 1971).
155. T.161/715/S.39889.
156. T.161/688/S.21568/06/1 to S.21568/06/5.
157. T.161/931/S.42339/1: note by Bridges, 15 July 1937; Minney, *Hore-Belisha*, pp. 53f. and 93.
158. T.161/949/S.49096/4: Hopkins to Fisher, 25 July 1938; T.161/931/S.42339/1: Gilbert to Mr. S. K. Brown, India Office, 11 Oct. 1938; T.161/949/S.49096/6: note by Fisher, 24 Oct. 1938; T.161/949/S.49096/3: Pownall Committee report; CAB.24/287: C.P.133(39).
159. T.161/949/S.49096/7: Sir Findlater Stewart, India Office, to Barlow, 4 May 1939.
160. CAB.23/100: Cabinet minutes, 28 June 1939, pp. 51 and 63ff.
161. *History of the Second World War, U.K. Military Series*: Major-General S. Woodburn Kirby, *War Against Japan* (1957), i. 15; *Pownall Diaries*, i. 190.
162. T.161/1055/S.18917/019/1 and S.18917/019/2.
163. CAB.24/274: C.P.24(38) and C.P.26(38).
164. T.161/855/S.48431/01/3: notes by Hopkins and Fisher, 11 and 15 Feb. 1938.
165. *Ibid.*, note by Bridges, 14 Feb. 1938.
166. CAB.23/92: Cabinet minutes, 16 Feb. 1938, pp. 155–7.
167. CAB.24/275: D.P.(P.) 21.
168. T.161/1071/S.42580/3: note by Bridges, 10 Mar. 1938.
169. CAB.2/7: C.I.D. minutes, 17 Mar. 1938, pp. 4–6, and conclusion 18.
170. CAB.23/93: Cabinet minutes, 23 Mar. 1938, p. 61.
171. T.161/1071/S.42580/3: Bridges to Bovenschen, 31 May 1938.
172. CAB.16/196: minutes, 28 Feb. 1938, p. 7.
173. *Ironside Diaries, 1937–40*, ed. Roderick Macleod and Denis Kelly (Constable, 1962), p. 55.
174. T.161/949/S.49094/1: T.I.S.C. minutes, 9 Sept. 1938, items 1 and 11.
175. *Ibid.*, Fisher's comment on memorandum by Compton, 12 Sept. 1938.
176. *Ibid.* This belief was not peculiar to Fisher – see CAB.64/3: Ismay's memorandum, 21 Sept. 1936.
177. T.161/949/S.49094/1: note by Simon, 13 Sept. 1938.
178. T.161/877/S.19907/5: Fisher to Simon, 25 Oct. 1938.
179. CAB.2/8: C.I.D. minutes, 6 Oct. 1938, p. 57.
180. CAB.27/648: D(38)3.
181. T.161/1071/S.42580/3: Hopkins to Fisher and Woods, with Fisher's comments, 31 Oct. 1938.
182. CAB.23/96: Cabinet minutes, 22 Nov. 1938, p. 246, and Gibbs, *Grand Strategy*, i. 493.
183. CAB.53/44: C.O.S.827. See also CAB.53/43: C.O.S.811.
184. T.161/1071/S.42580/4: Fisher to Simon, 1 Feb. 1939.
185. CAB.24/282: C.P.27(39).
186. T.161/1071/S.42580/4: note by Compton, 1 Feb. 1939. As an example of how the price of an individual item might rise, the cost of a light tank was given by the War Office in March 1938 as £4000, as against £3250 in October 1936 (T.161/822/S.35177/38: Oram to Compton, 23 Mar. 1938).
187. T.175/104(Part 2): note by Hopkins and Phillips on C.O.S.827.
188. *Ibid.*, note by Simon on Cabinet of 2 Feb. 1939; CAB.23/97: Cabinet minutes, pp. 173ff., 306f., 311.
189. Minney, *Hore-Belisha*, p. 186f.
190. PREM.1/296: Wilson's memorandum, 29 Mar. 1939.

191. T.175/104(Part 2): Barlow's memorandum, with Hopkins' comment, 28 Mar. 1939.
192. CAB.23/99: Cabinet minutes, 24 Apr. 1939, p. 10.

CHAPTER V

1. ADM.205/3: Backhouse to Sir Percy Noble, 14 Nov. 1938.
2. Treasury Supply files, esp. T.161/770/S.40467: Fisher's note, 5 June 1935.
3. T.161/923/S.40760/03/1: Bridges' note, 12 Apr. 1938; T.162/430/E.20456/4 and E.20456/5.
4. Swinton, *I Remember*, p. 118; Winterton, *Orders of the Day*, p. 233. Winterton, as Chancellor of the Duchy of Lancaster, acted as Swinton's deputy in 1937–38.
5. Hancock and Gowing, *British War Economy*, p. 69f.
6. T.161/950/S.53066.
7. T.161/671/S.40019: Bridges to Barlow, 4 July 1935.
8. T.161/754/S.35170/37: Swinton to Chamberlain, 13 Jan. 1937.
9. *Ibid.*, Bridges to Barlow, 15 Jan. 1937. For underspending see Appendix III, Table B.
10. Swinton, *Sixty Years of Power*, p. 119, and *I Remember*, p. 110.
11. PREM.1/252: Wood to Chamberlain, 14 Oct. 1938; CAB.27/508: Ministerial D.R.C. minutes, 10 May 1935, pp. 147 and 150.
12. Roskill, *Hankey*, iii. 320, n. 2.
13. AIR.6/26: minutes of Secretary of State's progress meeting, 15 Sept. 1936, p. 1.
14. AIR.6/30: minutes of Secretary of State's progress meeting, 8 June 1937, item 1.
15. PREM.1/236: Wilson to Chamberlain, 15 Mar. 1938 and again, no date, after 21 Apr.
16. Swinton, *Sixty Years of Power*, p. 118.
17. T.172/1830: Fergusson to Chamberlain, 9 May 1935.
18. T.161/778/S.41735: Bridges to G. Ismay, Treasury Officer of Accounts, 3 Feb., and to Banks, 24 Feb. 1937.
19. AIR.6/30: minutes of Secretary of State's progress meeting, 1 June 1937, item 2(iii).
20. T.161/850/S.42994.
21. PREM.1/252: Fisher to Chamberlain, 2 Apr. 1938; R. J. Overy, 'German pre-war aircraft production plans', *E.H.R.* (1975), xc. 781.
22. T.161/923/S.40760/03/1: Simon to Fisher, 25 Apr. 1938; AIR.6/34: minutes of Secretary of State's progress meeting, 24 Apr. 1938.
23. T.161/923/S.40760/04/1: minutes of Air Council Committee on Supply, 26 May, p. 1; 9 June, p. 15, and 13 June, p. 3 (all 1938).
24. T.161/949/S.49096/4: Bridges to Wilkie, 21 July 1938.
25. T.161/923/S.40760/03/2: T.I.S.C.–A.M. Memo. No. 242, 25 July 1938.
26. T.161/950/S.53066: Bridges to Fisher and Woods, 18 July 1938.
27. *Ibid.*
28. AIR.6/35: minutes of Secretary of State's progress meeting, 18 Oct. 1938, item 2(b).
29. Postan, *British War Production*, pp. 40, 471 and 484.
30. T.161/923/S.40760/03/2: Fisher to Freeman, 30 Sept. 1938, and T.I.S.C.– A.M. Memo. No. 242; T.161/1322/S.40700/39: T.I.S.C. minutes, 10 Mar. 1938, and A. M. Memo. No. 185. AIR.6/34: minutes of Secretary of State's progress meetings, 24 Apr., p. 2, and 11 July, 1938, p. 7.
31. T.161/949/S.49094/2: Gilbert to W. R. Fraser (Treasury), 12 Nov. 1938.
32. T.161/923/S.40760/03/3: note of meeting at Treasury, 9 Dec., and Gilbert to Barlow, 15 Dec. 1938.
33. PREM.1/236: Wilson to Chamberlain, 13 Dec., and 'Note on the Size of Bomber Aircraft', with Fisher's comments, 22 Dec. 1938; T.161/923/S.40760/ 03/3: Barlow to Hopkins, 19 Dec. 1938, and Gilbert to Barlow and Hopkins, 10 Jan. 1939.
34. T.161/923/S.40760/03/3: Self (A.M.) to Barlow, 21 Mar. and 13 July 1939.
35. *Ibid.*, Gilbert to Barlow, 15 Dec. 1938. Postan, *British War Production*, p. 484.

36. Gibbs, *Grand Strategy*, i. 598f.
37. See Appendix III, Table A2.
38. T.161/719/S.41109. T.161/1316/S.40700/7: T.I.S.C. minutes, 9 Sept. 1936, pp. 5ff.
39. T.161/989/S.42212: memorandum by Rowan, 25 Aug. 1937.
40. T.161/754/S.35171/37: Chamberlain to Hoare, 9 Feb. 1937. T.161/822/ S.35171/38: Bridges' note, 10 Feb. 1938.
41. CAB.16/112: D.R.C. 37, p. 40; CAB.16/123: D.P.R.(D.R.) 9.
42. T.161/713/S.36130/36/01: Hopkins to Bridges, 24 June, and to Fisher and Fergusson, 25 June 1936.
43. CAB.16/136: D.P.R.C. minutes, pp. 256f. and 260.
44. T.161/755/S.36130/37: Bridges' note, 6 Jan. 1937.
45. *Ibid.*, Fisher's note, 11 Jan., and Bridges' notes, 18 Jan. and 15 Feb. 1937.
46. ADM.116/3596: note by C. B. Coxwell, 27 Nov. 1936.
47. ADM.116/3631: Phillips' note, 22 Dec. 1937.
48. T.161/783/S.48431/02/1: Hopkins' note, 19 Jan. 1937.
49. T.161/755/S.36130/37: Bridges' note, 17 June 1937.
50. CAB.16/112: D.R.C. 37, p. 31; T.175/97: Hopkins to Fisher, 19 Jan. 1938.
51. T.175/97: Hopkins to Fisher, 19 Jan. 1938.
52. T.161/855/S.48431/04: minutes of Fourth Meeting, 12 Nov. 1937.
53. ADM.116/3631: Phillips' note, 10 Nov. 1937.
54. T.175/97: Hopkins to Fisher, 19 Jan. 1938.
55. PREM.1/346: Hopkins' note, 28 Apr. 1938.
56. T.161/852/S.43240: Rowan to Bridges, 27 May 1938.
57. T.161/909/S.36130/39: Stanhope to Simon, 22 Dec. 1938.
58. See pp. 114–6.
59. T.161/909/S.36130/39: Rowan's note, 3 Jan., and Gilbert to Barlow, 28 July 1939.
60. Chatfield Papers 4/3: Chatfield to Churchill, 10 Mar. 1942.
61. T.161/755/S.36130/37: Chamberlain to Hoare, 11 Dec. 1936.
62. Chatfield, *It Might Happen Again*, p. 62.
63. Chatfield Papers 3/1: 'Naval Policy and the Sketch Estimates', 30 Aug. 1932.
64. CAB.16/123: D.P.R.(D.R.) minutes, 20 Jan. 1936, p. 144; *H.C. Deb.*, 5th series, 1935–36, vol. 310: 70.
65. T.161/909/S.36130/39: Treasury Letter, 15 Dec. 1938; Fisher's comment on note by Gilbert, 10 Jan. 1939; Gilbert's note, 13 July 1939.
66. Milward, *Germany Economy at War*, p. 24.
67. T.161/783/S.42663: Bridges to Barlow, 1 Dec. 1937.
68. Roskill, *Naval Policy Between the Wars*, i. 109.
69. Chatfield Papers 6/1: Chatfield's memorandum on *Royal Oak*, 20 Nov. 1939.
70. ADM.116/3637: 'Most Secret Draft Review of Defence Measures Taken in the Recent Crisis'.
71. Sir Winston Churchill, *Second World War* (Cassell, 1948), i. 324.
72. T.161/580/S.35164/33: Hailsham to Chamberlain, 13 Dec., and Grieve to Strohmenger, 21 Dec. 1932.
73. W.O.163/39: Army Council minutes, 20 Nov. 1933, p. 48f.
74. Ismay, *Memoirs*, p. 68; Minney, *Hore-Belisha*, p. 67; Grigg Papers 9/6: Grigg to Fisher, 25 May 1939.
75. W.O.163/47: Informal Army Council minutes, 28 Oct. 1937, p. 7.
76. See p. 32f.
77. *Parl. Papers*, 1937–38, xvii. *Cmd.* 5681; 1938–39, xvii. *Cmd.* 5948.
78. T.161/842/S.41210: Compton's note, 3 Sept. 1936.
79. *Ibid.*, Bridges to Barlow, 22 Sept. 1936.
80. W.O.32/10326: Gort's memorandum, 18 July 1938.
81. T.161/836/S.40063/2: extract from T.I.S.C. minutes.
82. *Ibid.*, extract from T.I.S.C. minutes.
83. T.161/718/S.40801: Bridges' note, 4 Mar. 1936.
84. *Pownall Diaries*, i. 111.
85. See p. 135f.
86. CAB.16/181: D.P.(P.)C. minutes, 13 July 1937, p. 26.

87. W.O.163/47: Informal Army Council minutes, 20 July 1937, item 2.
88. T.161/850/S.43011: comment, 3 Mar. 1938, on note by Compton.
89. *Ibid.*, T.I.S.C. minutes, 10 Mar., p. 15, and 28 Apr. 1938, p. 1; Compton's note, 2 July 1938.
90. T.161/877/S.19907/4: Bridges to Fisher and Woods, 18 Nov. 1936.
91. Postan, *British War Production*, p. 33f.
92. T.161/753/S.34884/35: Creedy to Treasury, 7 Mar. 1936 (enclosure).
93. T.161/773/S.40949 and T.161/754/S.35164/37.
94. Appendix III, Table B.
95. W.O.32/4601: note by Creedy, 4 Apr. 1938.
96. CAB.64/35: C.P.99(38).
97. *Pownall Diaries*, i. 166; T.161/856/S.49094/02: Hopkins to Simon, 5 Nov. 1938; CAB.23/96: Cabinet conclusions, p. 170; T.161/1328/S.40700/68: T.I.S.C. minutes, 4 Nov., item 1.
98. *Pownall Diaries*, i. 166; CAB.2/8: C.I.D. minutes, 19 Jan. 1939.
99. T.161/1329/S.40700/76: T.I.S.C. minutes, 17 Jan. 1939, item 1; T.161/1329/ S.40700/78: T.I.S.C. minutes, 2 Feb. 1939, item 13.
100. *Pownall Diaries*, i. 175.
101. PREM.1/241: Hore-Belisha to Chamberlain, 31 Jan. 1938; W.O.32/4441: T.I.S.C.-W.O. memorandum No. 343, 2 May 1938, and Brown to Bovenschen, 23 July 1937; Gibbs, *Grand Strategy*, i. 525.
102. CAB.16/141: D.P.R. 128; W.O 163/47: Informal Army Council precis No. 8.
103. W.O.163/47: Informal Army Council minutes, 27 July 1937, item 6.
104. See p. 49f.
105. CAB.2/8: C.I.D. minutes, p. 200.
106. T.161/949/S.49094/3: Gilbert to Barlow, 29 Mar. 1939.
107. *Ibid.*, note attached to Gilbert to Bovenschen, 4 Apr. 1939.
108. T.161/1332/S.40700/91: T.I.S.C. minutes, 1 May 1939.
109. T.161/1072/S.42580/6: T.I.S.C. minutes, 4 May, and Bovenschen to Barlow, 10 May 1939.
110. *Ibid.*, Barlow to Bovenschen, 12 May 1939.
111. W.O.32/9581: Bartholomew Committee Report, 1940; Gort's Despatches, *London Gazette*, No. 35305 (1941), 5900ff.

CHAPTER VI

1. Mr. A. V. Alexander, former Labour First Lord, *H.C. Deb.*, 5th series, 1935–36, vol. 310: 79.
2. *Fontana Economic History of Europe*: B. R. Mitchell, *Statistical Appendix 1920–1970* (Collins, 1974), p. 85.
3. Klaus Knorr, *War Potential of Nations* (Princeton, New Jersey, University Press, 1956), p. 190.
4. Appendix III, Table A2.
5. Appendix III, Tables A1 and A2.
6. Robertson, *Hitler's Pre-War Plans*, pp. 79 and 108; Sir Basil Liddell Hart, *Other Side of the Hill* (Cassell, 1951), pp. 20, 47ff. and 144ff.
7. R. J. Overy, 'German pre-war aircraft production plans', *E.H.R.* xc. 796; Parker, *Europe 1919–45*, p. 340.
8. Carroll, *Design for Total War*, pp. 177f. and 213.
9. Ismay, *Memoirs*, p. 104; Slessor, *Central Blue*, pp. 166, 183 and 204–8.

Appendix I

Treasury Organisation, 1936
(Based on T.199 files and *Parl. Papers* 1935–6, v. 633)

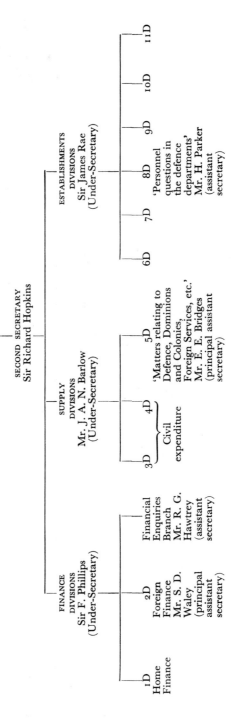

CHANCELLOR OF THE EXCHEQUER
Mr. Neville Chamberlain

PERMANENT SECRETARY
Sir Warren Fisher

SECOND SECRETARY
Sir Richard Hopkins

FINANCE
DIVISIONS
Sir F. Phillips
(Under-Secretary)

1D
Home
Finance

2D
Foreign
Finance
Mr. S. D.
Waley
(principal
assistant
secretary)

Financial
Enquiries
Branch
Mr. R. G.
Hawtrey
(assistant
secretary)

SUPPLY
DIVISIONS
Mr. J. A. N. Barlow
(Under-Secretary)

3D   4D
Civil
expenditure

5D
'Matters relating to
Defence, Dominions
and Colonies,
Foreign Services, etc.'
Mr. E. E. Bridges
(principal assistant
secretary)

ESTABLISHMENTS
DIVISIONS
Sir James Rae
(Under-Secretary)

6D   7D   8D   9D   10D   11D

'Personnel
questions in
the defence
departments',
Mr. H. Parker
(assistant
secretary)

Appendix II

Treasury representatives in the C.I.D. organisation
(selected sub-committees), C. 1937

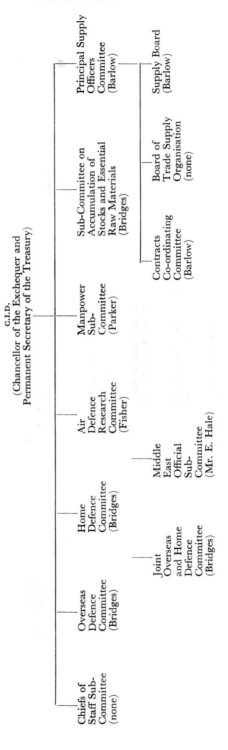

C.I.D.
(Chancellor of the Exchequer and
Permanent Secretary of the Treasury)

Chiefs of Staff Sub-Committee (none)

Overseas Defence Committee (Bridges)

Home Defence Committee (Bridges)

Joint Overseas and Home Defence Committee (Bridges)

Middle East Official Sub-Committee (Mr. E. Hale)

Air Defence Research Committee (Fisher)

Manpower Sub-Committee (Parker)

Sub-Committee on Accumulation of Stocks and Essential Raw Materials (Bridges)

Contracts Co-ordinating Committee (Barlow)

Board of Trade Supply Organisation (none)

Principal Supply Officers Committee (Barlow)

Supply Board (Barlow)

Appendix III

Table A1: Forecasts of annual expenditure if full D.R.C. recommendations accepted

First D.R.C. Report, 28 Feb. 1934 (CAB.16/109: D.R.C.14) £000s

Financial Year	Admiralty	Air Ministry	War Office	Total
1934	56,249	17,650	44,639	118,538
1935	60,978	18,665	44,946	124,589
1936	63,323	20,300	45,243	128,866
1937	63,844	21,300	45,468	130,612
1938	65,081	21,275	45,684	132,040

Third D.R.C. Report, 21 Nov. 1935
(CAB.16/112: D.R.C.37)

1936	74,900	45,000	54,000	173,900
1937	89,000	60,000	62,000	211,000
1938	90,650	64,000	72,000	226,650
1939	90,700	50,000	72,000	212,700
1940	83,300	44,000	82,000	209,300

Table A2: Actual expenditure by departments £000s

Financial Year	Admiralty	Air Ministry	War Office	Civil Defence	Total
1932	50,164	17,057	35,978	—	103,199
1933	53,443	16,700	37,468	—	107,611
1934	56,616	17,670	39,603	—	113,889
1935	64,887	27,515	44,515	—	136,917
1936	80,976	49,996	54,529	679	186,180
1937	101,892	81,799	78,141	3,365	265,197
1938	127,295	133,800	121,361	17,783	400,239
1939	149,339	248,561	243,638	59,000	700,538

[*Parl. Papers*, 1933–7, Air, Army and Navy Appropriation Accounts; T.161/999/ S.46095: 'Defence Expenditure before and during the present war.']

Table B: Expenditure by Votes. £000s

Air Vote 3A
(aeroplanes and spares)

Financial Year	Sum Voted	Underspent	Overspent
1934	5,985	31	—
1935	9,621	614	—
1936	19,600	665	—
1937	30,100	—	121

Army Vote 9C
(warlike stores)

1934	2,470	177	—
1935	4,943	208	—
1936	9,073	46	—
1937	25,032	5,981	—

Army Vote 9E
(machine tools for manufacture of warlike stores other than at Royal Ordnance Factories)

| 1936 | 1,000 | 700 | — |
| 1937 | 3,297 | 1,490 | — |

Royal Ordnance Factories Vote E
(works carried out by contract or by Office of Works)

1934	103	16	—
1935	103	36	—
1936	458	197	—
1937	5,991	2,677	—

Navy Vote 9F
(naval armaments stores – guns)

1934	395	—	27
1935	630	—	10
1936	1,427	246	—
1937	2,082	535	—

[*Parl. Papers* 1935–9, Air, Army and Navy Appropriation Accounts.]

Appendix IV

Economic indicators mentioned in text

Table A1: Government accounts for financial years

	Central Government Receipts (£ millions)	Central Government Expenditure (£ millions)	Published Surplus or Deficit (£ millions)
1932	745	777	−32
1933	724	693	+31
1934	709	701	+8
1935	749	746	+3
1936	797	803	−6
1937	873	844	+29
1938	927	940	−13
1939	1,049	1,817	−768

Receipts include £65 million borrowed in 1937, and £128 million borrowed in 1938, under the Defence Loans Act.

Table A2: Standard rate of income tax

1919	6s. in £
1925–9	4s.
1931	5s.
1932	5s.
1933	5s.
1934	4s. 6d.
1935	4s. 6d.
1936	4s. 9d.
1937	5s.
1938	5s. 6d.
1939 (Apr.)	5s. 6d.
1939 (Sept.)	7s.

Table B: Unemployment (annual average)

	Number (000s)	Percentage
1932	2,829	22·1
1933	2,567	19·9
1934	2,171	16·7
1935	2,027	15·5
1936	1,749	13·1
1937	1,482	10·8
1938	1,859	13·5
1939	1,582	11·6
1940	1,022	9·7

Table C: Board of Trade wholesale price indices
1930 = 100

	Total Index	Iron and Steel
1930	100	100
1931	87·8	92·8
1932	85·6	91·5
1933	85·7	94·3
1934	88·1	98·7
1935	89·0	100·5
1936	94·4	106·6
1937	108·7	129·6
1938	101·4	139·1

Table D: External finance (£ millions at end of financial year)

	Current balance of payments excluding gold	Gold and convertible currency reserves
1930	+28	148
1931	−104	121
1932	−51	206
1933	0	372
1934	−7	415
1935	+32	493
1936	−18	703
1937	−56	825
1938	−55	615
1939	−250	545
1940	−804	108

Exchange rate against U.S. Dollar

Year	Highest	Lowest
1936	5·041	4·888
1937	4·997	4·885
1938	5·018	4·671
1939	4·687	4·030
1940	4·035	3·275

Table A1 is derived from *H.C. Deb.*, 5th series, 1932–40, vols. 277, 288, 300, 311, 322, 335, 346 and 360. Table C is from B. R. Mitchell, *Abstract of British Historical Statistics* (Cambridge U.P., 1962), p. 477.

The current balance of payments figures for 1930–8 in Table D are from Sayers, *Bank of England*, iii. 309, and are contemporary Board of Trade estimates. All other figures are from London and Cambridge Economic Service, *British Economy: Key Statistics 1900–1970* (Times Newspapers Ltd., 1971). The balance of payments figures in particular should be regarded as very approximate, and indicative only of the main trends. For example, C. H. Feinstein, in his *National Income, Expenditure and Output of the United Kingdom 1855–1965* (Cambridge U.P., 1972), p. 113, has re-estimated the current balance of payments figures as follows: 1935—+23; 1936—−27; 1937—−47, and 1938—−55.

Note on Sources

The writer was fortunate in that a number of Treasury officials allowed him to interview them, and these interviews proved extremely useful in helping to understand the significance of various documents. To enable these former civil servants, who would not normally record their memories, to speak freely, all interviews were 'off the record', and subsequently, when it was desirable to quote a former civil servant as a source, the relevant portion of the draft manuscript was submitted to him, or to her, as a check on that passage's accuracy. Besides Treasury papers, Cabinet Office and defence departments' papers were examined for Treasury and other influences on policy, and much relevant material was found scattered through private papers. The most important private papers were those of Neville Chamberlain, and here again an interview with one of Chamberlain's private secretaries helped to bring the 'dry bones' of the documents to life. It should be made clear, however, that conclusions drawn from documents are the sole responsibility of the author.

The Chamberlain papers were essential reading, linking as they do the world of the departmental Treasury with the wider world of politics. Fisher's papers, though few in number, and mainly duplicates of papers to be found in the files of the Treasury or the Prime Minister's Office, nevertheless contain one or two very important memoranda which do not seem to have survived elsewhere. Every aspect of rearmament is touched upon in the Treasury Supply files, but the economic rationale behind the Treasury's military arguments can be understood only with reference to Treasury Finance files, together with the papers of the Chancellor of the Exchequer's Office and the ample collections of Hopkins and Phillips. Hawtrey's papers contain interesting additional information on Treasury economic thought. The Leith-Ross papers, on the other hand, provide little of direct interest on the subject of rearmament. Treasury Establishment files are also of marginal importance, but Treasury Establishment Officer's Branch files contain much useful information about the Treasury's internal organisation. Among the papers of people outside the Treasury the most useful information was gleaned from those of Baldwin, Chatfield, Hankey, Liddell Hart and Weir. The papers of the Cabinet Office dealing with defence, and the papers of the defence departments themselves, had to be studied extensively, if only because examples of Treasury influence are to be found therein at almost every turn.

Unpublished Documents

Public Record Office:
  References given are P.R.O. series numbers. In footnotes these are
followed by a volume number, or a box or file number.

Admiralty:
  ADM.1, Admiralty and Secretariat papers.
  ADM.16, Admiralty and Secretariat, cases.
  ADM.205, First Sea Lords' papers.

Air Ministry:
  AIR.6, minutes of Secretary of State's progress meetings.

Cabinet Office:
  CAB.2, C.I.D. minutes.
  CAB.4, C.I.D. memoranda.
  CAB.12, Home Defence Committee.
  CAB.13, Home Defence sub-committees.
  CAB.16, C.I.D. sub-committees, including A.D.R., D.R.C.,
    D.P.R.C., D.(P.)P.C., and S.A.C.
  CAB.21, Cabinet Secretariat files.
  CAB.23, Cabinet minutes and conclusions.
  CAB.24, Cabinet memoranda.
  CAB.27, Cabinet committees.
  CAB.29, London Naval Conference (1935) memoranda.
  CAB.36, Joint Home and Overseas Defence Committee.
  CAB.50, Oil Board.
  CAB.51, sub-committees on Middle East questions.
  CAB.53, Chiefs of Staff Committee.
  CAB.55, Joint Planning Sub-Committee.
  CAB.57, Manpower Sub-Committee.
  CAB.58, Economic Advisory Council Committee on Economic
    Information.
  CAB.60, Principal Supply Officers Committee and its sub-committees.
  CAB.63, memoranda and drafts by Hankey.
  CAB.64, Minister of Co-ordination for Defence papers.
  CAB.65, War Cabinet conclusions.

Prime Minister's Office:
  PREM.1, correspondence and papers.

Treasury:
  T.160, Finance files.
  T.161, Supply files.
  T.162, Establishment files.
  T.171, Chancellor of the Exchequer's Office, Budget papers.
  T.172, Chancellor of the Exchequer's Office, miscellaneous papers.

T.175, Sir Richard Hopkins papers.
T.177, Sir Frederick Phillips papers.
T.188, Sir Frederick Leith-Ross papers.
T.199, Establishment Officer's Branch files.
T.208, Sir Ralph Hawtrey papers.
War Office:
W.O.32, general files.
W.O.163, Army Council minutes and memoranda.
W.O.197, British Expeditionary Force papers.

Private Collections

Names are as in text, e.g. Sir Thomas Inskip, and not Lord Caldecote, his later title.
Birmingham University Library:
  Mr. Neville Chamberlain papers.
British Library of Political and Economic Science:
  Sir Warren Fisher Papers.
Cambridge University Library:
  Mr. Stanley Baldwin papers.
Churchill College, Cambridge:
  Sir James Grigg papers.
  Sir Maurice Hankey papers.
  Sir Thomas Inskip diary.
  Lord Swinton papers.
  Sir Robert Vansittart papers.
  Lord Weir papers.
King's College, London:
  Captain Liddell Hart papers.
  Lord Ismay papers.
Leeds University Library:
  Sir Graham Vincent, unpublished memoir.
National Maritime Museum, Greenwich:
  Lord Chatfield papers.

Interviews

The following were interviewed in their homes, unless otherwise stated:

Mrs. Catherine Charlton, on 22 November 1974.

Mr. George Oram, 21 March 1975, at Sundridge Park Golf Club, London.

Sir Thomas and Lady Padmore, 15 March 1975.

Sir Edward Playfair, 21 April 1975.

Lord Trend, 26 June 1975, at Lincoln College, Oxford.

Sir John Winnifrith, 31 January 1975.

Mrs. Charlton, as Miss Catherine Campbell, was a secretary on Chamberlain's private staff from December 1937 to May 1940, and was his only private secretary thereafter until his death in November 1940.

Mr. Oram joined the Treasury in 1919 at the age of 20, and, while a staff officer, was transferred to Mr. Edward Bridges' division dealing with defence expenditure in February 1936. During the next three years he regularly attended T.I.S.C. meetings, acting as secretary on twenty-two occasions.

Sir Thomas Padmore was born in 1909, and is a graduate of Cambridge. He transferred to the Treasury from the Board of Inland Revenue in 1934. For just over a year in 1936–7 he was private secretary to Hopkins, Second Secretary of the Treasury, and from May 1939 until the end of 1941 he was private secretary to Sir Horace Wilson, the Permanent Secretary.

Lady Padmore is the former Miss Rosalind Culhane. She was attached to the Chancellor of the Exchequer's Office for much of the inter-war period, and from 1934 was assistant private secretary first to Chamberlain and then to Sir John Simon. She was, in Sir Thomas Padmore's words, 'much confided in by all Chancellors – as young and attractive women in such positions commonly are. And she was a close friend of Warren [Fisher]'s.' Sir Thomas also became a 'pretty close friend' of Fisher's after the latter retired.* Both Sir Edward Playfair and Sir John Winnifrith are of the opinion that the Padmores are the most important living witnesses regarding Fisher.

Sir Edward Playfair was born in 1909, and is a graduate of Cambridge. He transferred to the Treasury from the Board of Inland Revenue in 1934. He was Hopkins' private secretary from 1934 to 1936, and, after two years as private secretary to the Financial Secretary of the Treasury, served under Mr. S. D. Waley in the Treasury division dealing with overseas finance.

Lord Trend was born in 1914, and is a graduate of Oxford. He transferred to the Treasury from the Ministry of Education in 1937, and worked on overseas finance under Waley in 1938–9, before becoming assistant private secretary to the Chancellor in 1939.

Sir John Winnifrith was born in 1908, and is a graduate of Oxford. He transferred to the Treasury from the Board of Trade in 1934 and

* Letter from Sir Thomas to Sir Edward Playfair, 4 Oct. 1974. A copy was given by Sir Thomas to the author.

served in Bridges' division dealing with defence expenditure until 1937. He was assistant private secretary to the Chancellor from 1937 to 1939.

Official Publications

Board of Trade Journal.

Documents on British Foreign Policy, 1919–39, Second Series, ed. E. L. Woodward and R. Butler, esp. vols. IV and V (1950 and 1956 resp.).

History of the Second World War, U.K. Civil Series:

William Ashworth, *Contracts and Finance* (1953),

Sir (W.) Keith Hancock and M. M. Gowing, *British War Economy* (1949),

William Hornby, *Factories and Plant,* (1958),

P. Inman, *Labour in the Munitions Industries* (1957),

C. M. Kohan, *Works and Buildings* (1952),

H. M. D. Parker, *Manpower* (1957),

M. M. Postan, *British War Production* (1952),

M. M. Postan, D. Hay and J. D. Scott, *Design and Development of Weapons* (1964),

R. S. Sayers, *Financial Policy, 1939–45* (1956),

J. D. Scott and Richard Hughes, *Administration of War Production* (1955).

History of the Second World War, U.K. Military Series:

Basil Collier, *Defence of the United Kingdom* (1957),

N. H. Gibbs, *Grand Strategy,* vol. I (1976),

Major-General S. W. Kirby, *War Against Japan,* vol. I (1957),

Major-General I. S. O. Playfair, *Mediterranean and Middle East,* vol. I (1954),

Stephen Roskill, *War at Sea,* vol. I (1954),

Sir Charles Webster and Noble Frankland, *Strategic Air Offensive Against Germany,* vols. I and IV (1961).

London Gazette, supplement to no. 35305, 17 Oct. 1941, for Lord Gort's Despatches.

Minutes of Evidence Taken Before the Committee on Finance and Industry (the Macmillan Committee), vol. I (1931), for Hopkins' evidence.

Parliamentary Debates.

Parliamentary Papers, Accounts, Committees.

Serial Publications

Daily Telegraph.
Economist.
Journal of the Royal United Services Institution.
The Times.

Contemporary Articles and Books

(Unless otherwise stated, all publishers listed have London offices.)

Works relevant mainly to Chapter II:

Duff Cooper, 'Spend to Rearm', London *Evening Standard*, 26 Oct. 1938.
Sir Oswyn Murray, 'The Admiralty', *Mariner's Mirror*, xxxiii (1937) to xxxv (1939).

Those relevant mainly to Chapter III:

Sir Ralph Hawtrey, *Economic Aspects of Sovereignty* (Longmans, 1929).
Hubert Henderson, *Inter-War Years and Other Papers*, ed. Sir Henry Clay (Oxford U.P., 1955).
John Maynard Keynes, *General Theory of Employment, Interest and Money* (Macmillan, 1936),
   'How to Avoid a Slump', *The Times*, 12, 13 and 14 Jan. 1937,
   'Borrowing for Defence: Is it Inflation?' *The Times*, 11 Mar. 1937,
   'Efficiency in Industry, a Measure of Growth', *The Times*, 13 Sept. 1938,
   'Crisis Finance', *The Times*, 17 and 18 Apr. 1939,
   'Will Rearmament Cure Unemployment?' *The Listener*, 1 June 1939,
   How to Pay for the War (Macmillan, 1940),
   Collected Writings vol. XIII (Macmillan, 1973), for Hawtrey-Keynes correspondence.

Those relevant to Chapters IV or V:

Captain Liddell Hart, *British Way in Warfare* (Faber and Faber, 1932),
   'An Unready Army', *Daily Telegraph*, 3 Oct. 1933,
   'Plans to Increase Our Defence Forces', *Daily Telegraph*, 25 June 1934,
   'The Army Today', *The Times*, 25, 26 and 27 Nov. 1935,
   'The Army Under Change', *The Times*, 30 Oct. and 2 Nov. 1936,
   Europe in Arms (Faber and Faber, 1937),
   'The Field Force Question', *The Times*, 17 June 1938.
Air Marshal Sir Cyril Newall, 'Expansion of the Royal Air Force', *Journal of the Royal United Services Institution*, May 1936.

Published Diaries and Memoirs

Ministers, civil servants and military men:

Action This Day: Working with Churchill, ed. Sir John Wheeler-Bennett (Macmillan, 1968), for memoirs by Lord Bridges, Sir Ian Jacob and Sir Leslie Rowan.

Lord Chatfield, *It Might Happen Again* (Heinemann, 1947).

Duff Cooper (Viscount Norwich), *Old Men Forget* (Rupert Hart-Davis, 1953).

Anthony Eden (Earl of Avon), *Memoirs, Facing the Dictators* (Cassell, 1962).

Sir Warren Fisher, 'Beginnings of Civil Defence', *Public Administration*, Winter 1948.

Sir (P.) James Grigg, *Prejudice and Judgement* (Jonathan Cape, 1948).

Lord Halifax, *Fulness of Days* (Collins, 1957).

Samuel Hoare (Viscount Templewood), *Nine Troubled Years* (Collins, 1954).

Sir Leslie Hollis, *One Marine's Tale* (Andre Deutsch, 1956).

Ironside Diaries, 1937–40, ed. Roderick Macleod and Denis Kelly (Constable, 1962).

Lord Ismay, *Memoirs* (Heinemann, 1960).

Marquess of Londonderry, *Wings of Destiny* (Macmillan, 1943).

Lord Eustace Percy, *Some Memories* (Eyre and Spottiswoode, 1958).

Diaries of Lt.-General Sir Henry Pownall, vol. 1, ed. Brian Bond (Cooper, 1972).

Sir Frederick Leith-Ross, *Money Talks* (Hutchinson, 1968).

Viscount Simon, *Retrospect* (Hutchinson, 1952).

Sir John Slessor, *Central Blue* (Cassell, 1956).

Lord Swinton, *I Remember* (Hutchinson, 1948), and *Sixty Years of Power* (Hutchinson, 1966).

Robert (Baron) Vansittart, *Lessons of My Life* (Hutchinson, 1943), and *Mist Procession* (Hutchinson, 1958).

Sir John Winnifrith, 'Edward Ettingdean Bridges – Baron Bridges', *Biographical Memoirs of Fellows of the Royal Society*, Nov. 1970.

Earl Winterton, *Orders of the Day* (Cassell, 1953).

Marquis of Zetland, *Essayez, Memoirs of . . .* (John Murray, 1956).

The Government's critics:

Leo Amery, *My Political Life*, vol. III *The Unforgiving Years* (Hutchinson, 1955).

Clement Attlee, *As It Happened* (Heinemann, 1954).

Robert Boothby, *I Fight to Live* (Gollancz, 1947).

Sir Winston Churchill, *Second World War*, vol. I, *The Gathering Storm* (Cassell, 1948).

Hugh Dalton, *Memoirs, 1931–45, The Fatal Years* (Muller, 1957).
Sir Basil Liddell Hart, *Memoirs*, 2 vols. (Cassell, 1965).
Harold Macmillan, *Winds of Change* (Macmillan, 1966).

Other Books and Articles

Those relevant mainly to Chapter II:

Samuel H. Beer, *Treasury Control* (Oxford U.P., 1956).
Sir Alexander Legge-Bourke, *Master of the Offices* (Falcon Press, 1950).
Lord Bridges, *Portrait of a Profession* (Cambridge U.P., 1950).
Lord Bridges, *Treasury Control*, Stamp Memorial Lecture (London U.P., 1950).
Lord Bridges, *The Treasury*, in New Whitehall Series (Allen and Unwin, 1966).
Sir Herbert Brittain, *British Budgetary System* (Allen and Unwin, 1959).
H. E. Dale, *Higher Civil Service* (Oxford U.P., 1941).
Geoffrey Fry, *Statesmen in Disguise* (Macmillan, 1969).
Sir Horace Hamilton, 'Sir Warren Fisher and the Public Service', *Public Administration*, Spring 1951.
Sir Thomas Heath, *The Treasury*, in First Whitehall Series (Putnam, 1927).
Franklyn A. Johnson, *Defence by Committee* (Oxford U.P., 1960).
Arthur Berriedale Keith, *British Cabinet System*, ed. N. H. Gibbs (Stevens and Sons, 1952).
Henry Roseveare, *The Treasury, The Evolution of a British Institution* (Allen Lane, 1969).
F. M. G. Willson, *Organisation of British Central Government, 1914–56* (Allen and Unwin, 1968).

Those relevant mainly to Chapter III:

B. W. E. Alford, *Depression and Recovery? British Economic Growth 1918–39* (Macmillan, 1972).
Andrew Boyle, *Montagu Norman* (Cassell, 1967).
Alan Bullock, *Life and Times of Ernest Bevin*, vol. I (Heinemann, 1960).
Sir (D.) Norman Chester, ed., *Lessons of British War Economy* (Cambridge U.P., 1951).
Sir Henry Clay, *Lord Norman* (Macmillan, 1957).
C. H. Feinstein, *National Income, Expenditure and Output of the United Kingdom 1855–1965* (Cambridge U.P., 1972).
Sir Roy Harrod, *Life of John Maynard Keynes* (Macmillan, 1963).
Ursula Hicks, *Finance of British Government, 1920–36* (Oxford U.P., 1938, reprinted 1970).

Susan Howson, *Domestic Monetary Management in Britain, 1919–38* (Cambridge U.P., 1975).

Susan Howson and Donald Winch, *The Economic Advisory Council, 1930–1939* (Cambridge U.P., 1977).

D. E. Moggridge, *Keynes* (Fontana, 1976).

London and Cambridge Economic Service, *British Economy: Key Statistics, 1900–1970* (Times Newspapers Ltd., 1971).

Sir Leslie Rowan *Arms and Economics: The Changing Challenge* (Cambridge U.P., 1960).

B. E. V. Sabine, *British Budgets in Peace and War, 1932–45* (Allen and Unwin, 1970).

R. S. Sayers, *The Bank of England, 1841–1944*, 3 vols. (Cambridge U.P., 1976).

J. D. Scott, *Vickers, A History* (Weidenfeld and Nicolson, 1962).

Susan Strange, *Sterling and British Policy* (Oxford U.P., 1971).

Those relevant mainly to Chapters IV or V:

H. R. Allen, *Legacy of Lord Trenchard* (Cassell, 1972).

Andrew Boyle, *Trenchard, Man of Vision* (Collins, 1962).

Peter Dennis, *Decision by Default* (Routledge and Kegan Paul, 1972).

N. H. Gibbs, 'British Strategic Doctrine, 1918–39' in *Theory and Practice of War: Essays Presented to Captain B. H. Liddell Hart*, ed. Michael Howard (Cassell, 1965).

Robin Higham, *Armed Forces in Peacetime* (Foulis, 1962).

Michael Howard, *Continental Commitment* (Temple Smith, 1972).

H. Montgomery Hyde, *British Air Policy Between the Wars, 1918–39* (Heinemann, 1976).

Keith Middlemass, *Diplomacy of Illusion* (Weidenfeld and Nicolson, 1972).

F. S. Northedge, *Troubled Giant, Britain Among the Great Powers, 1916–39* (Bell and Sons, 1966).

Stephen Roskill, *Naval Policy Between the Wars*, 2 vols. (Collins, 1968 and 1976).

Christopher Thorne, *Limits of Foreign Policy* (Hamish Hamilton, 1972).

Ann Trotter, *Britain and East Asia, 1933–37* (Cambridge U.P., 1975).

D. C. Watt, 'The Air Force View of History', *Quarterly Review*, October 1962.

Derek Wood and Derek Dempster, *Narrow Margin* (Arrow Books, 1969).

Those relevant to all chapters:

Sir Keith Feiling, *Life of Neville Chamberlain* (Macmillan, 1946).

Iain MacLeod, *Neville Chamberlain* (Muller, 1961).

Keith Middlemass and John Barnes, *Baldwin, A Biography* (Weidenfeld and Nicolson, 1969).

R. J. Minney, *Private Papers of Hore-Belisha* (Collins, 1960).

R. A. C. Parker, 'Economics, Rearmament and Foreign Policy: The United Kingdom Before 1939 – a Preliminary Survey', *Journal of Contemporary History*, October 1975.

W. J. Reader, *Architect of Air Power, the Life of the First Viscount Weir of Eastwood* (Collins, 1968).

Stephen Roskill, *Hankey, Man of Secrets*, vol. III (Collins, 1974).

D. C. Watt, *Personalities and Policies* (Longmans, 1965), for Sir Warren Fisher.

For comparisons with Germany:

Berenice A. Carroll, *Design for Total War: Arms and Economics in the Third Reich* (Mouton, the Hague and Paris, 1968).

Sir Basil Liddell Hart, *Other Side of the Hill* (Cassell, 1951).

Alan S. Milward, *German Economy at War* (Athlone Press, 1965).

R. J. Overy, 'The German pre-war aircraft production plans, November 1936–April 1939', *E.H.R.* (1975), xc. 778ff.

R. A. C. Parker, *Europe 1919–45* (Weidenfeld and Nicolson, 1967).

E. M. Robertson, *Hitler's Pre-War Policy and Military Plans* (Longmans, 1963).

Index